READING MERLEAU-PONTY

Maurice Merleau-Ponty's *Phenomenology of Perception* is widely acknowledged to be one of the most important contributions to philosophy of the twentieth century. In this volume, leading philosophers from Europe and North America examine the nature and extent of Merleau-Ponty's achievement and consider its importance to contemporary philosophy.

The chapters, most of which were specially commissioned for this volume, cover the central aspects of Merleau-Ponty's influential work. These include:

- Merleau-Ponty's debt to Husserl
- Merleau-Ponty's conception of philosophy
- perception, action and the role of the body
- consciousness and self-consciousness
- naturalism and language
- social rules and freedom.

Reading Merleau-Ponty is an indispensable resource for understanding Merleau-Ponty's path-breaking work. It is essential reading for students of phenomenology, philosophy of mind and psychology, and anyone interested in the relationship between phenomenology and analytic philosophy.

Contributors: A. D. Smith, Sean D. Kelly, Komarine Romdenh-Romluc, Hubert L. Dreyfus, Mark A. Wrathall, Thomas Baldwin, Simon Glendinning, Naomi Eilan, Eran Dorfman, Françoise Dastur.

Editor: Thomas Baldwin is Professor of Philosophy at the University of York, UK.

READING
MERLEAU-PONTY

On *Phenomenology of Perception*

Edited by Thomas Baldwin

Routledge
Taylor & Francis Group

LONDON AND NEW YORK

First published 2007
by Routledge
2 Park Square, Milton Park, Abingdon, Oxon OX14 4RN

Simultaneously published in the USA and Canada
by Routledge
270 Madison Ave, New York, NY 10016

Routledge is an imprint of the Taylor & Francis Group, an informa business

Typeset in Goudy by Taylor & Francis Books
Printed and bound in Great Britain by
TJ International Ltd, Padstow, Cornwall

British Library Cataloguing in Publication Data
A catalogue record for this book is available from the British Library

Library of Congress Cataloging in Publication Data
Reading Merleau-Ponty : on Phenomenology of perception / edited by
Tom Baldwin.
p. cm.
Includes bibliographical references.
1. Merleau-Ponty, Maurice, 1908-1961. Phénoménologie de la
perception–Congresses. 2. Perception (Philosophy)–Congresses.
3. Phenomenology–Congresses. I. Baldwin, Thomas, 1947-
B2430.M3763P4736 2007
142'.7–dc22
2006102517

ISBN10: 0-415-39993-9 (hbk)
ISBN10: 0-415-39994-7 (pbk)

ISBN13: 978-0-415-39993-7 (hbk)
ISBN13: 978-0-415-39994-4 (pbk)

CONTENTS

CONTENTS

CONTRIBUTORS

Thomas Baldwin is Professor of Philosophy at the University of York. Recent works include *Contemporary Philosophy* (Oxford University Press, 2001), *The Cambridge History of Philosophy* (ed.) (Cambridge University Press, 2003) and *Maurice Merleau-Ponty: Basic Writings* (ed.) (Routledge, 2004).

Françoise Dastur is Emeritus Professor of Philosophy at the University of Nice. Recent works include *Chair et langage: essais sur Merleau-Ponty* (Encre Marine, 2001), *Heidegger et la question anthropologique* (Peeters, 2003), *La phénomenlogie en questions: langage, altérité, temporalité, finitude* (Vrin, 2004) and *Philosophie et différence* (Chatou, 2004).

Eran Dorfman has recently completed his doctorate on Merleau-Ponty at the University of Paris XII and is currently at the University of Tel-Aviv. He has published articles on Merleau-Ponty in English, French and Hebrew, and has translated some of Merleau-Ponty's writings into Hebrew.

Hubert L. Dreyfus is Professor of Philosophy at the University of California (Berkeley). He has published many articles on phenomenology, including several on Merleau-Ponty. His numerous books include *Being-In-The-World* (MIT Press, 1991), *What Computers Still Can't Do: A Critique of Artificial Reason* (MIT Press, 1992) and *Thinking in Action* (Routledge, 2002).

Naomi Eilan is Professor of Philosophy at the University of Warwick, where she is Director of the Consciousness and Self-Consciousness Research Centre. She has published many papers on philosophical psychology and edited several collections of papers in this field, including *Spatial Representation* (Oxford University Press, 1993), *Agency and Self-Awareness* (MIT Press, 2003), and *Joint Attention* (Oxford University Press, 2005).

Simon Glendinning is Fellow in European Philosophy at the European Institute, London School of Economics. His works include *On Being with Others*

(Routledge, 1998) and the *Edinburgh Encyclopedia of Continental Philosophy* (ed.) (Edinburgh University Press, 1999).

Sean D. Kelly is Professor of Philosophy at Harvard University. He is the author of *The Relevance of Phenomenology to the Philosophy of Language and Mind* (Routledge, 2000), and of several papers on non-conceptual content and Merleau-Ponty's account of perception.

Komarine Romdenh-Romluc is Lecturer in Philosophy at the University of Nottingham. She is currently working on a guide to Merleau-Ponty's *Phenomenology of Perception* for Routledge.

A. D. Smith is Professor of Philosophy at the University of Warwick. His recent works include *The Problem of Perception* (Harvard University Press, 2002) and *Husserl and the Cartesian Meditations* (Routledge, 2003).

Mark A. Wrathall is Associate Professor of Philosophy at Brigham Young University. He is the author of *How to Read Heidegger* (Granta, 2005) and, with Herbert Dreyfus, has edited *A Companion to Phenomenology and Existentialism* (Blackwell, 2005), and *Heidegger Re-examined* (Routledge, 2002).

PREFACE

In 2003 Eran Dorfman and I met to talk about Merleau-Ponty's philosophy, and as we talked we sketched a plan for an Anglo-French colloquium in Paris, where Eran was then working, to be held in 2005 in order to celebrate the sixtieth anniversary of the publication of Merleau-Ponty's *Phenomenology of Perception* in 1945. In order to convert this sketchy plan into a serious project we needed support from a French academic institution, and thanks to the support of Professor Ian Hacking we were exceptionally fortunate to receive this in generous measure from the Collège de France, where of course Merleau-Ponty was Professor of Philosophy from 1952 until his death in 1961. So it was that on 17–18 June 2005 the participants of the colloquium, British and French philosophers with a shared enthusiasm for Merleau-Ponty's philosophy, gathered at the Collège de France for two days of intensive discussion. We were much honoured that the proceedings were started off by Claude Lefort, Merleau-Ponty's friend and editor, and that Madame Merleau-Ponty attended for much of the time. My anxiety that the audience might evaporate on the second day turned out to be quite unjustified: over a hundred people were there on a hot Saturday afternoon to listen to the papers and join in the discussion.

This volume includes most of the papers given at the colloquium. One of the main purposes of the colloquium was to demonstrate to French philosophers the high esteem in which Merleau-Ponty's philosophy is held by a growing number of British philosophers. Equally it was our hope that the colloquium would provide a way of acquainting British philosophers with recent French work on his philosophy. In the event two rather different but complementary traditions were in play – the critical analytic approach to Merleau-Ponty of the British participants and the more faithful elucidations of his texts favoured by the French, though the papers in the collection show that these stereotypes should not be exaggerated.

We were fortunate that among those able to take part in the colloquium was Hubert Dreyfus, who has for many years played a prominent part in promoting the value of Merleau-Ponty's philosophy in the United States of America. When he agreed that his contribution to the colloquium should be included in this volume, he suggested that I should also include papers by two of his former students, Sean Kelly and Mark Wrathall, as representatives of a younger group of American enthusiasts for Merleau-Ponty's work. I was very glad to be able to do this, and thus to demonstrate further the way in which Merleau-Ponty's work is valued within the broader Anglophone philosophical community.

Thomas Baldwin

ABBREVIATIONS OF TITLES OF WORKS BY MERLEAU-PONTY

SB	*The Structure of Behaviour*
PhP	*Phenomenology of Perception*
SNS	*Sense and Non-Sense*
VI	*The Visible and the Invisible*
PofP	*The Primacy of Perception and Other Essays*
PW	*The Prose of the World*
IPP	*In Praise of Philosophy and Other Essays*
T&D	*Texts and Dialogues*
NC	*Notes de Cours*
HLP	*Husserl at the Limits of Phenomenology*

All page references in the text to Merleau-Ponty's works are to pages of the English translations specified in the bibliography, except in the case of *Notes de Cours* for which there is no English translation. In the case of *Phenomenology of Perception*, page references are provided for both editions of Colin Smith's translation (1962 and 2002) in the form '*PhP*, x/y', where x is the page number in the 1962 edition, and y is the page number in the 2002 edition (incidentally: the page numbers of the 2002 edition are generally close to those of the single French edition).

1

THE FLESH OF PERCEPTION

Merleau-Ponty and Husserl

A. D. Smith

We are here to celebrate Merleau-Ponty's *Phenomenology of Perception* (*PhP*). Its publication sixty years ago is the occasion of our being here. That is the occasion; but what is the *reason* for our being here? If we have a reason, it must be that something *new* in philosophy appears in the pages of that work: something that is still worth remembering and celebrating today. The task that I set myself here is to discern what it is that is original in that work. Because of Merleau-Ponty's situation, and because of various pronouncements of his own, I shall raise this question in a particular way: What is there to be found in the *Phenomenology of Perception* that is not already to be found in the work of Edmund Husserl? It is not uncommon for admirers and followers of Merleau-Ponty to expound his work by contrasting it with that of Husserl. Unfortunately, as often as not, what we are then presented with is but a caricature, or at best a one-sided view, of Husserl. But how do matters stand when the *real* Husserl is taken into account?

Before proceeding I should say that I shall be concerned with only one aspect of Merleau-Ponty's book, albeit the central one. For despite its title, the *Phenomenology of Perception* is a wide-ranging book, covering such issues as culture, history, art, freedom. I shall here be concerned only with the account of perception and our fundamental relation to the world that we find in its pages.[1]

I

Merleau-Ponty situates his own philosophical position in relation to two others – which he terms 'empiricism' and 'intellectualism'. The former he also characterises as 'realism' or 'objectivism', and the latter as 'idealism'. Repeatedly, when he broaches a subject, he lays out how these two positions treat it, and then expounds his own position in opposition to them. If anywhere, it is here, in his carving out a position that is different from both intellectualism and empiricism, that we shall find what is fundamentally new in Merleau-Ponty.

Although intellectualism and empiricism, idealism and realism, may seem, and indeed are, radically opposed to each other, Merleau-Ponty can stake out an alternative, third position for himself because, as he repeatedly points out, these two positions actually agree on certain issues; and it is precisely this source of agreement that underlies the inadequacies of both, in Merleau-Ponty's view. One fundamental thing they have in common is presupposing an initial, at least notional, separation between the physical and the mental. They then privilege one side of this division. Realism starts with objects in the world as given, and tries to understand the mental in terms of them. Even when such realism, or empiricism, is avowedly dualist in character, so that there is no question of a *reduction* of the mental to the physical, the mental is conceived along the same general lines as the physical. Mental laws of association, for example, are patterned on the character of physical causality. Intellectualism, or idealism, starts with the mental as what is given, and then tries to explicate the physical in terms of it – by reference to such things as forms of intuition and categories of the understanding. Merleau-Ponty seeks to overcome what these two schools of thought have in common by *starting* with an irreducible involvement of subject and world. He encapsulates this new starting point by asserting that it is *the body* that perceives. The 'subject' of perception is the body. Here we have two things that both empiricism and intellectualism would regard as separate and in need of being related. *Perception* is a 'mentalistic' notion; and the *body* is 'physical'. Merleau-Ponty, however, unifies them as the subject and the predicate of his fundamental assertion: *the body perceives*.

In this paper I shall be concerned with Merleau-Ponty's relation to intellectualism, since I am concerned with his relation to Husserl. For given the two options, it is clearly with the intellectualists that Husserl would be classed – and commonly is by interpreters of Merleau-Ponty. So in this section I shall consider how Merleau-Ponty distinguishes his own position from intellectualism.

In contrast to Merleau-Ponty's central claim, intellectualism places perception firmly in the hands of 'consciousness': of a 'constituting', understanding consciousness that contains within itself the a priori structure of the world. Merleau-Ponty's fundamental objection to this is that it overlooks the *opacity* of the world and our relation to it. 'If a universal constituting consciousness were possible,' he writes, 'the opacity of the fact would disappear' (*PhP*, 61/70–1; cf. 325/378). It is in opposition to such a perspective that he asserts that we do not 'possess' the world (*PhP*, xvii/xix). 'I am not', he writes, 'a constituting thought, and my "I think" is not an "I am", unless by thought I can equal the world's concrete richness, and re-absorb facticity into it' (*PhP*, 376 n1/437 n16). The world cannot, even in principle, be intelligibly laid out before consciousness. Even as regards its basic structures it has no 'ideal model' (*PhP*, 53/61). This is because we are ourselves caught up in the world, inextricably bound to it. The world is opaque because we are opaque to ourselves. There is no 'cognitive' subject, nor even a set of cognitive principles, above or prior to the world. We do, indeed, Merleau-Ponty accepts, carry the basic structures of the world with us (*PhP*, 326/380); but that is because we are essentially *of* the world. There is no 'form' that is the a priori condition of possibility of the world; rather, form arrives with the world (*PhP*, 61/70).

Merleau-Ponty's claim that we perceive with the body is explicitly posited as an alternative (and antidote) to intellectualism. At one point, for example, after criticising intellectualism, he sums up his critique by writing, 'We have expressed this by saying that I perceive with my body' (*PhP*, 326/380). Elsewhere he says that what he has done is to 'substitute for consciousness, as the subject of perception, existence, or being in the world through a body' (*PhP*, 309 n1/360 n22). And it is precisely the opacity of the world that this substitution is meant to enshrine. It is in the interests of doing justice to such opacity that Merleau-Ponty can deny that basic intentionality, the intentionality that fundamentally relates us to the world, is any kind of *thought*: 'What is meant by saying that this intentionality is not a thought is that it does not come into being through the transparency of any consciousness, but takes for granted all the latent knowledge of itself that my body possesses' (*PhP*, 233/270).

What is of primary importance in all this is that the body operates pre-personally and anonymously: 'My organism, as a pre-personal cleaving to the general form of the world, as an anonymous and general existence, plays, beneath my personal life, the part of an inborn complex' (*PhP*, 84/97). It is in virtue of this pre-personal level of existence that we fundamentally exist *in* the world:

> My personal existence must be the resumption of a prepersonal tradition. There is, therefore, another subject beneath me, for whom a world exists before I am here, and who marks out my place in it. This captive or natural spirit is my body.
>
> (*PhP*, 254/296)

My body, as it were, perceives the world for me. My body is already at grips with the world, before the offices of understanding: 'The thing . . . is not first of all a meaning for the understanding, but a structure accessible to inspection by the body' (*PhP*, 320/373).

The immediate objects of perception, for Merleau-Ponty, are meanings, or structures (e.g. *PhP*, 58–62/68–73). Perhaps we should say meaningful, structured objects and scenes. The world has a perceptual 'syntax' (*PhP*, 36/42). Indeed, it has a logic and a language. Significantly, however, it is a 'wordless' logic and a 'silent' language (*PhP*, 48–9/56). By this Merleau-Ponty means that the meaningful structures of the world are not originally for the understanding, but for the body. The logic of the world is a logic that we 'live through' (*PhP*, 49/57), a logic that my gaze 'understands', and to which my body in its entirety conforms (*PhP*, 326/381). It is, we might say, a 'vital language': for Merleau-Ponty certainly characterises a sensory quality as having a *vital value*, the meaning of which is first grasped by the body (*PhP*, 52/61). You can perceive a world because (and only because) your body is already attuned to the world.

Because, and only because, of this can sense experience be what it is: a 'vital communion' with the world (*PhP*, 52/61). We are in the world because we, in our bodies, are *alive to* the world. Indeed, we live the world: 'In order to perceive things, we need to live them' (*PhP*, 325/379).

This is, in part, what the term 'flesh' in my title is meant to express. We are vulnerable to the world, and affected by it, because our bodies are of a piece with the world. But the body is also what *fleshes out* a world for us: it is the living interpreter of the world. So we must begin our philosophising, not with self *or* world, but their intertwining and reciprocal conformation. In this way, for Merleau-Ponty, the body overcomes the divide between the 'physical' and 'mental'. This is possible, of course, only because the body that is here in question is not the 'objective' body of the realists – something that would already be on one side of the supposed divide. 'The eye is not the mind, but a material organ. How could it ever take anything into account?' Merleau-Ponty asks at one point. And the answer is immediately forthcoming: 'It can do so only if we introduce the phenomenal body beside the objective one, if we make a knowing body of it' (*PhP*, 309 n1/360 n22). Merleau-Ponty raises this issue of how the mental-physical divide is to be overcome on a number of occasions in the pages of the *Phenomenology of Perception*, and he always answers in two equivalent ways: by starting with *existence* or *being in the world*. He writes, on one occasion, for example, of 'this third term between the psychic and the physiological, between the for itself and the in itself ... which we call existence' (*PhP*, 122 n1/140 n55). And he states that he has found such 'existence' *in the body* (*PhP*, 89/102).

Such 'existence' *is* 'being in the world'; and so he can characterise the latter, too, as what allows us to unify the psychic and the physiological (e.g. *PhP*, 80/92). Existence of this kind is possible only because my body is already *familiar* with the world:

> My act of perception ... takes advantage of work already done, of a general synthesis constituted once for all; and this is what I mean when I say that I perceive with my body or my senses, since my body and my senses are precisely this familiarity with the world born of habit, that implicit or sedimentary body of knowledge.
>
> (*PhP*, 238/277; cf. 326/380)

We have an environment through 'stable sense organs and pre-established circuits' (*PhP*, 87/100). Because of this Merleau-Ponty can claim that the body 'is better informed than we are about the world' (*PhP*, 238/277).

II

The preceding section has highlighted what I take to be the principal features of Merleau-Ponty's 'third' position. What, however, is there in it that is new – in the sense that it is not to be found in Husserl? Well, essentially, nothing. The language is certainly different; but in so far as the essential points are concerned, it is all already there in Husserl, as I shall briefly indicate in this section.

For Husserl the body – the 'lived' body (*Leib*), not the 'objective' body (*Körper*) – is essential for perception of the world and for being in the world. Husserl writes quite explicitly that the body 'is *necessary* in all perception' (*Hua*, IV, 56, original emphasis; cf. *Hua*, IX, 107).[2] 'The constitution of nature', he writes elsewhere, 'is from the start indissolubly interwoven with the constitution of a body' (C 17 II, 45).[3] Indeed, the body is *co-constituted* whenever anything is perceived (*Hua*, XI, 298). Sensible appearances can be appearances of physical things – or even *as of* physical things – only as they are coordinated with our bodily movements. Only through 'holding sway' (*walten*) in my body through active movement can I have experience of objects in the world (e.g. *Hua*, VI, 108–9, 220 [106, 217]; *Hua*, XI, 13–15). Hence, Husserl can refer to the perceiving subject as the '*Ichleib*': the I-body (e.g. *Hua*, XIII, 43). Indeed, he can even say that 'the study of the intentionality in which things come to perceptual givenness cannot be carried out without the study of the *corresponding intentionality of one's own body*' (*Hua*, IX, 197, my emphasis). In this same context he says that body *is* a 'perceptual function'. We should not misconstrue talk of constitution, Husserl warns us elsewhere, as if it were a matter of a 'supramudane' (*überweltlich*) ego constituting a world external to itself. 'Much rather', he writes, 'is the world so constituted that the I itself steps forth as embodied. As a bodily I, as an I that truly lives in the world [*in der Welt leibt und lebt*], it is itself a worldly being' (*Hua*, XV, 286–7). This, however, is just the beginning of Husserl's agreement with Merleau-Ponty. We can begin to explore the full range of the agreement by looking at Husserl's view of the relation between a self and the world.

Despite what some have claimed, on the basis of Husserl's well known, indeed notorious, employment of the *epoché* (the 'bracketing' or 'putting out of play' of belief in the real world), Husserl believed that it is not possible for a conscious self – at least one of the sort we can comprehend and know ourselves to be – to exist without experiencing a world. 'Every ego', he writes, 'must build up a real world' (C 17 V, 24).[4] And again: 'It is inconceivable that, in reflection, I do not discover myself as experiencing a world in my experiences' (C 7 II, 19). But how, one might ask, can Husserl say such things, given his commitment to the possibility of the *epoché*? For Husserl always justifies the *epoché* by insisting that a dissolution of experience into a non-harmonious 'tumult', in which no world would be experienced, is thinkable. Moreover, it is thinkable that consciousness should persist despite such dissolution (e.g. *Hua*, III, 91). The answer to this is that, in Husserl's view, such a dissolution of the world for a subject would be equivalent to – *the dissolution of the I* (K IV 3, 57). Radically to lose our grip on the world would be to lose our grip on ourselves. Indeed, given only such a tumult of experiences, Husserl flatly says, 'there is no I' (*Hua*, VI, 289). Elsewhere Husserl allows that such a world-less experience would still have an 'I-pole'; but he characterises the descent into such a condition as the *death* of the self (A VI 30, 52).[5] The self – not a mere I-pole, something that Husserl says 'is not an I' (A VI 30, 54), but a genuine self – is at the mercy of the world.

In order to understand this we need to appreciate that Husserl's transcendental ego, or transcendental 'I', is not to be equated with the all-constituting subject of 'consciousness' of Merleau-Ponty's intellectualists. For Husserl, the transcendental ego is not what is absolute. What is absolute is transcendental consciousness as such – more precisely, the 'standing-streaming primal present', characterised as an 'originally streaming constituting' – not any cognising 'ego' (e.g. *Hua*, XV, 590, 668; C 2 I, 15; C 3 I, 3–4). By contrast, the transcendental ego is itself constituted, indeed founded. This emerges from Husserl's writings at a number of points. First, the *unity* of a pure I, and the unity of its transcendental life, are constituted (*Hua*, IV, 112; *Hua*, XI, 98). Second, Husserl states that the transcendental I is 'something perpetually constituted as an identical pole of all acts' (*Hua*, XXXIV, 158). Third, the standing-streaming present is temporalised, producing what Husserl calls 'pre-time' (*Vorzeit*); and Husserl says that 'the I itself ... is constituted ... in this pre-time' (C 17 IV, 65). Elsewhere, similarly, he characterises absolute streaming life as 'primal being' (*Ursein*), and says of it that it necessarily contains a synthesis 'that constitutes the I' (*Hua*, XV, 287).[6] Moreover, every *act* of the ego is constituted (*Hua*, IV, 118). Finally, not only is the life of the transcendental ego constituted, it is *founded*: it is a 'founded intentional accomplishment' (C 2 I, 11). One response in the face of such statements by Husserl is to suggest that what he means is that the transcendental ego *constitutes itself* in the respects mentioned – something that would preserve an all-constituting status for the transcendental ego. Husserl certainly does employ the concept of self-constitution (e.g. *Hua*, I, 100, marginal note; C 17 II, 30; C 17 V 2, 85).[7] However, he also gives us more details about the constitution of the ego that are simply incompatible with such a suggestion.

Let us begin by considering Husserl's claim that the *unity* of the life of the transcendental ego is constituted. If this is constituted by the transcendental ego, then this ego must, in itself, have a 'prior' unity that it then bestows on its temporalised life. But this is not at all what Husserl says. What he says, rather, is that the unity of the pure ego is itself constituted as a unity *in relation to the unity of the stream of experience*, and that a persisting I cannot be constituted unless a persistent stream of experiences is constituted (*Hua*, IV, 112–3). Now, and this is what is crucial, the unity of a stream of consciousness is itself *passively* constituted: 'The individual egological life, taken as immanent temporality, is passively constituted in immanent time' (B I 32 I, 16).[8] This passive constitution is a 'passive, primal-associative temporalisation within the lasting streaming' (C 16 VI, 29). Such passivity is important in the present connection, because by characterising something as passive Husserl means that *the ego is not involved* (e.g. *Hua*, XI, 323). Hence he can designate this domain of constituting, temporalising association as the 'non-ego' (B III 9, 23). When he discusses the various levels of constitution, Husserl says that 'on the lowest level we do not yet have an ego' (D 13 XXI, 124). In short, an I emerges from, and is constantly sustained by, 'pre-egoic' processes in consciousness. There is a lower-level ego-less 'streaming' that *founds* the structure of the ego, a lower level that Husserl characterises as 'radically pre-egoic' (*radikal Vor-Ichliche*) (*Hua*, XV, 598). It is on this pre-egoically constituted stream of experiences that the transcendental ego *depends* (E III 2, 18). Hence, Husserl can speak of a *passive genesis* in which the ego is constituted (B IV 12, 2–3).

The transcendental ego is dependent not only on its passively synthesised stream of consciousness, it is also dependent on the objects that are constituted (or 'pre-constituted') in that flowing life. 'The I', writes Husserl, 'is only possible as the subject of an "environment", only possible as a subject that has opposite it, as pre-given, things, objects, indeed temporal objects, realities in the widest sense' (E III 2, 22–3). And again, 'The transcendental ego ... is what it is only in relation to intentional objects. ... It is, therefore, an essential property of the ego constantly to have ... systems, and indeed harmonious systems, of intentionality' (*Hua*, I, 99–100). The life of the transcendental ego depends upon objects being constituted for that life, and the coherence of that life depends upon the harmoniousness of the objects so constituted. If these objects are themselves constituted passively and pre-egoically, once again the ego will be seen to be dependent upon what is simply *prior* to it. At the lowest levels of constitution this is certainly the case. The first 'object-like' things are hyletic unities.[9] These are constituted in what Husserl calls a 'primal consciousness' (*Urbewusstsein*), which all I-related consciousness presupposes and to which it is originally directed; a primal consciousness that Husserl locates in an 'extra-egological [*ausserichlich*] sphere of inwardness' that constitutes an 'environment' for the I. This primal consciousness is 'hyletic primal consciousness', and is characterised as 'alien to the I' (*ichfremd*) and as prior to every *cogito* and every comportment of the I (*Ich-Verhalten*). It is what first 'affects' the I (E III 2, 22).[10] If the domain of passive synthesis extends beyond these hyletic unities and encompasses *worldly* objects, Husserl's claim that the transcendental ego is dependent on its world will be justified and fully integrated into his philosophy as a whole. And extend beyond them it does, as we shall now see.

Husserl's transcendental ego does not *impose* rational ordering on neutral material, but *finds itself* already in a world. Although Husserl often writes of the transcendental ego as constituting the world, this is not, for him, strictly true.[11] For the world, too, is constituted through *passive synthesis*: 'What in life confronts us as, so to say, a finished existent merely physical thing ... is given in the originality of the *it itself* in the synthesis of passive experience' (*Hua*, I, 112). Elsewhere he writes that the manifold of experience results in a unity of an experiential object through 'passive synthesis' (*Hua*, IX, 99). As I have said, by 'passive' Husserl means that which is without the participation of the ego. Husserl re-states this point in the present connection: every turning of attention on to an object presupposes that 'a passive intentionality, in which the I does not yet hold sway, has already in itself constituted an object by which the I-pole has been affected and determined to activity [*actus*]' (*Hua*, IX, 209). That is why Husserl says that passively constituted worldly objects are 'pre-given' to the ego (e.g. *Hua*, I, 112). Perhaps, however, it will be suggested that, although the I is not specifically active in the constitution of worldly objects, the processes of passive synthesis in which such objects are constituted are yet governed by the categories of the understanding: a thesis that would still amount to a form of intellectualism. Not even this can be said, however; for what governs passive synthesis is not the 'understanding'. The understanding, rather, presupposes such synthesis; passive synthesis functions as a 'support' for possible, later conceptualisation and categorial formations (*Hua*, IX, 99). What governs passive synthesis is, rather, mere *association*, the 'universal principle of passive genesis' (*Hua*, I, 113), something that, Husserl insists, 'could not be more different from causality in the sense of the "category"' (*Hua*, XI, 386). It is, he plainly says, 'sub-personal' (ibid.). Causality proper rests upon this pre-personal 'support'. Moreover, causality itself is not a 'category' that understanding imposes on experience, but a 'style' that the world is experienced as having (e.g. *Hua*, IX, 102). For Husserl, as for Merleau-Ponty, 'form' arrives with the world.

To be sure, physical objects in the full sense, as identifiable and re-identifiable particulars, are not constituted solely through passive synthesis. They are, rather, constituted in what Husserl calls 'receptivity', which is a form of 'activity' involving the ego, a form of 'I-spontaneity', albeit at the lowest level (Husserl 1973b, 79; *Hua*, IV, 335). Husserl calls receptivity a form of spontaneity because it involves the ego turning its attention on to something that has 'affected' it. It involves the ego *grasping* (*erfassen*) an object. 'Apprehending' (*auffassen*) something as an object presupposes grasping it; indeed, apprehension is an 'intentional derivation' from grasping (*Hua*, IV, 23). As I say, according to Husserl the constitution of worldly objects involves not sheer passivity, but such receptivity: 'Space is the form of sensibility, having developed through receptivity, and so is already not pure sensibility. Sensible nature is constituted in mere receptivity, the world of sensible things with their sensible forms: time, space, substantiality-causality' (*Hua*, IV, 335).[12] Our ability to apprehend any fundamental type of object *as* such presupposes that there has been a 'primal establishment' (*Urstiftung*) of such a type of object in our experience: an occasion when such an object was constituted for us for the *first* time. Our apperceptions have a *genesis*. Such a primal establishment will not be a matter of sheer passivity; it will, as we have just seen, involve receptivity. But the *synthesis* through which the object is constituted will be wholly passive. For although receptivity involves the active turning of attention on to an object, this is the sum total of the ego's contribution: it explicitly 'takes in' as an object something that, even as regards its unity, is synthesised in sheer passivity or sensibility. As the term itself implies, in receptivity the ego simply *receives* what is passively synthesised. Even when we are fully attending to an object, perhaps even 'explicating' it in terms of its parts and features, the object appears in the 'clearly passive synthesis' of its manners of appearing (*Hua*, I, 112). Hence, Husserl characterises the genesis of our apperceptions as a *passive genesis* (*Hua*, I, 113). Cognition, as an *act* of an *ego*, is for Husserl, as much as it was for Heidegger, a secondary, founded intentional accomplishment, since it presupposes the existence of objects on to which its attentive regard can be directed. As Husserl says, 'I can know the world only if I am myself already in the world' (C 17 II, 7).

Although, at the sub-personal level of sensibility, all *synthesis* is entirely passive, everything is not sheer passivity, even apart from the issue of attentional advertence. Two sorts of 'activity' are necessary for the pre-constitution of worldly objects at this fundamental level, though neither is an activity specifically of the ego. The first is that of *instinctive striving* and instinctive *drives*. 'In the beginning', writes Husserl, 'there is instinctive striving' (C 13 I, 6). All constitution presupposes instinctive drives (E III 9, 4). Intentionality proper arises out of what Husserl calls 'drive-intentionality' and 'instinct-intentionality' (A VII 13, 20; C 8 II, 1). What will later become fully fledged 'objects' for a fully fledged intentional subject operating at the level of 'being', are first disclosed, at a level of 'pre-being' (e.g. A VI 34, 34), in the *satisfaction* of instinctive desires (e.g. C 13 I, 6; C 16 IV, 36; E III 3, 5).[13] The first unities that are there *for* a developing consciousness are 'interest-formations' (C 13 I, 6). Consciousness's fundamental relation to the world is to be found at this level of instinctive striving. What Husserl calls the 'primal child' (*Urkind*) is already 'instinctively oriented towards the world' (E III 3, 5); the fulfilment of instinct-intentionality is already 'world-directed' (C 8 II, 16). One could not wish for a more 'engaged', 'existential' relation between the self and the world than we find here at the basis of Husserl's account of intentionality.

An essential precondition for the constitution of fully fledged worldly objects – and this brings us to our second essential form of activity – is the role of *kinaesthesis* in perception. Kinaesthesis is our sense of actively moving our bodies. Although it is an expression in consciousness of activity, the movements that they express are not 'willed [*willkürlich*] actions' (Husserl 1973b, 84). Originally they are instinctive (C 16 IV, 16; E III 9, 23). What is essential here is that there be a dependence of the position of elements in a sensory field on such movements. The sort of thing Husserl has in mind is the fact that when I move my head from side to side, the elements in my visual field are laterally displaced, and that when I approach an object, it comes to occupy a larger portion of my visual field. Only when there is such dependence, Husserl repeatedly insists, are sensory appearances constituted as appearances *of* physical objects. Kinaestheses therefore play an 'absolutely necessary' role in the constitution of physical objects (*Hua*, V, 121; cf. *Hua*, XI, 14–5, *Hua*, VI, 108,

164, 220 [106, 161, 217]). Conversely, nothing more is needed for the constitution of a thing in space than such an interplay between sensory data and the kinaestheses. Given that the lowest level of passive synthesis has done its work in constituting both a stream of consciousness and different sense-fields with their sensory unities and discontinuities (Husserl 1973b, 75), an (attentive) appreciation of the sensory-kinaesthetic dependencies *suffices* for the original constitution of spatial objects. As Husserl says, the 'apprehension' of sensory data as exhibiting aspects of a thing in space is *motivated* by the interrelated kinaestheses, which, by the same token, themselves receive an apprehension (*Hua*, IV, 57). Apprehensions of sensory data as 'adumbrations' of physical things 'result from' the kinaestheses on which the flow of the data depend (*Hua*, XIII, 332).[14] All that is now required for the constitution of physical objects is an interrelation between the various senses to produce an 'inter-sensory thing' – which is a matter of association – and the appreciation of the way such objects causally interact – which is simply a mater of observation. A good indication of all this is Husserl's lecture series *Ding und Raum* (*Hua*, XVI). Here he gives a detailed account of the constitution of physical objects; and although the account is complex, it never exceeds the bounds I have just outlined. At no point is any reference made to anything remotely resembling categories of the understanding. The constitutions involved in the account are all 'extra-egologically' driven. So when Husserl's analysis of the perception of worldly objects postulates an 'apprehension' or 'apperception' of sensory data, or 'intentional *morphé*' in addition to sensory '*hylé*', this should not be read in an intellectualistic manner.[15] Apperception, at least at the level of the constitution of the physical world, is, Husserl repeatedly affirms, constituted through association (*Hua*, XI, 445).[16]

Because the world is constituted pre-egologically, it does not have the transparency to understanding that Merleau-Ponty's intellectualists ascribe to it. In the first place, there is no guarantee that the world will match up to the dictates of the understanding or reason. As Iso Kern pointed out long ago, Husserl's often derided *epoché* is actually one aspect of Husserl's anti-intellectualism.[17] Husserl regarded his own commitment to the possibility of a dissolution of the world, and, therefore, the mere contingent possibility of a scientific understanding of nature, as being in opposition to neo-Kantianism. At one point Husserl characterises neo-Kantianism as holding that 'nature is a necessary product of consciousness as rational consciousness. Science not only exists as a fact: there should and must be science' (B IV 9, 21, cited in Kern 1964, p. 297). Husserl consistently distances himself from any such idea. It is not possible to know with insight (*einsehen*) that consciousness must unfold in a harmonious, rational way, for no such thing is determined by the essence of consciousness (*Hua*, III, 91). 'That consciousness must be rational', he writes elsewhere, 'admits of no proof ... [I]t is not "necessary"' (B I 4, 2).[18] Hence, he repeatedly refers to the reality of the world and, correlatively, the harmoniousness of experience, as a Faktum – a sheer given fact (e.g. *Hua*, VII, 220).

Indeed, he can even write of it as an 'irrational fact' (*Hua*, XVI, 289; cf. VII, 188). That consciousness constitutes a world, and thereby conscious subjects, is, as Husserl repeatedly says, a 'wonder' (e.g. *Hua*, VII, 394). Now, the wonder is that the course of experience, which is beyond the control of the subject and appears as wholly contingent, is harmonious and indefinitely harmonisable; or, as he puts it in the passage just cited, that reason has a 'field of application'. Husserl did, indeed, believe that this was so. For the actual perceiving subject, however, such ultimate rationality is a mere presumption and pretension. Indeed, our cognitive life, Husserl says, is a matter of pretension from beginning to end (e.g. K III 2, 9). This is because the rational harmonisability of experience has an infinite scope, which we cannot possibly plumb even in principle. We are, as Husserl remarks at one point, finite amidst infinite horizons, so that everything is hidden from us – even our own being. All cognition exists in a relativity (A V 10, 22).[19] The world is one of 'vague and flowing typicality' (Husserl 1973b, 44). 'There is', Husserl writes elsewhere, 'no fixed world for us – though another world than the world for us, with all its vague ... horizons, has for us not the least sense' (*Hua*, XV, 212). Our life, therefore, is not 'ideally constructible': it is not a 'logical' life (B I 32 I, 19).[20]

Our life is not a 'logical' life because it, and its world, are constituted before an ego possessed of understanding and reason is on the scene. Husserl endorses the traditional distinction between 'reason' and 'sensibility', and gives the prior, determining role to the latter:

> In the sphere of sensibility ... we have associations, perseverances, determining tendencies etc. These 'make' the constitution of nature. But they go yet further ... all mental life [Leben des Geistes] is pervaded by the 'blind' operation of associations, drives, and feelings that are stimuli and determining grounds for drives, tendencies that emerge in obscurity, etc., which determine the subsequent course of consciousness according to 'blind' rules.
>
> (*Hua*, IV, 276–7)

So Husserl was no intellectualist. In particular, according to him, 'before' or 'beneath' the ego we have an existence that has, in Merleau-Ponty's words, 'already sided with the world' (*PhP*, 216/251), and has done so in and through the body. This should come as no surprise if we believe Merleau-Ponty himself. For he refuses to characterise Husserl as an intellectualist, at least after his early period. The mature Husserl's position was, in Merleau-Ponty's own words, that of 'existentialism' (*PhP*, 274 n1/320 n46). Given that Merleau-Ponty has staked out his own position as the only alternative to both empiricism and intellectualism, and given that Husserl subscribed to neither of these, it straightforwardly follows that Husserl already occupied the position that Merleau-Ponty has staked out for himself.

III

So what, then, *is* new in the *Phenomenology of Perception*? The answer, I suggest, is a certain emphasis on the autonomous unity of the body, the way this is explicated, and the centrality that is given to it in Merleau-Ponty's account of perception.

I remember, when I first read the *Phenomenology of Perception*, being particularly struck by two passages. The first is the following:

> If I stand in front of my desk and lean on it with both hands, only my hands are stressed, and the whole of my body trails behind them like the tail of a comet. It is not that I am unaware of the whereabouts of my shoulders or back, but these are simply swallowed up in the position of my hands, and my whole posture can be read, so to speak, in the pressure they exert on the table.
>
> (*PhP*, 100/115)

A similar point is made in the following passage:

> If I am sitting at my table and I want to reach the telephone, the movement of my hand towards it, the straightening of the upper part of the body, the tautening of the leg muscles are superimposed on each other. I desire a certain result and the relevant tasks are spontaneously distributed amongst the appropriate segments.
>
> (*PhP*, 149/172)

The second passage that originally struck me was the one in which Merleau-Ponty discusses what typically happens when you pull off an insect's leg: in terms of its moving around, it immediately accommodates to the situation. If, however, two of the insect's legs are tied together, its movement is considerably encumbered (*PhP*, 78/90). Although Merleau-Ponty is here discussing an insect, he clearly thinks that we, too, are like this in essential respects. What such passages bring out is the way in which the body *takes care of itself*. It has, as it were, a *life of its own*: one, moreover, that possesses an *organic unity*.

The account of human action that such passages suggest is radically anti-'Cartesian'.[21] One does not have to hold, like Descartes himself, that when we act we stand to our bodies like a pilot to his ship in order to find such passages challenging.[22] Any theory (and they are legion) that attempts an exhaustive and exclusive classification of body-movements into 'mere' physical movements on the one hand and 'voluntary' actions on the other on the grounds that the former lack and the latter possess some controlling, conscious mental process, is seriously challenged by such examples. A good, scientifically documented example, to supplement Merleau-Ponty's own, that brings out the same problem for such theories is the fact that when we reach to grasp an object, as soon as our arm begins to move our fingers take up a posture that is adapted to the final act of grasping (see Jeannerod 1986). In such cases we are typically *wholly* unaware of this incipient movement of our fingers; no 'intention' or 'pro-attitude' is directed towards it. And yet it is not a 'mere' physical movement. Particularly striking in this connection are the cases where such proleptic bodily adjustments are found in an appropriate form in subjects who, as a result of brain damage, have no conscious 'cognitive' awareness of the shape, size or orientation of the objects towards which such movements are directed.[23] One is reminded of Merleau-Ponty's remark that such bodily movement is 'magically at its completion' (*PhP*, 104/119).

This issue is sometimes discussed these days in terms of the contrast between *body-image* and *body-schema*.[24] Shaun Gallagher has done as much as anyone to bring out the importance of the distinction between these two (see Gallagher 1986). Of the two, only the former is consistent with a 'Cartesian' account of action as that which is under the control of 'consciousness'. For the body-image is a matter of our body being *mentally represented*. The body-schema, by contrast, as Gallagher puts it, 'plays an active role in monitoring and governing posture and movement' (Gallagher 1995, 228). It plays this role independently of our conscious awareness of our body. Not only do we commonly act, and act 'voluntarily', without our mind being on what we are doing; not only are there aspects to any bodily performance that, even when we are consciously intent upon our performance, escape our conscious attention or monitoring; it is also the case that consciously attending to the details of a bodily performance typically inhibits the smooth execution of it. The body-schema operates 'anonymously'. Moreover, the body-image is *partial*, whereas the body-schema, being concerned with the active powers of our body as such, is holistic. Merleau-Ponty's discussions of the body, taken as a whole, clearly show a recognition of the body-schema so understood. Its holistic character is stated in connection with Merleau-Ponty's first reference to the body-schema, when he says that we are in 'undivided possession' of our bodies (*PhP*, 98/113). The three examples that I used to inaugurate this discussion themselves embody an appreciation of the body-schema. And in more discursive vein Merleau-Ponty can explicitly deny that the body-image is a collection of sensations or mental 'contents': it is, rather, a 'law of constitution', anterior to such sensations, that makes any association among bodily sensation possible (*PhP*, 99/114).

Is any such recognition of the body-schema to be found in Husserl's writings? As I have said, I have turned to this topic because, here, I believe, we can find in Merleau-Ponty a significant development of Husserl's thought. Shaun Gallagher, however, has argued both that Husserl did not recognise anything approximating to the body-schema, and also that he was in principle precluded from doing so. This I certainly want to contest. According to Gallagher, the body-schema, since it is essentially a non-conscious ability, is undiscoverable by the methods of transcendental phenomenology, since the latter is restricted to examining *consciousness*. For Husserl, according to Gallagher, intentionality appears *ex nihilo*, a pure spontaneity that begins at the noetic act of consciousness and moves in the direction of the noema. Everything of importance happens in full phenomenological view, 'out in front' of the noetic act. Husserl ignores the 'from whence' of the act ... [T]he body is reduced to a perceived object and appears to have no role in the production of perceptual experience.

Hence 'the prenoetic role of the body schema is impenetrable to phenomenological reflection' (Gallagher 1995, 232–3). This, however, as the previous section of this paper demonstrates, is a serious misrepresentation of Husserl's position. Much of what Husserl refers to as 'consciousness' is *unconscious*. For example, the most fundamental 'accomplishment' of consciousness, that on which all other constitution is founded, is the synthesis of inner time. Is this conscious? Obviously not, since it is the pre-condition for the consciousness of anything at all, even oneself. Indeed, all 'passive synthesis', of which this is but one example, is accomplished behind the back of 'consciousness' in the everyday sense. Such synthesis occurs without any involvement by the ego, and serves to constitute whatever is 'pre-given' to the ego. Husserl also discusses many states of consciousness that are unconscious: such as our reservoir of memories, sleep, and the 'involuted' condition of monads prior to and subsequent to their 'waking', conscious life (see Smith 2003, 92–5, 202–3). It should come as no surprise, therefore, when we find Husserl referring to a 'phenomenology of the unconscious' (*Hua*, XI, 154). Moreover, and most pertinently to our present enquiry, Husserl emphasises, over and over again, the centrality to transcendental consciousness of *abilities*. Let just one passage serve to illustrate this: 'Effective subjectivity is necessarily more than actual intentional life ... it consists also, and continually, in its abilities' (*Hua*, XVII, 218). In defence of his interpretation Gallagher does cite Husserl as stating that 'somatology' can be based only on 'the direct somatic perception that every empirical investigator can effect of his own body' (Gallagher 1995, 232). But 'based on' is not the same as 'limited to'. Gallagher's own claims about the nature of the body-schema are certainly 'based on' explicit perception of the body, for otherwise he would know nothing of it. Abilities can only be recognised through their exercise; and we must be conscious of their exercise if we are to become cognisant of the abilities.

So Husserl *could* recognise the body-schema. Is there any evidence that he did? Husserl does often refer to the body as a unity. Although sometimes what he seems to have in mind is just the body-image (e.g. *Hua*, XIII, 44), sometimes this is not the case. It is not the case, for example, when he discusses the unity of the body in relation to kinaesthesis. The body, he writes, is a *system* of members, a *system* of organs (*Hua*, XIII, 331), a *unity* of perceptive organs (*Hua*, IX, 196–7); and something counts as an organ for Husserl only thanks to kinaesthesis (*Hua*, VI, 109 [107]). Each of us has *one* kinaesthetic system, in which all individual kinaestheses are 'bound together' in a unity (*Hua*, VI, 108

[106]). Our bodily movements are 'amalgamated into the unity of a complete system' (*Hua*, IX, 197). The term *gesamt* – 'complete' or 'total' – is very frequently employed by Husserl in this context. He writes again, for instance, of the 'availability of the systematically constituted total kinaestheses' (*Hua*, XI, 428), and says of the 'familiar, total system of kinaestheses' that it is 'actualised' in each particular kinaesthetic situation (*Hua*, VI, 109 [107]). This emphasis on the kinaesthetic unity of the body is significant not so much because we are not normally aware of kinaestheses – though that is true, and Husserl stresses the fact (e.g. *Hua*, V, 122). For it is not that the body-schema is just attentionally recessive; it is essentially non-conscious. It would, indeed, be a 'category mistake' to suppose it to lurk at the fringe of consciousness. Such kinaesthetic unity is significant, rather, in two respects. First, Husserl explicates the *scope* of kinaesthesis in terms of *abilities*. The unitary 'system' of kinaesthesis is, Husserl says, the system 'of my kinaesthetic "I can"' (*Hua*, IV, 330). One's original relation to one's body consists, in essential part, in the fact that one actively 'governs' or 'holds sway over' one's body in a way that is expressed by kinaesthesia. So something is part of the unitary system of my body if I *can* move it (*Hua*, IX, 107; *Hua*, VI, 220 [217]). So the unity of the body, for Husserl, consists in a set of *abilities*, not in any supposed body 'image'. Second, such 'governed' actions need not be consciously controlled. For one thing, many actions are *habitual*. Husserl often characterises the I as an I of habits (e.g. *Hua*, I, §32, *Hua*, XIV, 59). Significantly, in the present connection, he can include *action* in this, characterising the 'habitus' of an I, in part, in terms of 'determinate habits of acting' (*Hua*, XIII, 244). We all have 'habitual kinaestheses' and 'familiar, habitual' systems of movements (D 13 I). We all have, as he also puts it, a *kinaesthetic habituality* (*Hua*, VI, 109 [107]). He also refers to 'kinaesthetic complexes' and their 'way of running off' (*Ablaufsweise*) (*Hua*, XIII, 331). Husserl does not, therefore, suppose that all 'voluntary' action is consciously supervised by the subject; many motor complexes have become for us 'second nature'. Indeed, and more generally, Husserl explicitly distinguishes between action that is *willkürlich* – involving the will, decision, 'consciousness' – from a prior, more basic form of activity: '*Before* the will and its active thesis of the "fiat"', he writes, 'lies action as instinctive action, e.g., the non-willed [*unwillkürlich*] "I move", the non-willed "I reach" for my cigar: I desire it and do it "without any further ado"' (*Hua*, IV, 258). And again: 'Some sensuous urge [*Trieb*] stirs, say the urge to smoke. I reach for a cigar and light it whilst my attention . . . is entirely elsewhere . . . Here we have "unconscious" I-affection and reaction' (*Hua*, IV, 338). And yet again:

> But what if I move my hand without intention [*unwillkürlich*]? Why does it move? Because the position of the hand is uncomfortable. Or 'I do not rightly know why', I was not paying attention to it, though the reason does lie in what is psychic and its obscure attractions and motivations.
>
> (*Hua*, IV, 260)

15

Husserl refers, in this connection, to a 'natural mechanism' that is a function of *drives*, one that sustains what he calls the 'mechanical I-do' – an I-do that is at the level of 'mere nature' (*Hua*, IV, 338). Interestingly, it is in this connection that Husserl employs the very image used by Merleau-Ponty, in a passage I cited earlier, to describe the body of the person leaning on a desk: that of the tail of a comet. 'Even each free act', he writes, 'has its comet's tail of nature' (*Hua*, IV, 339).[25]

Nevertheless, none of this receives the kind of central emphasis that we find in Merleau-Ponty. Moreover, various other elements in Merleau-Ponty's thinking cluster around this account of the body in a way that is absent from Husserl's thinking; and the concept itself is expounded in a way that significantly differs from Husserl. One of the most salient aspects of this is the 'existential' characterisation of the body and its unity.

IV

For Merleau-Ponty the unity of the body is an *existential unity*. Indeed, it is this that his term 'body-schema' primarily expresses. One thing that Merleau-Ponty means when he characterises the body in terms of 'existence' is that the body is defined by its 'tasks', its 'projects'. He writes, for example, that my body 'appears to me as an attitude directed towards a certain existing or possible task' (*PhP*, 100/114). Hence, the spatiality of the body is not one of 'location', but of 'situation'. The 'here' of the whole body is its 'situation in face of its tasks' (*PhP*, 100/115); and a situation is delimited in terms of objects offering themselves as 'poles of action' (*PhP*, 106/122). To have a body-schema is to *be in the world* (*PhP*, 101/115). And conversely: the body is what it is by being 'polarised', in the face of objects, by its tasks – which is the same as having (or being) an 'existence towards' objects (*PhP*, 101/115).

This repeated reference to *tasks* when expounding the nature of the body schema may bring to mind one of one of the most obvious superficial differences between Husserl's and Merleau-Ponty's accounts of perception: namely, that whereas Husserl standardly takes *sight* as his principal example of perception, and often uses visual terms metaphorically to stand for perception as such, Merleau-Ponty assigns such a role to *grasping* things.[26] He often uses this term to stand for our relation to the world – our being in the world, or 'existence' – as such. Through my body I am 'at grips with the world' (*PhP*, 303/353); and he characterises the body as 'a comprehensive hold on the world' (*PhP*, 303/353). This difference is, however, more than superficial. By reference to Gelb and Goldstein's accounts of their patients, Merleau-Ponty argues that concrete movements and acts of grasping enjoy a 'privileged position' in our commerce with the world (*PhP*, 103/118). The body 'surges' towards objects to be *grasped* (*PhP*, 106/121). Our environment is a set of *manipulanda*; our surrounding world is 'a collection of possible points upon which ... bodily action may operate' (*PhP*, 105/121).

What is therefore at the heart of Merleau-Ponty's philosophy of perception, in a way that it is not in Husserl's, is existence, or being-in-world, conceived of in terms of *motility*. 'Already motility, in its pure state, possesses the basic power of giving a meaning' (*Sinngebung*) (*PhP*, 142/164). Motility gives us 'a new meaning of the word "meaning"' (*PhP*, 146/170). Such motility is not just active movement – something that is certainly at the heart of Husserl's account of perception, as we have seen – but action *on* or *towards* objects, the primary example of which, as I have said, is grasping things. In this connection Merleau-Ponty famously writes of *motor intentions* and *motor intentionality* (e.g. *PhP*, 110/127, 317/370). Motility is, he states, 'basic intentionality'. Consciousness is 'in the first place not a matter of "I think that" but of "I can"' (*PhP*, 137/159). He often quotes Grünbaum with approval, particularly for making motility 'into an original mode of intentionality or meaning': something that, he says, 'amounts to conceiving man, no longer in terms of consciousness, but in terms of existence' (*PhP*, 191 n1/222 n19).

As I have said, movement, in the form of kinaesthesis, is absolutely central in Husserl's account of perception. But he, in contrast to Merleau-Ponty, tends to focus on the role of movement in getting different perspectives on objects, rather than on cases of active movement *towards* objects – cases where, as Merleau-Ponty says, movement is 'magically at its completion' (*PhP*, 104/119). Nevertheless, such activity directed towards objects is not only not ignored by Husserl, he actually gives it a foundational role in his account of intentionality. For, as I briefly indicated in the second section above, according to Husserl instinct and drives are at the basis of consciousness. What is important in this, in the present connection, is not only that the kinaestheses are essentially involved at this level, but that they are so involved in virtue of the fact that drives are drives to *satisfy* innate, instinctive needs. For such needs can, of course, be satisfied only by *acting on* what attracts us. What prefigures fully object-directed intentionality is what Husserl calls the 'disclosure' of an instinctive tendency in satisfaction. Still, although this is certainly there in Husserl's thought, and, as I say, at a fundamental level, it can hardly be said that it takes centre-stage as it does in the philosophy of Merleau-Ponty.

Moreover, Merleau-Ponty spells out the unity of the body, in a way that Husserl does not, in terms of the unitary nature of the tasks themselves as they present themselves to the subject. The unity of the body, he says, is the unity of an open set of equivalences in relation to possible action:

> The normal subject has his body not only as a system of present positions, but besides, and thereby, as an open system of an infinite number of equivalent positions directed to other ends. What we have called the body schema is precisely this system of equivalents, this immediately given invariant whereby the different motor tasks are instantaneously transferable.
>
> (*PhP*, 141/163)

The unity of the body with its body-schema therefore presupposes objects to be acted upon, objects that are presented *as* targets of possible action, in relation to which our body can be polarised and unified: 'We grasp the unity of our body only in that of the thing; and it is by taking things as our starting point that our hands, eyes, and all our sense-organs appear to us as so many interchangeable instruments' (*PhP*, 322/375).

<h1 style="text-align:center">V</h1>

For Merleau-Ponty the unity of the body extends, however, beyond such dynamic task-oriented equivalences between the various parts of the body. There is also a unity to the various senses in virtue of the existential unity of the body. The unity of the senses, writes Merleau-Ponty, is not a matter of their 'subsumption under a primary consciousness, but their never-ending integration into one knowing organism' (*PhP*, 233/271). By the 'body' Merleau-Ponty means all our perceptual faculties as integrated into a project towards the world. The body is an 'intersensory system', and different senses can communicate because they are 'inseparable constituents' of that system (*PhP*, 119 n2/ 137 n48). This is explicitly related by Merleau-Ponty to the notion of the body-schema: 'With the notion of the body-schema we find that not only is the unity of the body described in a new way, but also, through this, the unity of the senses and of the object' (*PhP*, 235/273). And in general, perceptual syntheses are 'supported by the prelogical unity of the body-schema' (*PhP*, 233/ 270). So, there are equivalences between the various senses just as, as we have seen, there are equivalences between the various parts of the body in relation to tasks: 'My body is a ready-made system of equivalents and transpositions from one sense to the other. The senses translate each other without any need of an interpreter, and are mutually comprehensible without the intervention of any idea' (*PhP*, 235/273). Furthermore, the unity of an object is correlative to the unity of the body:

> The sensory 'properties' of a thing together constitute one and the same thing, just as my gaze, my touch and all my other senses are together the powers of one and the same body integrated into one and the same action. ... Any object presented to one sense calls upon itself the concordant operation of all the others. ... I perceive a thing because I have a field of existence, and because each phenomenon, on its appearance, attracts towards that field the whole of my body as a system of perceptual powers.
>
> (*PhP*, 317–18/370)

Husserl, too, of course, emphasises that a physical object is an 'inter-sensory thing'; but this unity is not explicated as correlative to the unity of the body understood in terms of perceptual equivalencies in the way that it is in

Merleau-Ponty. Moreover, it is against this background that Merleau-Ponty can give weight to the phenomenon of *synaesthesia* in a way that is absent from the thought of Husserl. 'There is', writes Merleau-Ponty, 'a sense in saying that I see sounds or hear colours' (*PhP*, 234/272). Such a thing is possible for Merleau-Ponty because for him the *content* of perception is 'existential' (*PhP*, 53/62) – in a sense that we have still not yet exhausted. The articulations of an object are, he writes, 'those of our very existence' (*PhP*, 320/373). A thing adumbrates a 'mode of existence'; and to understand a thing is to take such a mode of existence up on our own account (*PhP*, 319/372). Sensory experience is 'the assumption of a form of existence' (*PhP*, 221/257). But what exactly do such assertions mean? Whenever we are active, we are so to a greater or lesser degree. When we are active we exercise and expend energy, to a greater or lesser degree. Any task calls for, and presents itself as calling for, a greater or lesser expenditure of effort and a greater or lesser accommodation to the task. Compare, for example, facing up to the task of shifting a table from one part of the room to another with picking up a teacup. Merleau-Ponty expresses this fact by saying that there is 'a certain energy in the pulsation of existence' (*PhP*, 80/92), a certain 'momentum' (*PhP*, 137/159), 'a certain rhythm of existence' (*PhP*, 213/248). Objects present themselves as possible foci of action, and their appearance calls for a certain accommodation in our 'rhythm of existence'. Since action always involves a certain level of energy, objects themselves are ultimately to be interpreted in terms of the way our existence is *modulated* in relation to them. The 'language', of which we saw Merleau-Ponty speak in the first section of this paper, is a language of *existence*, for our perception of the world, our primordial contact with being is, 'the assumption by the sentient subject of a form of existence to which the sensible points' (*PhP*, 221/257). The shapes and sizes of things, for example, 'merely provide a modality for this comprehensive hold on the world' (*PhP*, 303/353). And the experience of a 'sensible quality' is that 'of a certain mode of movement or of a form of conduct' (*PhP*, 234/272). Or, as he says more fully,

> When we say that red increases the compass of our reactions, we are not to be understood as having in mind two distinct facts – a sensation of redness and motor reactions – we must be understood as meaning that red, by its texture as followed and adhered to by our gaze, is already the amplification of our motor being.
>
> (*PhP*, 211/211)

The sensible not only has 'a motor and vital significance'; it is, writes Merleau-Ponty 'nothing other than a certain way of being in the world suggested to us from some point in space, and seized and acted upon by our body, provided that it is capable of doing so, so that sensation is literally a form of communion' (*PhP*, 212/246). From this perspective synaesthesia makes sense, since a quality in two different 'sense modalities' can elicit the same sort of existential modulation in the subject. If redness is a certain 'amplification of my motor being', so, too, could a certain musical chord be. 'When I say that I see a sound, I mean that I echo the vibration of the sound with my whole sensory being, and particularly with that sector of myself which is susceptible to colours' (PhP, 234/272). The essence of a colour, and more generally, the essence of any feature of the world, is, Merleau-Ponty is claiming, indissociable from the reaction it calls forth from us. Indeed, it is nothing other than such a call. Hence, he can describe the world as the 'congealed face of existence' (PhP, 234/272). It should hardly need saying that in all this, as compared with Husserl, we hear a distinctively new philosophical voice.

To conclude: I have suggested that there is nothing *radically* new in Merleau-Ponty, as compared with Husserl. They occupy essentially the same terrain in philosophical space. But over the last few sections we have, I believe, found in the pages of the *Phenomenology of Perception* a number of significant and original developments of the basic outlook that Merleau-Ponty and Husserl share: developments that are, I believe, sufficient reason, indeed, for us to celebrate Merleau-Ponty's achievement here today.

Notes

1 Heidegger was another important philosophical influence on Merleau-Ponty, of course. And so one could perhaps raise the question of originality in relation to Heidegger. In this paper, however, I am concerned solely with the issue of perception and the fundamental role that it plays in our relation to the world. Heidegger is not really relevant here, since he did not give perception such a foundational role. Indeed, as I have argued elsewhere, he did not really have an account of perception as such: see Smith 2002, 103–6.

2 All translations from Husserl are my own. References to *Hua* are to volumes of Husserl's works in the *Husserliana* series (see bibliography for details of volumes referred to and of English translations, where they exist). Page references are always to the *Husserliana* editions, which pagination is, with the exception of the *Crisis* (VI), indicated in the margins of the English translations. When I make reference to the *Crisis* I give two page references, the first being to the *Husserliana* edition, the second (in square brackets) to the English translation.

3 References such as this are to Husserl's unpublished manuscripts. I warmly thank the director of the Husserl Archives in Leuven, Professor Rudolf Bernet, for permission to consult manuscripts held there and to cite them in print.

4 This, and the following quotation, are cited in Mensch 1988, 151–2.

5 This and the previous passage from Husserl's manuscripts are both cited in Kern 1964, 294.

6 I should say that the sentence in question is grammatically ambiguous: it could conceivably mean that the I constitutes such a synthesis. But not only is this the less natural reading – thanks to Tanja Staehler for telling me this – I know of nowhere (else) where Husserl writes of *syntheses* being constituted. What are constituted are, rather, the products of such syntheses.

7 These passages are more significant than the fact that Husserl often uses the reflexive form of the verb 'to constitute' – 'X constitutes itself' – when discussing aspects of the transcendental ego. (Some of the passages I have cited above use this verbal form, though I have translated using the simple passive.) For Husserl uses this

reflexive verbal form as a mere stylistic variant for the passive 'is constituted'. This is borne out by the fact that he freely uses the reflexive form of the verb when he is dealing with the constitution of things – such as senses, physical objects, the world – that clearly cannot, as transcendental egos supposedly do, constitute *themselves*. (For senses, see A VII 13, 62; for physical objects, see *Hua*, XIV, 50 or XI, 292; for the world, see C 17 II, 30.)

8 This and the next five quotations from Husserl's manuscripts are cited in Mensch 1988, 93, 103, 86, 97, 126 and 84.

9 My 'object-like' translates '*objectives*' with scare-quotes.

10 Although it is beyond dispute that such unities are constituted without any contribution by the ego, I should say that there is a question whether they can be so constituted without them at least exercising some degree of affective attraction (*Reiz*) on the ego. (See, for example, *Hua*, XI, §34, and for a discussion of this issue see Steinbock 1995, 153–6 and Bégout 2000, 191–5). Even if such affective attraction is necessary for such constitution, this has no intellectualistic implications at all.

11 So why, it may be asked, does Husserl say it? Because in a broad sense it is true. The experiences in which objects are passively constituted are the ego's experiences, in the sense that the ego is the 'pole of identity' to which these experiences belong.

12 It is not the case that *all* constitution involves the attentional advertence of the ego. The most fundamental forms of passive constitution – such as those of the immanent temporality of the stream of consciousness, and of the unity of different sense-fields – do not. It is the constitution of *objects* that requires the subject's attention.

13 I have discussed this aspect of Husserl's though at somewhat greater length in Smith 2003, 149–56. For more extensive discussion see Lee 1993.

14 Elsewhere Husserl says that such kinaestheses condition (*bedingen*) both the course of appearances and appearing nature (*Hua*, XV, 580).

15 In his earlier writings Husserl did, indeed, model perceptual apprehension on the 'sense' that is involved in linguistic understanding. For a good account of how Husserl gradually 'de-intellectualised' his account of perception, see Welton 1983).

16 Husserl can, indeed, employ the term 'apperception' when he is dealing with constitution at a very basic level, before intentionality proper has even emerged: e.g. *Hua*, IV, 335.

17 Kern 1964, 293–303.

18 To show its necessity, he writes in this same manuscript, would be to prove the existence of God and His (necessary) teleological governance of the world. Now, Husserl did firmly believe in both these things – but only, as he says in this same passage, '*ex post*'. I take this to mean that God's existence is implied by the world (ultimately experience) being teleologically ordered, and that this is implied by there being an actual world. But our 'knowledge' that there is a world, although 'empirically apodictic' is, ultimately, a 'pretension'. All we ultimately have is the '*Urdoxa*': our practically unshakable belief in the reality of the world. As Husserl says, 'Experience is the force that vouches for the existence of the world' (*Hua*, XVI, 290).

19 This and the next quotation from Husserl's manuscripts are cited in Mensch 1988, 154 and 118 respectively.

20 Cited in Mensch 1988, 118.

21 I employ scare-quotes here because Descartes himself would have had no problem with Merleau-Ponty's examples. According to Descartes, when our mind is not intent upon what we are doing, the body operates purely mechanically – in the way that mere animal bodies always do: see, for example, Descartes' letter to Plempius for Fromondus, 3 October 1673. Merleau-Ponty's objection to this would not be, of course, that it over-intellectualises bodily action, but that it ignores the 'lived body' in favour of the realists' 'objective' body.

22 Descartes is well known for writing in the *Sixth Meditation* that we are *not* in our bodies as a pilot is in a ship. He makes this claim, however, in connection with *sensation*. What is less well known is that when it comes to our relation to our bodies in intentional action, Descartes *endorses* the image: see the final paragraph of the *Discourse on the Method*, Part V.

23 Such cases are reported and discussed in Milner and Goodale 1995, ch. 6.

24 When Merleau-Ponty discusses this aspect of the body's functioning, he himself employs the term *schéma corporel*. This term is, however, regularly translated by Colin Smith as 'body image'. I shall employ the translation 'body-schema': not only because that is closer to what Merleau-Ponty actually wrote, but, more importantly, given the distinction between the two concepts that I am about to discuss, it is clearly the body-*schema* that Merleau-Ponty has in mind.

25 In this passage, I should say, Husserl is primarily concerned with cognitive acts; but I take it that his claim has more general application.

26 The *gaze* is a very important notion in Merleau-Ponty, of course, but he often describes this in terms of bodily action on objects. The gaze, for example, is 'at grips with a visible world' (*PhP*, 351/409). Indeed, according to Merleau-Ponty, to look at an object is 'to plunge oneself into it' (*PhP*, 67/78).

2

WHAT DO WE SEE (WHEN WE DO)?[1]

Sean D. Kelly

The philosophical problem of what we see

My topic revolves around a very basic question. In its leanest, most economical form, this is the question: 'What do we see?' In this form, however, the question admits of at least three different interpretations. We can call these the epistemological, the metaphysical, and the intentional (or phenomenological) interpretations. In this introductory section I would like briefly to distinguish these ways of interpreting the philosophical problem of what we see; in the rest of the paper I will focus exclusively on problems that arise out of the intentional interpretation. In particular, I will try to show how, if the intentional question is answered properly, two important psychological theories of perception – one empiricist and the other cognitivist – both fail to account for what we see. Along the way I will suggest that a combination of phenomenological and analytic resources is necessary for a satisfactory treatment of the central philosophical problems concerning perception.

The basic question, 'What do we see?' has a rich history in modern philosophy, and so has a variety of interpretations. In the first place, one might understand it to be an epistemological question, perhaps one with sceptical overtones. On this reading, it is short for something like 'What things in the world are we justified in believing we see, given the possibility of evil demon scenarios and all the other impedimenta to genuine sight that have become the working tools of epistemologists over the last 350 years?' I shall not be concerned with the question in this sceptical sense. I intend the parenthetical addition to the question, namely, 'What do we see (when we do)?' to rule out discussion along these sorts of epistemological lines, at least for the purposes of this paper. In order to make this perfectly clear, I want to highlight at the start a certain bald-faced assumption I am making – the assumption that we do, at least sometimes, succeed in seeing things. Whether or not this assumption is true, however, will not affect the position I am defending.

Another (though related) way one might understand the question focuses on what the proper objects of perception are.[2] This is also a traditional interpretation of the philosophical problem of perception, and on this interpretation, the question 'What do we see?' leads eventually to debates about whether we perceive the things of the world directly or only indirectly and by means of some perceptual intermediary. A subsidiary question in traditional debate focuses on what the 'things in the world' really are anyway, so we might call this a metaphysical interpretation of the question. I will not be primarily interested in this interpretation of the problem of perception either, although I will, for the purposes of this paper, take a more or less undefended position with respect to it. Let me say, very briefly, then, what some of the going positions are.

In the first place, the ordinary person, who is sometimes called a 'direct or naive realist', is generally thought to believe that our perceptual experiences, if not infallible, are nevertheless trustworthy, by and large. On the whole, then, such a person typically believes that we are in some kind of direct or unmediated relation to the objects of perception. Furthermore, the naive realist is committed to the view that the proper objects of perception are just the familiar objects in our everyday world, the 'moderate-sized specimens of dry goods' that J. L. Austin so famously discussed.[3] This is the most straightforward of the metaphysical views about what we see.

Bishop Berkeley, in contrast to the naive realist, extends the ordinary notion of direct perception to the more radical view that the proper objects of perception are things about which the perceiver could not be mistaken – not just things about which he is generally correct.[4] This radical notion of the infallibility of perception, however, leads Berkeley rather quickly to the peculiar brand of idealism that he advocates, according to which physical objects – the 'things in the world' – are just collections of sensible ideas. Berkeley's kind of direct perception, then, when combined with his idealism, constitutes a second kind of metaphysical view about what we see.

Finally, both Berkeley and the naive realists might be contrasted with a kind of Lockean position that is sometimes called indirect realism. According to the indirect realist, the proper objects of perception are internal things – in the Lockean terminology, sensations or ideas. About this issue the indirect realist agrees with Berkeley. Unlike Berkeley, however, he believes further that it is possible, by means of these perceptual intermediaries, actually to perceive the objects of the everyday world. About this issue the indirect realist agrees with the ordinary Joe. This combination of Berkeley and naive realism, then, constitutes a third metaphysical view about what we see – one that is in some very general ways consonant with the cognitivism I will discuss in the fifth and sixth sections below. There is, of course, a wide variety of other possible positions on the metaphysical question concerning what we see. I shall not attempt to enumerate them here. Rather, for the purposes of this paper, I intend to side somewhat dogmatically with the naive realists, the people who believe both that we have a direct, unmediated relation to the objects of perception and that the proper objects of perception are just the familiar objects of the world. Although I will not attempt to defend this naive realism, I will highlight some passages that indicate it is a natural position for a phenomenologist to hold.

24

A third interpretation of the question 'What do we see?' understands it to be a question about the contents of perception. This is the intentional or phenomenological interpretation that I prefer. To ask about the contents of perception is different from asking about the objects of perception because often merely to say what object or property one is perceiving does not fully specify one's experience. If I see the wall to be white, then in some sense it seems right to say that the object of my perception is the whiteness, or more generally the colour, of the wall. But the whiteness of the wall seems to me different in different lighting contexts – now shady, now more shady, and now brightly lit – and although all of these are perceptions of the whiteness of the wall, they are qualitatively (and hence with respect to content) distinct. To put it in a phrase, I believe that our normal perceptual experience consists not only of seeing the world to be a certain way (properly specified in terms of the objects we perceive), but also of its seeming to us a certain way. To give a complete and accurate description of the way the world seems to us throughout a variety of different experiences of our seeing it to be a certain way – that project just is, as far as I can tell, the project of specifying the content of perceptual experience.

I want to take up that project here, albeit in a very limited form. In particular, I want to talk about what the relation is in our perceptual experience of them between (as one normally says) the objects we see and the properties we see those objects to have. By object and property, here, I mean nothing fancier than what we normally call things (tables, chairs, books, and the like) and what we normally understand to be their features (size, shape, and colour, to name a few). The analytic philosophical tradition agrees that to talk about how these are presented to us in experience is to give an account of 'perceptual content'. Christopher Peacocke's paper of the same title forms perhaps the locus classicus for the discussion (see Peacocke 1989). My main technique for approaching the problem, however, will be phenomenological; I take my clues here from the work of Martin Heidegger and above all Maurice Merleau-Ponty. The goal of the paper will be to show that a proper account of perceptual content invalidates two important psychological theories of perception.

What we see: the phenomenological interpretation of the question and the psychological theories that succumb to it

The starting point for my project, and indeed for (almost) any phenomenological project, is found in what might be called the anti-Cartesian belief that our primary relation to the ordinary world is direct and unmediated. This is the undefended naive realism I mentioned earlier; it can sometimes seem difficult to find a philosopher who actually holds this view (despite the fact that it was against this view that Berkeley and especially Russell and Ayer rebelled), but I believe the phenomenologists are sympathetic to at least some form of naive realism. As Heidegger says in *Being and Time*, it is clear that when I experience an object, '[I have] in view the entity itself and not, let us say, a mere "representation" of it' (Heidegger 1962, 196). And this is what Merleau-Ponty means when he says, 'I aim at and perceive a world ... [T]he world is what we perceive' (*PhP*, xvi/xvii, italics added).

That our perception of the ordinary world is direct and unmediated is something the phenomenologist believes on strictly phenomenological grounds, which is to say, in this case, strictly on grounds of descriptive accuracy. For there is no doubt that it would be a grossly inaccurate description of my experience to deny either that I often see, for instance, tables, or that I often see those tables to be, for instance, square. To paraphrase the English philosopher J. J. Valberg, when I look carefully at my experience I find nothing that defines it as an entity separate from the thing that it is an experience of; indeed, when I look carefully at my experience I find nothing but the ordinary world (Valberg 1992).[5]

But even if one accepts this kind of naive realism, there is still an important question about the way perceiving the things in the world seems to us. This problem is especially important in cases of so-called perceptual constancy, because different descriptions of the experience of these phenomena lead to widely varying psychological theories of perception. Following Merleau-Ponty, I hope to explain how two classic theories of perceptual constancy – one empiricist and the other cognitivist – are based on inaccurate descriptions of the phenomena involved.

I will approach this project in two stages. First, I will consider two related empiricist theories of perception – one from Bertrand Russell in *The Problems of Philosophy* (Russell 1959), and the other from the late-nineteenth-century German psychologist Ewald Hering. I will argue that these empiricist theories of perception fail to recognize an important aspect of perceptual experience: the dependence of a perceived property on the context in which it is perceived. This interpretation will make sense of a puzzling distinction that Merleau-Ponty emphasizes between a colour and the way the colour looks.

Next, I will consider a classic cognitivist account of perceptual constancy that is based on a notion of unconscious inference. I will argue that this account fails to recognize another important aspect of perceptual experience: the dependence of a perceived property on the object it is perceived to be a property of. This interpretation will make sense of the puzzling way in which Merleau-Ponty characterizes the phenomena of perceptual constancy: rather than understanding constancy as the maintenance of a constant property, Merleau-Ponty describes it as the phenomenon whereby an object maintains its colour, its shape, and its size. This sense of the belonging of the property to the object, I will argue, is central to any proper phenomenological account of what we see.

In what follows I will try to present and clarify these observations against the background of some familiar or updated versions of the traditional psychological views that Merleau-Ponty considers. In doing so, I hope to do justice to

Merleau-Ponty's observation that 'Nothing is more difficult than to have a sense for precisely what we see' (*PhP*, 58/67, translation modified).

The empiricist account of perceptual constancy

The phenomenon of perceptual constancy arises for a variety of perceptible properties like size, shape, colour, and many others that we see as constant for a given object throughout a variety of different perceptual contexts. A common example of perceptual constancy is found in the fact that there are many different viewpoints from which I see a table as square, for instance, even though the image projected from the table onto my retina from each of these perspectives is different, and in fact is rarely itself a square image. Similar examples can be found in the perception of colour under various lighting conditions, and in the perception of the size of an object as viewed from a variety of distances. A typical example in the case of colour is that coal looks black even in sunlight, and chalk looks white even in shadow, even though in these conditions the eye may receive much stronger light from the coal than it does from the chalk. Likewise, in the case of size constancy, a man continues to look the same size as he walks away from me, even though the size of the image his body casts onto my retina decreases with distance. With these descriptions in mind, let us take a took at the empiricist account of perceptual constancy and the theory of perception that arises from it.

The early sense-data views, like the one that Russell presents in the first chapter of *The Problems of Philosophy*, are not so much accounts of the phenomenon of perceptual constancy as they are denials of it. Or at least they are denials of it as a strictly perceptual phenomenon. Although Russell denies the phenomenon of perceptual constancy, however, he admits that we ordinarily speak as if we see objects to be the same colour, size, shape, and so on, throughout a variety of perceptual contexts. Russell's explanation of why we speak that way is similar to the empiricist account of perceptual constancy that I will consider in a moment, so I would like to start out with the more familiar Russellian view.

To begin, Russell denies that I see the table to be a constant colour throughout lighting contexts, insisting, rather, that I only believe it to be so. He says:

> Although I believe that the table is 'really' of the same colour all over [brown, in the example that Russell chooses], the parts that reflect the light look much brighter than the other parts, and some parts look white because of reflected light.
>
> (Russell 1959, 8)

On Russell's account, then, the colour we actually see the table to have can change dramatically depending upon the lighting context. If the light is very

27

bright, then even a brown table may look white; if the light is very low, then even a white table may look black. Furthermore, different parts of the table may be lit differently, and if this is the case, then each part will appear to be a different colour.

Russell admits that 'for most practical purposes these differences [across context] are unimportant' (Russell 1959, 9), but he thinks that for the philosopher they point toward a crucial insight about what we see when we see the colour of the table. 'It is evident from what we have found', he says, 'that there is no colour which pre-eminently appears to be the colour of the table, or even of any one particular part of the table – it appears to be of different colours from different points of view' (Russell 1959, 9).

Of course, this is not the way we ordinarily speak about the colour of the table, or even the way we ordinarily take ourselves to perceive the colour of the table; even Russell admits that one has to 'learn the habit of seeing things as they appear' (Russell 1959, 9) in order to see the colour of the table this way. But, nevertheless, he thinks that the way things appear in this special, detached attitude[6] tells us something important about what we really see, and therefore when he talks about the colour we normally attribute to the table, and, by extension, the colour we ordinarily believe ourselves to be seeing, he describes it as derivative from what we perceive from the detached perspective. The colour we normally believe the table to have, according to Russell, is just the colour we see it to have from the detached perspective when the perceptual context is normalized. Russell writes: 'When, in ordinary life, we speak of the colour of the table, we only mean the sort of colour which it will seem to have to a normal spectator from an ordinary point of view under usual conditions of light' (Russell 1959, 9–10).

Strictly speaking, then, it is clear that Russell's account entails the denial of the phenomenon of perceptual constancy as a perceptual phenomenon, since if we are considering what we actually see, according to Russell, then we do not see the table to have a constant colour in different lighting contexts. But since he admits that his account does not accord with what we normally believe about the world, or even with what we ordinarily believe about our own perceptual experience of the world, Russell has to postulate a relation between detached perception and ordinary belief. By postulating that the colour we ordinarily believe the table to have is just the colour of the table as seen from the detached perspective under normalized conditions, Russell independently discovered the basic principle behind the empiricist explanation of perceptual constancy that I will consider next.

The standard empiricist account of perceptual constancy was first proposed by the German psychologist Ewald Hering, writing at the end of the nineteenth century. At the centre of the account was a concept of 'memory colour' that is very much like the ordinarily perceived colour of an object as Russell understood it. The memory colour of a thing, according to Hering, is just the colour we see the thing to have in normal perceptual circumstances, where the normal circumstances are the ones in which we have most often seen the object's colour. Hering claimed that using the concept of memory colour, along with the fact that we have clues for determining whether the current perceptual context is a normal one, he could explain how it is that we are able to see the colour of an object as constant throughout a variety of perceptual contexts. If the context is normal, he claimed, then we experience the colour as it is presented to us currently. But if the context is perceivably abnormal – it is too dark, say, or too light – then we substitute our memory of the colour of the thing as seen in the normal context for our current perceptual experience of the colour. In this way, Hering argued, we see an object to have its memory colour even in situations where, from the detached perspective, it does not appear to have that colour at all. That is to say, the colour is seen as constant throughout perceptual contexts, because in every case it turns out to be the memory colour that, in the end, we experience.[7]

Criticism of the empiricist account

This is an ingenious but, in the end, an inaccurate account of colour constancy. The central problem with the account is that it depends on an inaccurate description of what we see when we see the colour of an object as constant. In particular, it wrongly tries to separate out the experience of the object's colour from the experience of the lighting context in which it is seen. In doing so, it fails to recognize a crucial, if puzzling, distinction that is insisted upon by Merleau-Ponty. This is the distinction between, as I will say, a colour and the way the colour looks. Let me try to clarify this distinction.

Colour constancy is the phenomenon whereby an object looks to be the same colour throughout a variety of different lighting contexts. Hering's explanation of colour constancy, on the other hand, depends on the preservation of a certain kind of experience – the experience of seeing the object's colour in normal lighting circumstances. If Hering's account were right, then whenever we see the colour of an object we would see it the way it looks in the normal lighting context. That is what the memory colour is. So on Hering's account, to see a piece of paper as white would be, in every lighting context, to see it the way it looks when the lighting is good. What we actually see, however, is that the object is a certain colour, and this colour will look different depending upon the light. For instance, a white piece of paper looks to be the same colour whether it is seen in the shade or in the light, but even though it looks to be the same colour, the colour looks different in the two lighting contexts.[8]

If we can really make sense of the distinction between a colour and the way the colour looks, then I think we will have the resources to explain some puzzling passages in *Phenomenology of Perception*. For instance, Merleau-Ponty says, somewhat mysteriously, 'The alleged constancy of colours does not prevent "an indubitable modification during which we continue to receive in our vision the fundamental quality'" (*PhP*, 305/355, quoting Gelb). If the distinction I am suggesting holds, then we can easily see that the 'indubitable modification' to which Merleau-Ponty refers is the change in the way the colour looks – different in the shade, for instance, than in the light. But to say that we continue to receive the same 'fundamental quality' throughout is simply to say that even though the colour looks different in different contexts, it continues to look like it is the very same colour. To see this distinction more clearly, consider the following example.

Imagine a situation in which a reasonably light shadow in the shape of a solid square is cast upon a white wall. Now, it is obvious that the shadowy part of the wall looks different from the lighted part; if it did not, the square would not be visually identifiable. But it seems odd to say that this difference is a difference of colour. It does not, after all, look as though a different colour paint was used for the square part of the wall than for the rest. In cases where different colour paints are used there is generally a sharp lack of continuity between the two areas, but this rarely occurs in cases of colour constancy.[9] Rather, in cases where constancy is preserved we seem to see the same wall, covered with the same paint, and therefore having the same colour, but nevertheless looking in one place shadowy, and in another place well lit. The best way to describe what we see seems to be to say that the shadowy part is not seen as a different colour; it is seen as the same colour but with a different look, a different, as we might say, qualitative appearance. And this difference in qualitative appearance is the contribution of the lighting context.

How would the empiricist respond to this claim? You might think he would just deny that the shadowy square and the white wall look to be the same colour. Perhaps every change in lighting really does correspond to a change in perceived colour; if so, then it would be true to say that the shadowy square looks grey, not white. But it is important to recognize that this response is not open to the empiricist, at least not if he is trying to give an explanation of the phenomenon of colour constancy. Hering, for instance, cannot deny that the white wall and the shadowy square look to be the same colour, because the fact that they do is precisely what he is trying to explain. The problem for Hering is that the explanation he gives of this phenomenon forces him to insist that they do not look any different from one another either. Since this fact is clearly false, the empiricist explanation of colour constancy fails.

It is possible, of course, to follow Russell in simply denying the phenomenon of perceptual constancy. This comes at a drastic cost both to our ordinary language use of colour terms and to our ordinary understanding of perceptual experience; nevertheless, I cannot see any knock-down argument against someone who, like Russell, simply denies the phenomenological facts. But even if he denies the phenomenological facts, a related problem arises for Russell, too. One way of highlighting this problem is to point out that even Russell admits we do not ordinarily perceive things the way they are seen in the detached perspective. Russell thinks we can explain our ordinary perceptual experience in terms of the detached experience, but he does not think that we ordinarily perceive in the detached mode. The problem for Russell, then, is that any explanation of the way our ordinary experience comes to be the way it is will have to depend on a concept like Hering's concept of memory colour. And once we force Russell to talk about ordinary experience, it seems as though he will fall into the very trap that Hering did.

I should note, briefly, that this way of putting the problem may not be quite fair to Russell, and I should also explain that this unfairness stems from what I think is a peculiar weakness of phenomenology. I was slipping, in the last paragraph, from talk (on Russell's behalf) of our ordinary beliefs about the colour of things into talk of the way we ordinarily perceive those colours. For Russell to fall into the trap that Hering does, he must be seen to be making a point about perception, not belief, because the trap depends upon a distinction in perception between a colour and the way the colour looks. My only defence for the slippage is to point out that since Russell says we must 'learn the habit of seeing things as they appear' (Russell 1959, 9), perhaps it is not egregious to attribute to him the view that ordinarily we see things some other way. If that is right, then why not think this other way of seeing things is what the phenomenologist is describing?

I am not happy with this way of gerrymandering Russell's view, though, and I suppose that if he steadfastly denies that he ever actually sees things the way I am describing them (instead of just believing them to be that way) then I really do not know what to do. In general I think this is a danger of phenomenology – that, in the end, it always comes down to descriptions, and descriptions do not have the normative force that arguments do. On the other hand, I also believe that arguments do not do any good on their own if they lead you to phenomenologically untenable positions. That is why I think the best philosophy of mind has to be found in knock-down arguments for phenomenologically motivated views. The arguments give you the normative force while the phenomenology guarantees this normative force is expended in defence of a viable philosophical position.[10]

Let me summarize, briefly, the criticism I have been making of the empiricist view. Roughly speaking, there are two phenomenological facts that need to be accounted for: first, that we see an object to be the same colour throughout changes in the lighting context and, second, that there is a difference in the way the colour looks in the different contexts. Russell denies the first in favour of the second, while Hering denies the second in favour of the first. The way to avoid this problem is to recognize that the phenomenon of colour constancy, properly described, requires a reference both to the colour of the object and to the way the colour looks in a context; no explanation of colour constancy in terms of only one or the other of these will get the phenomenon right. What we recognize in making this clarification is that, for instance, a white piece of paper never merely looks white; it looks like a white-piece-of-paper-in-the-shade or a white-piece-of-paper-in-the-sun, and these are different but equally viable ways of looking like it is the very same colour. It is this distinction that Merleau-Ponty is pointing to when he says, 'We shall not succeed in understanding perception unless we take into account a colour function which may remain even when the qualitative appearance is modified' (PhP, 305). What we see, then, is never merely the colour of an object, it is always the colour as it looks in the context.[11]

The cognitivist account of perceptual constancy

We have seen that in order to give a complete and accurate description of what we see when we see an object to have a property, we have to include in the description something about the perceptual context in which the object and its property are seen. In the case of the perception of colours, we need to include something about the lighting context, and, though I did not explicitly talk about these, it should be obvious that in the case of the perception of size, we need to include something about the distance to the object, and in the case of the perception of shape, we need to include something about the orientation of the object with respect to the viewer. In general, you might say, we need to take the perceptual context into account in order completely and accurately to describe our experience of an object and its properties. One popular cognitivist explanation of the phenomenon of perceptual constancy is based on an interpretation of what it is to take the context into account, and the failure of this explanation points to the second important observation about what we see.

This second observation is a little harder to formulate than the first one was. The basic idea is that in normal perception we always see a property to be a property of a particular object, and that this belonging of the perceived property to the perceived object creates a peculiar intimacy between them that is not normally recognized. It is often difficult to follow Merleau-Ponty on this obscure point, but I think that this intimacy is most easily expressed in the observation that we cannot completely and accurately describe a perceived property of an object without some reference to the object it is perceived to be a property of. In the case of colour, as Merleau-Ponty says, 'A colour is never merely a colour, but the colour of a certain object, and the blue of a carpet would never be the same blue were it not a woolly blue' (PhP, 313/365).

If this is right then it means that, strictly speaking, we do not in normal perception see properties as such, at least not if properties are independently specifiable attributes that can be found in many different objects. But this does not mean that we never see the colour of the carpet. In order to clarify this point, I will say that we see the carpet under its colour aspect, or that we see the colour aspect of the carpet. In general, I will use the term 'aspect' to indicate that the colour we see is not completely and accurately describable independently of the fact that it is the colour of a particular object, and not some other. That we see aspects instead of properties is the central component of my second observation. I think the cognitivist explanation of perceptual constancy by means of unconscious inference neglects this fact, so let me turn to that explanation now.

The Unconscious Inference explanation of perceptual constancy originated in the late nineteenth century with the German physiologist Helmholtz. Recently it has been revived by the late American psychologist Irvin Rock, and some version of this explanation is accepted by many perceptual psychologists for at least some of the perceptual constancies. It is easiest to get hold of the general approach of this explanation if we consider the case of size constancy, so let us begin there. The central claim of the explanation of size constancy by unconscious inference is that the brain unconsciously infers the perceived size of an object on the basis of information about how far away the object is perceived to be and what the size of the retinal image it casts is. The motivation for this claim is the observation that the information directly available to the brain is given by the size of the retinal image, but that, by itself, this information does not tell us anything about how big the object is: it could be an object that is six feet tall and ten yards away, or it could be an object that is six hundred feet tall and a thousand yards away. Each of these would cast a retinal image of the same size. Unless we take into account the distance, the theory argues, the brain does not have enough information to calculate any perceived size at all.

Given this general view about perceived size, an explanation of size constancy follows directly. Think of two trees, both of which are sixty feet tall, and imagine that one is one hundred yards away while the other is two hundred yards away. If the visual angle of the object (a measure of the size of the retinal image) were the only factor governing the perceived size of the tree, then the farther tree would appear to be half as tall as the closer one, since it subtends a visual angle that is half the size.[12] But if we take the perceived distance into account then this diminution is exactly compensated for. By defining perceived size as the product of perceived distance and visual angle, the Unconscious Inference theory explains how the perceived size of the tree remains the same despite changes in the size of the retinal image it casts.

It should be clear that the general approach of the Unconscious Inference theory could be applied to the problems of colour constancy and shape constancy as well. The details are not important for our purposes here, but the basic idea in the case of colour constancy would obviously be to calculate the colour of the object as a function of the surrounding illumination and the amount of light it is giving off, while the idea in the case of shape constancy would be to calculate the shape of the object as a function of shape of the retinal image and the orientation from which the object is seen. I said before that this kind of explanation is based on a particular interpretation of what it is to take the perceptual context into account in determining the perceived properties of an object. The characteristic feature of this interpretation is that it implicitly understands the elements of the perceptual context to be seen as determinate, measurable quantities on the basis of which we can infer, in accordance with a simple algorithm, the perceived property of the object, also understood to be seen as a determinate, measurable amount. Merleau-Ponty claims, however, that in perception, 'We must recognize the indeterminate as a positive phenomenon' (PhP, 6/7). I want to try to say now what I think this means.

Criticism of the cognitivist account

The central problem with the Unconscious Inference theory is that it fails to recognize, when it treats perceived distance determinately, that not all perceived distances ought to be treated equally. The Unconscious Inference theory assumes that there will be no perceivable difference at all between what I see when I see the size of an object that is one hundred yards away, and what I see when I see the size of the same object at ten yards, except that one of them will be perceived to be ten times farther away than the other. To see the object at one hundred yards is no better or worse than to see it at ten yards since, in both cases, according to this theory, I will perceive the object as having the same determinate, measurable size – that is what size constancy amounts to on this view.

But of course intuitively, at least, there is an important difference between what we see in these two cases, since a man who is one hundred yards away, although he appears to be a constant size, is nevertheless, as Merleau-Ponty says, 'not real and present in the sense in which [he] is at 10 yards' (PhP, 302/351). The most extreme example of this lack of reality and presence is seen from an aeroplane when the cars below look like moving toys. This is not exactly the kind of example I want to consider, since at this distance the phenomenon of size constancy breaks down altogether. But it does give a sense for the phenomenon that Merleau-Ponty is pointing out. Even when a person is close enough for me to be able to see that she is person-sized, so to speak, say at one hundred yards, she may nevertheless still be too far away for me to see her as well as I want to, i.e. to see her in the most real and present sense.

This fact leads Merleau-Ponty to claim that each object has its own optimum viewing distance, the distance one ought to stand from the object in order to see it best. Merleau-Ponty's presentation of this claim is helpful. He says:

> For each object, as for each picture in an art gallery, there is an optimum distance from which it requires to be seen, a direction viewed from which it vouchsafes most of itself: at a shorter or greater distance we have merely a perception blurred through excess or deficiency.
>
> (PhP, 302/352, translation modified)

The claim, then, is that there is a right context in which to view an object, and when the object is seen in a context that is not the right one, you will not be able to see its features as well as you might. Notice, incidentally, that there is no single context that will allow you to see all the features perfectly, since seeing some better means seeing others worse. If I want the best look at the texture of my sports coat, then I can only do this at the expense of getting a proper look at its shape. Merleau-Ponty thinks that this is one of the important ways in which being embodied viewers is essential to the way we see things, but I do not want to say more about this here.

The important thing I want to point out about the privileged perceptual context is that it is not just a descriptive norm – it is not just, as in Hering's view, the context in which we have in fact most often seen the object. Rather, on my interpretation of Merleau-Ponty's view, this privileged context has a normative component to it – it is the distance one ought to stand from the object, the orientation in which the object ought to be with respect to the viewer, the amount of surrounding illumination that ought to be present. This privileged perceptual context is in fact the one in which the size, shape, and colour of the object are best seen, but it is more than that, too – I experience it as the context in which the object ought to be seen, a context particular to that very object.

This normative component also separates Merleau-Ponty's view from the Unconscious Inference view, since it shows the sense in which not all perceived distances are to be treated similarly. Perceiving someone at one hundred yards is not just perceiving them as ten times farther away than they were when they were at ten yards. Perceiving someone at a distance of one hundred yards is not as good as perceiving them at ten, and so to say that I perceive their distance from me simply as a determinate, measurable amount does not properly describe the experience. Rather, according to Merleau-Ponty, I perceive this distance as a deviation from a norm. What he means by this, I think, is that I perceive that the distance I am now at gives me a less good view of the person than it might, but if I move this way it will be a little bit better, and some other way will make it better still. What I perceive when I perceive the distance to an object is the need to move closer or farther away in order to see the object better. Distance is perceived not as an amount, but, as Merleau-Ponty says, 'in terms of the situation of the object in relation to our ability to get a grasp on it' (PhP, 261/304–5, translation modified). And in another place, 'The distance from me to the object is not a size which increases or decreases, but a tension which fluctuates round a norm' (PhP, 302/352).

The idea that the distance to an object is experienced in terms of how conducive it is to seeing the object properly is an idea that holds for the other contextual factors as well. About orientation, for instance, Merleau-Ponty says, 'An oblique position of the object in relation to me is not measured by the angle which it forms with the plane of my face, but felt as a lack of balance, as an unequal distribution of its influences upon me' (PhP, 302/352). And we can imagine a similar claim about lighting.

If this is right, then what we take into account when we perceive the distance to an object is not that it is a distance of two hundred yards, but that it is not a very good distance to see the object well and that I would have to do this (move closer, say) in order to see the object better. As Merleau-Ponty says, 'One can only say that the man 200 yards away is a much less distinguishable figure, that he presents fewer and less identifiable points on which my eyes can fasten, that he is less strictly geared to my powers of exploration' (*PhP*, 261/ 304). And in particular one cannot say, he might have added, that he is 200 yards away.[13]

So let us assume that Merleau-Ponty is right to say that in taking into account the distance to an object we do not perceive that distance as a determinate amount. And further, let us assume that Merleau-Ponty is right to say that what we do experience is a deviation from a norm. How does this affect our description of what we see when we see an object to have a certain property throughout variations in context? How should I describe what I see, for instance, when I see a man 200 yards away to be the same size I see him to be at five yards away?

Well, to begin with, on this view, it cannot be the size itself that I see to be constant, at least not if size is considered as a determinate property independent of the man. After all, as Merleau-Ponty and Peacocke both insist, the perceived size of an object is no more determinate than the perceived distance to it. In normal vision, the man is 'neither smaller nor indeed equal in *size*: [the way I perceive his *size*] is anterior to equality and inequality' (*PhP*, 261/304, my emphasis). Perceived size is not a determinate quantity at all. But I do, nevertheless, see the man to be the same size at both distances. How is this possible?

Well, there is one thing that remains constant in the two experiences, namely, that they are experiences of a person as a person who ought to be seen in a particular, privileged, context. But does not this tell us something about his size? After all, the reason he ought to be seen in that context is because that is the context that gives me the best view of him, given that, among other things, he is the size he is. So my experience of the right context in which to view him is at the same time an experience of his size (along with an experience of his other aspects). But it is not just an experience of some determinate property size that any object could have; it is an experience of the size of the guy I am looking at now, given that I would have to do this (move closer, turn up the lights, stop him from standing on his head, etc.) to see him better. To use the terms from the fourth section above, in addition to being an experience of the size I see him to be, it is also an experience of the way that size looks to me when I see it manifested in him. It is an experience, in other words, of his very particular kind of tallness or shortness. Moreover, this particular kind of tallness or shortness is an aspect of him as a perceptible object that is not identifiable outside of my experience of him as that visual object.[14]

When I emphasize that I experience him as that object, I mean to be pointing out something beyond just the fact that I do not experience his aspects determinately. I mean to be pointing out further that I do not experience his aspects separately, because after all there is a whole privileged context in which I ought to see him, not just a privileged distance at which I ought to stand. So to see him as that object is not just to see him as the object having that size, experienced non-determinately; it is also to see him as having, inextricably, a bunch of other aspects as well. Therefore, for example, if I see the man as tall, it is because I see him as tall the way tall is manifested in him, and this will be different if he is tall and skinny, or tall and hefty, or even tall and handsome. In perceptual experience these aspects of him are not clearly separated.

As an aside, I will just point out briefly that if this is right, then it explains a puzzling fact about perceptual experience that Christopher Peacocke notices. Peacocke says (changing his example slightly) that even if I see a tall skinny man to be the same height as a tall hefty man, I can always rationally wonder if they are in fact the same height. We now see that the reason for this is that what I really see is not that they are each a particular height, but that they each manifest tallness in the way that is appropriate to them. Even if they are the same height, they will manifest that height differently given that one is skinny and the other fat.

The upshot of all this is that the perceived size of an object is indeterminate in the sense that the object is seen to have the size that is proper to it, given that it has all its other aspects, too. A perceived object has its shape, its size and its colour, rather than a constant determinate shape, a constant determinate size, and a constant determinate colour. That is why, when Merleau-Ponty describes the phenomenon of perceptual constancy, he does not say that an object maintains a constant property, he says, 'A thing has in the first place its size and its shape throughout variations of perspective' (PhP, 299/348). But then, if this is right, the proper explanation of perceptual constancy follows immediately: insofar as I see a constant thing, I see it as having all the aspects proper to it, no matter what context I see it in. I see the man at 200 yards to be the same size I see him to be at five yards because I see him to be the same man in both instances, first at a distance and then close up, and in each case I see him as having the size proper to him, the size proper to the very guy I am seeing. Perceptual constancy, then, is not a matter of seeing properties to be constant, it is a matter of seeing objects to have the aspects they should. As Merleau-Ponty says, 'The constancy of colour [or shape or size] is only an abstract component of the constancy of things. ... It is ... in so far as my perception is in itself open upon a world and on things that I discover constant colours [or shapes or sizes]' (PhP, 313/365).

Phenomenology and analysis

I said earlier that I believe the best way to approach philosophical problems about perception is by means of a combination of phenomenological and analytic techniques. This is because each approach on its own has a weakness it cannot overcome. Phenomenology, being primarily descriptive, has insufficient normative force, while analysis, being primarily argumentative, runs the risk of losing touch with the phenomenological facts. I want to develop this point briefly here by considering the relation between Peacocke's claim that perceptual content is nonconceptual and Merleau-Ponty's claim that perceptual content is indeterminate. What we will see is that Peacocke gives us a good, clear argument for his position, though the position itself insufficiently characterizes the phenomenology. Merleau-Ponty, on the other hand, gives a great description of the phenomena but no argument that one has to see things his way. Together, however, these two views begin to present a story about perception that is both forceful and complete.

Peacocke gives the following intuitive argument that perceptual 'manners of presentation' are not conceptual. By conceptual, here, he means having the features of Fregean 'modes of presentation' or *Sinne*, and in particular the feature of meeting the Fregean criterion of informativeness. This is the criterion according to which for any two modes of presentation m and m', if $m = m'$, then the thought that the thing presented by m is identical with the thing presented by m' is uninformative. Roughly, Peacocke's argument is that it makes perfect sense to imagine two things looking to be, for instance, the same length, even though it would be informative to discover that they in fact are the same length. To the extent that this is true, the content of the perceptual experiences of the two lengths must not be assimilable to the same Fregean mode of presentation. Perceptual 'manners of presentation' are not the same as Fregean 'modes of presentation', in other words, and so perceptual content is not conceptual. Here is Peacocke's presentation of the argument:

> Suppose you see both a line and a bar on a wallpaper pattern. Suppose too that they look as if they are the same length: they match in respect of apparent length. Now suppose that in fact not merely do they match in this way, but that they are in fact in exactly the same length [sic]; and that they are presented in exactly the same manner. We will also assume that once the subject's context is fixed, there is for each distance presented in a given manner a unique demonstrative mode of presentation of it of the form 'that distance.' ... Under the suppositions of our example, this implies that the modes of presentation (m.p.'s – 'that distance') used in connection with the line and the bar are identical. Nevertheless, it is consistent with everything in this example so far that you, the perceiver, suspect that the line and the bar are not precisely the same length (and not because your perceptual systems are malfunctioning). You suspect that there could, as things actually are, be objects matching the bar in length which do not match the line in length. For all you believe, a few moments later you may notice something in the wallpaper which matches the bar but not the line in length. So you are not willing to judge, concerning the apparent length of the line and the bar, that the former is identical with the latter. But this is incompatible with the identity of the

demonstrative modes of presentation in question, in the presence only of Frege's Principle that if m.p.'s m and m' are identical, the thought that the thing presented by m is identical with the thing presented by m' is uninformative. So we have a contradiction.

(Peacocke 1989, 307–8)

Now, the strength of this argument is that it is an argument, and so has compelling normative force. However, although there is some phenomenological data at the heart of the argument – namely, the observation that we could see two objects to be the same length while the contents of the two perceptions remain distinct – nevertheless, the complete phenomenological story about the relation between these two aspects of perception remains undiscussed. Only in Merleau-Ponty's story about the indeterminateness of perception do we find a complete discussion of the distinction between the length an object looks to be and the way that perceived length is manifested in the object perceived. All the phenomenological observations that enable us to distinguish aspects from properties, discuss aspects in terms of normative contexts for viewing, and describe contexts as inseparable wholes are lacking in Peacocke's analysis of perception. It is not that Peacocke's account of perception is wrong, it is just that it is incomplete. Whereas Peacocke simply argues for a distinction between concepts and percepts, Merleau-Ponty tries to describe fully the nature of the content of perceptual experience. Both of these projects, I believe, need to be tackled in order to get both a forceful and a complete story about perception.[15]

Conclusion

Let me summarize briefly, and then conclude. I have been concerned with the problem of how properly to describe what we see when we see an object's features to remain constant throughout a variety of perceptual contexts. In approaching this problem I have identified two phenomenological facts about what we see, and then shown how each of these facts renders invalid an important psychological theory of perception. In the first place, the empiricist explanation of perceptual constancy failed to recognize that we cannot accurately describe the property we see an object to have unless we include in the description some reference to the context in which the experience takes place. The cognitivist Unconscious Inference theory is an advance on the empiricist theory because it explicitly recognizes the important role that the context plays in my perception of an object's properties. But the Inference theorist assumes that we see the contextual factors as determinate, measurable quantities, and therefore that perceptual constancy is just a matter of seeing an object's property to have the same determinate measurement throughout contexts. By making this assumption the theory misses the important normative component of the privileged perceptual context, and in doing so it fails to recognize that we cannot accurately describe a perceived property of an object without some reference to the object it is perceived to be a property of. The proper phenomenological account of perceptual constancy, I have argued, is that we see an object, throughout contextual variations, to have the aspects appropriate to it, given that it is an object that ought to be seen in a given perceptual context. The seeds of this view may be found in Peacocke's argument that perceptual content is non-conceptual, but the view is not complete until it is supplemented with a full phenomenological account.

As a speculative concluding note, I will mention briefly an apparent connection between Merleau-Ponty's view of perception and a famous problem concerning language: the so-called problem of the unity of the proposition. Recall that the problem of how to get a subject and predicate glued together is particularly difficult for Russell, because he insists that each of the elements of the proposition must be capable of being named, and therefore must be understood as independent logical entities. Frege gets around the problem of unity, but he does so only at the cost of admitting an 'incomplete' or 'unsaturated' concept. I think this manoeuvre leads him to a conception of the relation between concepts and objects in philosophical logic that is closely allied with Merleau-Ponty's conception of the relation between objects and aspects in perception. In particular, like Merleau-Ponty's perceptual aspect, the defining feature of Frege's logical concept is that it so depends upon its object for completion that it can never, as such, be named itself.

When Merleau-Ponty claims that the blue of the carpet would never be the same blue were it not a woolly blue, he is saying, essentially, that the perceived colour blue is, by itself (in Frege's terms), unsaturated. I think that this points to an important connection between the content of our perceptual experiences and the content of our linguistic utterances, although this connection has not been my central concern here. It is interesting to note, however, that the relation between perception and language is a problem that has been at the centre of the phenomenological movement almost from the start, and it has become an important area of research in recent analytic philosophy as well in the work of people like Strawson, Evans, Peacocke, and McDowell. The issues I have discussed here seem to me to be a precursor to the adequate study of that difficult issue, and what I have said above suggests that a good solution will require a combination of analysis and phenomenology.

Notes

1 This paper was first published in *Philosophical Topics* 27 (1999): 107–28.
2 John McDowell, among others, is concerned to articulate the relation between the question of what we are justified in believing we see and the question of what the proper objects of perception are. I see this concern both in McDowell (1994) and in his earlier paper (McDowell 1986).
3 See Austin 1962, 8, *passim*: Austin argues that an analysis of our ordinary use of language shows how much more sophisticated the ordinary person is than the

philosopher generally gives him credit for being. Consequently, 'naive realism' may be a misleading name for his view.

4 This is at least one standard interpretation of Berkeley's view. For an argument against this interpretation, see Pappas (1987). Pappas argues (p. 202) that the so-called 'epistemic interpretation of immediate perception', the view I have attributed to Berkeley above, is not general enough to account for all the details of his theory of vision. Whether this is Berkeley's view or not, however, such a position has held an historically important place in the philosophy of perception. The sense-datum theorists, of course, are often understood to hold a view related to this one, and its basic motivations are typically taken to derive from Descartes. Cheryl Chen has recently pointed out to me a passage in the second of Descartes' *Meditations* where Descartes switches from an ordinary or naive use of the verb 'to see', according to which seeing is fallible, to a more radical use of the same verb, according to which it must be infallible. Descartes, therefore, seems to be genuinely conflicted about the issue; Berkeley, on the standard interpretation of his view, can be understood to have highlighted the more radical of the conflicting positions in Descartes.

5 Gil Harman makes the same point in his influential paper (Harman 1999, 251):

> When you see a tree, you do not experience any features as intrinsic features of your experience. Look at a tree and try to turn your attention to intrinsic features of your visual experience. I predict you will find that the only features there to turn your attention to will be features of the presented tree.

6 I will use the phrase 'detached attitude' or 'detached perspective' to indicate that the perceiver is looking at things in such a way as to 'see them as they appear'.

7 What I have presented here is an application of Hering's idea to the problem of colour constancy, but it is interesting to notice that nothing in this account depends on the fact that colour is the property being preserved throughout perceptual contexts. Similar accounts could be given, and were given, of the phenomena of size and shape constancy as well. In these cases we simply need to define a memory size, which is the size of the object as seen from a normalized distance, and a memory shape, which is the shape of the object as seen in a normalized orientation. Then we can explain the fact that the property is experienced as constant throughout perceptual contexts by postulating that, in non-normal contexts, the memory of the property as seen in the normalized context is substituted in.

8 It is important to emphasize that both of these are aspects of the perceptual experience – that the object appears *to be* a certain colour and that that colour looks different in different lighting contexts. In this section I want to emphasize that accounts of perception that try to explain perceptual content solely in terms of the colour the object appears *to be* will fail completely to describe the content of experience. But, at the same time, I do not want to deny that we do see the object to be a certain colour – that is just not the entirety of the experience. Now, there is a further question about how we can come to categorize presentations of the same colour *in different contexts* as presentations of the same colour, and I will have something to say about that in the sixth section. Roughly, it will be because we see them to be presentations of the same object, and we see objects to maintain constant colours. But I do not want to pretend that this is a complete answer to the problem. Indeed, a complete answer would require a subtle, convincing, and phenomenologically adept account of the problem of universals, which I do not at this point have.

9 In fact, it seems to me that the sharper the boundary between the shadow and the rest of the wall, the less likely it is that colour constancy will be preserved. For an

example of this, think about the sharp contrast engendered by difference of colour, even when the shades of colour are relatively close, in the experimental colour paintings of Mondrian or in the dichromatic paintings of Ellsworth Kelly. To the extent that there looks to be a boundary, it fails to look like a case of colour constancy.

10 My best attempt so far at this kind of methodological approach is in a paper called 'Why Perception Might Not Be Like Thought; or, The Return of Romanticism to the Philosophy of Mind' (unpublished).

11 Of course, this is only true for the colours *of objects* (as opposed to pure colours not manifested in any object), and in this observation might lie the final demise of the sense-datum theory. For if it were really true that we perceive colours the way Russell says we do, then every change in lighting (as we have already said) would constitute a change in colour. Now there is one place where a change in lighting does have this effect – in the clear sky as the sun begins to set. There, as the lighting context changes, so too does the colour – no phenomenon of constancy obtains. But surely this change is different, perceptually, from the way we experience changes in the lighting context when viewing the colour of an object. Surely the change in the look of the colour of my carpet, as the setting sun casts a shadow upon it, is nothing like the change in the colour of the sky as the setting sun turns it from blue to orange to red to black. Or will Russell put his foot down even here?

12 Half as tall because, as a little bit of simple geometry will confirm, the visual angle of an object is inversely proportional to distance, so an object that is 200 yards away will subtend a visual angle that is half the size of an object that is 100 yards away.

13 Perhaps this is a good place to note in passing that the fact that we do not perceive distance as a determinate measurement is central to Christopher Peacocke's work on perceptual content as well. He seconds Merleau-Ponty's observation when he says, forty years later, 'It seems that there is a way of perceiving distance, and a way of thinking of distances based on perception of them, neither of which are captured by specifications of distance in feet and inches' (Peacocke 1986, 1). I will say something briefly in the seventh section about the relation between Merleau-Ponty's characterization of perceptual experience as indeterminate, and Peacocke's characterization of perceptual content as nonconceptual.

14 See also note 7. I do not want to deny, of course, that it is possible to see the man to be a certain size – say, six feet tall. Perhaps I can put him next to a six-foot-tall measuring stick and see that he is roughly the same size as that. I do think that we can see things this way, of course, and I even think that when we see the more particular size-as-manifested-in-the-object we also see the object to be a certain size. Both kinds of things are part of the perceptual experience. What I do want to deny, and what the cognitivists seem committed to, is that *all* I see when I see his height is that he is six feet tall. In this section I deny this because the determinate size leaves out the normative aspect of the experience, and in the next section I will give a different kind of argument from Peacocke to the effect that determinate size cannot be all we see. To the extent that we do see determinate size, however – to the extent, that is, that we see six-foot-tall objects to be about the same size – there must be a way we can abstract back to this information from the more particular information that fully specifies our experience. I have just given part of the story about how this works, but a more complete story will have to deal with the problem of universals, which I am not prepared to do here.

15 For more on the relation between Peacocke and Merleau-Ponty, see Kelly 2001. There I argue not only that Peacocke underspecifies the perceptual content, but also that in doing so he is led to say false things about it. Indeed, it is possible that even here Peacocke is emphasizing a different point than the one that I mean to be attributing to him. It may be that although Peacocke agrees that we do not see the

height of an object as a determinate value, that is just because our powers of perceptual acuity are not great enough to ascertain things like determinate height (which, after all, are real numbered values). When I argue that we do not see determinate heights, I mean not just that we see height approximations, but moreover that we see *heights-as-manifested-in-objects*, in ordinary perception, not height *simpliciter*. This is more a point about the unity of perceived objects than a point about the limitations of perceptual acuity.

3

MERLEAU-PONTY AND THE POWER TO RECKON WITH THE POSSIBLE

Komarine Romdenh-Romluc

The things we do – our actions – can be contrasted with the things that merely happen to us.[1] Orthodox accounts hold that actions are essentially brought about by states of the agent that represent their performance, and can be distinguished from mere happenings on this basis. Dreyfus (2000) puts forward Merleau-Ponty's view of action as an alternative, arguing that his model captures the human capacity for action better than the orthodox accounts, and should be adopted by anyone seeking to understand human action. As a matter of fact, I agree with Dreyfus' claims. However, my purpose in this paper is not primarily to try and convince others of their truth. Instead, my aim is as follows. Dreyfus' interpretation of Merleau-Ponty is problematic. He does not address a capacity that, for Merleau-Ponty, is essentially involved in the human ability to act. Consequently, the account he presents is both incomplete as a reading of Merleau-Ponty, and independently problematic as it cannot adequately explain how conscious deliberation gives rise to action. My aim in this paper is to remedy the situation by presenting the capacity that Dreyfus overlooks. I will not attempt to defend Merleau-Ponty's model of action here – I will merely provide an interpretation of it. But by presenting it in its complete form, I hope to pave the way for further research into his model as a serious alternative to the orthodox account.

'Absorbed coping'

Dreyfus is primarily interested in Merleau-Ponty's account of unreflective behaviour. What counts as unreflective behaviour depends upon how one understands what it is to reflect. In this context, to call an instance of behaviour 'unreflective' is to describe an aspect of one's experience of engaging in it. Behaviour is unreflective in this sense if the subject experiences her behaviour as occurring without the guidance of thought. Examples will help to get the phenomenon in clear view. Someone who drifts absentmindedly into the kitchen and makes a cup of tea whilst thinking about what to eat for lunch

44

behaves unreflectively. Merleau-Ponty gives the example of modifying one's behaviour to suit one's social situation (*PhP*, 106/122) – I unthinkingly modify my fruity language, e.g. when talking to the vice chancellor. The martial artist who is sparring in a kung fu competition also behaves unreflectively. Although the activity requires the subject's complete concentration – successful sparring requires that she be fully absorbed in what she is doing – the subject does not experience her behaviour as guided by thought. Indeed, it is well documented that consciously thinking about what one is doing interferes with one's ability to do it; thought interrupts the 'flow' of the action. Unlike orthodox accounts which take unreflective behaviour to be initiated and controlled by states of the agent that represent the movements it involves, Merleau-Ponty holds that unreflective behaviour is brought about by the agent's perceptions of her surroundings.

The direct objects of perception, on Merleau-Ponty's account, are things that have a value or meaning for the perceiver in terms of her capacities to interact with them. One's surrounding environment is immediately presented in perception as 'requiring' or 'suggesting' a certain sort of behaviour such that the perceiver is not confronted with things that have merely objective qualities such as size, shape, etc., but with entities that are edible, throwable, kickable, and so on. The behaviour that one perceives one's environment as requiring will be behaviour that relates to one's current task. Consider this example,

> For the player in action the football field is not an 'object'. ... It is pervaded by lines of force (the 'yard' lines; those which demarcate the 'penalty area') and articulated into sectors (for example the 'openings' between the adversaries) which call for a certain mode of action.
>
> (SB, 168)

Here, Merleau-Ponty claims that to the player engaged in a game of football, the pitch is presented as a space, delimited by certain entities, that offers the player opportunities to perform certain actions. The yard lines and those that mark out the penalty area are not perceived simply as white lines with a particular location in space. They are perceived as real boundaries that mark out areas of the pitch that have significance for the player's behaviour. The spaces between the players on the opposing team are not perceived as simply areas of the pitch where no people are standing but as 'openings', i.e. opportunities to progress towards the goal, or opportunities to pass the ball to another member of one's team. Moreover, it is only when playing football that the agent perceives the pitch like this. If, for example, she is walking her dog and accidentally wanders onto the pitch during a game, she will not see the ball as to-be-intercepted, but as to-be-avoided.

It is the perceived opportunities for action that initiate and control unreflective behaviour on Merleau-Ponty's account. The agent simply perceives an opportunity to behave, and responds by so behaving, without the need for any intervening states that represent her engagement in the activity. Thus in the above examples, when I drift absentmindedly into the kitchen and make a cup of tea, I perceive the kettle as for-boiling-water, the mug as for-holding-tea, the teabag as for-brewing, and so forth. These perceptions 'pull forth' the act of tea-making from me and guide its execution whilst I think of other things. Similarly, when talking to the vice chancellor, I have a perceptual grip on my social situation constituted by a sense of formality that permeates the proceedings, and which immediately regulates my language so that I do not swear. The martial artist likewise perceives her situation as requiring a certain sort of behaviour. Her opponent's fist is seen as an opportunity to duck, an unguarded chest presented as an opportunity to deliver a kick, etc., and the martial artist simply responds to these perceptions by acting.[2] Dreyfus calls action that is immediately brought about by the agent's perception of her environment 'absorbed coping'.

Merleau-Ponty holds that the capacity for absorbed coping is underpinned by the possession of motor skills. These are physical abilities, capacities to engage in forms of behaviour or modes of activity. They range from very basic skills, such as scratching one's nose, to more complex skills such as driving a car. Motor skills are acquired by practice. One has to launch oneself into attempts to do the thing in question, and keep practising until one becomes proficient. Practice is a process of familiarising oneself with the activity in question so that it comes to feel natural. To illustrate these points, consider what it is like to acquire the ability to roller-skate. Clearly, I cannot learn to roller-skate by sitting in a chair and thinking about doing so, I have to launch myself into attempts to roller-skate. When I first put on a pair of roller-skates they feel alien. I am very much aware of the skates being strapped to my feet, and I feel encumbered. My feet feel heavy, I am aware of being taller than usual and I feel that I might fall over at any minute. The sensation of being on wheels and the bodily movements required to propel myself along feel strange and awkward. I move tentatively and without confidence. I often fall over. But as I practice, wearing roller-skates starts to feel more natural; I cease to be constantly aware of the skates attached to my feet, and of being taller. I no longer feel that I might fall over at any moment, and I manage to stay upright. The bodily movements needed to move on the skates also start to feel less awkward and I start to move with confidence. The more I skate, the better I become at making minute adjustments to my posture to keep my balance. I start to crouch down and lean forwards slightly when I am skating along. As I move my legs to propel myself forward, I learn to shift my weight just enough to aid propulsion without overbalancing. Through practice, I become familiar with roller-skating so that it feels natural to me. The same is true of other motor skills. As Merleau-Ponty says, the body has to '"catch" the movement' (PhP, 143/165) for one to acquire a motor skill.[3]

It is very easy to see one way in which motor skills are implicated in absorbed coping: to execute an action – to perform the bodily movements it involves – the agent must possess the necessary skills. To block an opponent's fist during a kung fu fight, for example, I must be skilled at kung fu. However, there is a further way in which the possession of motor skills contributes to absorbed coping. They also play an important role in perception. The objects of perception, for Merleau-Ponty, are things that invite the perceiver to interact with them in various ways. Merleau-Ponty holds that the opportunities for action that one perceives in the world around one are determined both by one's current task, and by what one can do. What a subject can do on any particular occasion depends both on what her environment is like, and her behavioural capacities, i.e. her motor skills. It follows that on Merleau-Ponty's account, what a subject *perceives* on any particular occasion will be dependent on her current task, the nature of her environment, and the motor skills she possesses.

Motor skills contribute to perception in the following way. A motor skill cannot be exercised in just any old environment. One cannot, for example, snowboard, unless one is in a part of the world that contains snow (real or artificial), a slope, and a snowboard. Thus part of what it is to be able to do x, is to be able to do x in appropriate environments (indeed, no sense can be given to doing x in an inappropriate environment – 'snowboarding' whilst lying in bed just isn't snowboarding – although some environments are more appropriate than others). Since engaging in an activity necessarily requires an environment of a particular sort, the ability to engage in that activity essentially involves the ability to pick out appropriate environments in which to do so. Merleau-Ponty holds that the ability to recognise certain environments as being appropriate for doing x is constituted by *perceiving* those environments as offering an opportunity to do x. Learning to do x is therefore partly a matter of learning to perceive opportunities to do so. Acquiring the skill of rock-climbing, for example, partly involves learning to see little cracks and ledges in the rock as hand and footholds. When one starts out, only the bigger ledges and wider cracks will look suitable, but as one gets better at rock-climbing, smaller ledges will be perceived as offering a passage up the rock-face. Thus one will progress from seeing a rock-face as an impassable mass of rock to seeing it as climbable. The better one gets at climbing, the better one will become at perceiving opportunities to do so, and thus different rock-faces will be perceived as more or less difficult to climb. We can see from this analysis that to perceive an opportunity to act is to exercise a motor skill on Merleau-Ponty's account.

Dreyfus and intention

Dreyfus' exposition of absorbed coping is illuminating. However, as a model of action, it is incomplete. On Merleau-Ponty's view as it has been expounded so far, the agent's perception of her environment as 'requiring' a certain sort of behaviour, immediately brings about that behaviour without the need for any intervening states that represent the actions she performs. However, there are cases where we want to say that the subject's *thoughts* – rather than her perceptions – bring about her behaviour. The clearest instances are cases where an episode of practical reasoning leads to action, for example, I deliberate about my monthly expenditure, decide I can afford to buy a television, form an intention to now go to the shop, which brings about my leaving the house. Merleau-Ponty needs to be able to accommodate this kind of case if his account of action is to be at all plausible.

Given what we know of Merleau-Ponty's account so far, cases like that of the television-buying described above seem to present him with an immediate difficulty. We want to say of the above case, that my action of leaving the house to buy a television is brought about by my intention to do so, which represents me leaving the house to buy a television. However, during the time that I form the intention and carry it out, I also perceive the world. Moreover, my perception of my environment plays some role in the execution of my intention – my action of going to the shop must be guided at least in part by my perceptions of the front door, the road, etc. The problem is that on Merleau-Ponty's account, perception has the power to immediately bring about behaviour, without the need for any states that represent it. But if this is so, then it is unclear what role intention can play in bringing about my behaviour. The relation between perception and action looks too tight; there seems to be no room for intention to intervene. Of course, Merleau-Ponty could simply stipulate that intention can alter the course of behaviour. However, as an explanation of how intention can initiate action, this leaves a lot to be desired, and it would be better if some fuller account could be given.

Dreyfus reads Merleau-Ponty as holding that intention initiates absorbed coping when the flow of behaviour has come to a standstill (2000, 300–1). He does not indicate when absorbed coping might cease, but there seem to be two options here: the flow of coping may stop when the subject is not perceiving, and with no perceptions to bring about behaviour, intention is required to 'kick-start' the process. Alternatively, the flow of absorbed coping may stop because perception is sometimes insufficient to bring about behaviour, and so the agent needs as it were, a nudge from intention, to continue interacting with the world. Both suggestions are problematic. Consider first the idea that intention brings about behaviour when perception ceases. There is an absence of perceptual experience when the subject is unconscious. Perhaps the subject also ceases to perceive when she is asleep. This is, however, controversial, since one still retains some sensitivity to one's surroundings whilst asleep. It is reported that people who live in lighthouses are not roused by the sound of the foghorn although another noise of a similar volume would wake them, and conversely, parents with small babies are immediately wakened by the sound of their children crying, even though they would sleep through a different sound of this volume. Nevertheless, let us accept for the sake of argument that the subject ceases to perceive when she is sleeping. Dreyfus reads Merleau-Ponty as holding that intention can initiate behaviour when the flow of absorbed coping stops. One way in which the flow of coping can cease is when there is an absence of perceptual experience to bring about behaviour. But if this is right, then the only time that thought can bring about behaviour is whilst the subject is asleep or unconscious. Clearly, this is inadequate as an account of how intention can initiate action.

According to the second suggestion, the flow of behaviour comes to a halt when the subject's perceptions are insufficient to bring about coping. In such cases, the subject still perceives the world, but her perceptions do not call forth any behaviour. When this happens, intention gets the process up and running again by initiating action. The first problem is to explain why perception is sometimes insufficient to bring about behaviour. Nothing in Dreyfus' reading of Merleau-Ponty provides any clue as to why this might be so. Perhaps we can make sense of the idea as follows. Suppose Celia has a hard day at work. She leaves the office, dashes round the supermarket, arrives home and sinks into a chair. One might suppose that Celia's flow of behaviour ceases when she sits down. She continues to perceive the world, but her perceptions no longer call forth any behaviour, and so coping stops. But on Merleau-Ponty's view as it has been expounded so far, this is incorrect. Although one may at first be inclined to think that sitting still involves doing nothing, this is not literally true. When sitting still, the agent's muscles are still working to keep her balance, stop her from falling out of the chair, hold her head upright, and so on. One has to learn how to sit in chairs and although this is a very basic skill, con-sisting merely of abilities to hold one's body upright and keep one's balance, being able to sit in a chair is nevertheless a motor skill. Thus, when an agent is sitting still in a chair, even for a length of time, she is exercising the skill of sitting still in chairs. Notice further, that the agent is exercising the skill in response to her perceived surroundings. An agent, for example, may sit still in the chair because it feels comfortable. When the chair starts to feel uncomfortable, the agent moves in response. Thus when Celia sits in the chair, there is still some low-level coping going on – the flow of her behaviour has not come to a complete standstill. The second, far more significant problem is that, even if we could make sense of the idea that the flow of absorbed coping sometimes grinds to a halt because perception is sometimes insufficient to generate behaviour, this would still leave us with an unsatisfactory account of how intention can bring about action. It would mean that practical reasoning could only generate action on those occasions when perception was insufficient to bring about behaviour. To act on the basis of some practical reasoning, the subject would thus have to wait until her perceptions stopped calling forth coping. But this is extremely counterintuitive; we want to say that the subject can decide to act and then do so. It follows that the account of action that Dreyfus attributes to Merleau-Ponty cannot adequately explain how intentions bring about behaviour.

49

Action generated by thought

One may accept that Dreyfus' account of how thought can generate action on Merleau-Ponty's model should be rejected. However, one might suppose that there is no problem with explaining how intentions can bring about behaviour given the analysis of absorbed coping presented above. As we have seen, unreflective behaviour is brought about by perceptual experience. The content of perceptual experience is determined by the agent's current project, in combination with her environment and the motor skills she possesses – the agent perceives her surroundings in the light of her current task, and so perceives opportunities to exercise those of her skills that are relevant to her current project. The proficient driver, for example, perceives a space-to-park because she can drive, is facing a space suitable for parking, and is engaged in the project of parking her car. Humans can *decide* to take on projects, and deciding to do x involves forming an intention to do x. I take on the task of playing football, for example, through deciding, or forming an intention to play football. Since one's current task affects the course of absorbed coping and one takes on one's current task by forming an intention to do so, it appears that the account of unreflective behaviour given above already explains how intention can generate action.

Although there is something right about this thought, there is more to Merleau-Ponty's account of how intentions can generate action than this. First, Merleau-Ponty can tell us more about what is involved in taking on a task. One might wonder what more there is to know about this matter. But consider the following. It was assumed above that one takes on the task of doing x in virtue of forming an intention to do x; however, this is not always so. Physical creatures have instincts to satisfy hunger, to avoid danger, to mate, to rest, and so forth. These instincts impose certain tasks upon the creature that possesses them. If a simple creature feels hungry, for example, the feeling of hunger imposes the task of procuring food. The creature does not need to form an intention to take on the task of satisfying hunger; it simply takes on the task in virtue of feeling hungry. Notice next that a creature can go from one task to the next without ever making any decisions. At any time, it is engaged in some task or other. Once that project is complete, another task is imposed by the creature's physical nature – for example, once it has completed the task of procuring and eating food, its hunger is satiated and it feels sleepy, and thus becomes involved in the project of resting. Human beings are physical creatures possessing instincts to satisfy hunger, to mate, to avoid danger, and so forth. Thus humans could go through life simply engaged in the tasks imposed by these instincts. Given that humans do have certain projects imposed upon them by the fact that they are physical beings, yet can also take on tasks in virtue of forming intentions to do so, one might wonder what opens up the possibility of a human *deciding* to do x, rather than simply finding food when hungry, resting when tired, and so on.

Second, although we have identified one way in which intention can bring about action – a subject's intention to engage in the project of doing x affects her perceptual experience and thus affects her behaviour – this does not account for all of the ways in which thought can guide action. To see this, consider the following case. Juan is a martial artist and film director. He is shooting a film starring himself. One scene depicts him fighting an alien adversary. After experimenting with various ways of shooting the film, Juan decides that the best effect will be achieved if the alien foe is computer-generated. Thus Juan has to mime fighting the alien foe who will be superimposed on the film later. In this case, Juan's action of miming a fight is initiated by his intention to do so. However, it is problematic to suppose that his intention to mime the fight brings about his behaviour by shaping his perceptual experience, so that he perceives opportunities to exercise those skills that are relevant to his project. The problem is that it appears the skill Juan exercises when he mimes the fight is his skill of fighting a real opponent. It is because he knows how to block a real punch, deliver a kick to the stomach of a real person, and so on, that he can mime these actions. The sort of worldly setting that is appropriate for exercising this skill is thus one where there is a real opponent – a person who is attacking the agent and against whom he has to defend himself. It is a setting of this sort that will be perceived as offering an opportunity to exercise the skill of fighting. A setting that does not contain a real opponent will not be perceived as offering an opportunity to exercise this skill. When Juan mimes fighting the alien, there is no real opponent, and so it cannot be the case that his intention to mime fighting an alien brings about this action in virtue of leading him to perceive an opportunity to exercise his skill at fighting. Some alternative analysis of this case is required.

The key to understanding Merleau-Ponty's account of how thought can generate action lies with his claim that the normal human agent has the power 'to reckon with the possible' (*PhP*, 109/125). To get to grips with what it is 'to reckon with the possible', we need a contrasting notion of 'the actual'. Merleau-Ponty's account of unreflective behaviour yields such a notion. It is the agent's *actual* environment and the project in which she is *actually* engaged – together with her motor skills – that shape the content of her perceptions, which initiate and control absorbed coping. In absorbed coping there is thus a sense in which the agent contends or reckons with 'the actual': her actual environment and actual task. Correlatively, 'the possible' with which the normal person has the power to reckon can be understood as encompassing possible projects that the agent could undertake, and/or possible environments in which she could be located.

Further examination of what it is to reckon with one's actual environment and task on Merleau-Ponty's account will enable us to understand what it is to contend with a possible task and/or environment on his view. Notice first that on Merleau-Ponty's view, to perceive is itself to exercise one's motor skills. An agent who possesses a motor skill is able to perform the bodily movements required to engage in some activity, and to recognise environments that are suitable for doing so. The recognition of places as suitable for doing x is constituted by the perception of those places as inviting one to do x. It follows that when the subject perceives the world as inviting her to act in various ways, she is exercising her motor skills. The content of perceptual experience is not, of course, just determined by the motor skills the subject possesses; it is also shaped by her environment and current task. Merleau-Ponty holds that the subject's surroundings and current task bring relevant motor skills 'online' making them available for the subject to use in perception and action; the subject accesses her motor skills via her actual environment in combination with her current task. The presence of a rock-face and the project of climbing it, for example, make the climber's ability to rock-climb available to her so that she can both perceive the rock-face as climbable and actually climb it. Since contending with 'the actual' involves accessing motor skills that are relevant to one's actual environment and current task, it follows that the power to reckon with 'the possible' should be understood as the power to access – and so use – motor skills that are relevant to merely possible tasks and environments.

One thing the power to reckon with the possible enables the agent to do is perceive more opportunities for action than just those that relate to her current project. It has so far been claimed that the content of perceptual experience is determined by the subject's environment, her motor skills, and her current task. However, this analysis does not yet accurately describe the perceptual experience of a normally functioning adult human. We can demonstrate this by comparing it with the pathological perceptual experience of Schneider, a man who sustained a brain injury during World War I. One of the many strange aspects of Schneider's case is that he never recognises the house of Goldstein (one of the psychologists who worked extensively with him) when he walks past it unless he sets out with the intention of going there (PhP, 134–5/155).

This case stands in stark contrast to the experience of a normal human agent who will recognise a house that she knows, even if she is engaged in a project that does not involve going to it. Merleau-Ponty analyses this as follows. To recognise something is to perceive it as familiar. Things appear familiar when one knows how to interact with them. Thus to perceive something as familiar is to perceive it as something for which a particular form of behaviour is appropriate. As we have seen, to perceive something as offering an opportunity to engage in a particular form of behaviour is to exercise a motor skill. It follows that to recognise something on Merleau-Ponty's account is to exercise a motor skill, or set of motor skills.

What Schneider cannot do is exercise those motor skills that *could* be used to interact with Goldstein's house, unless he is *actually* engaged in some project which involves interacting with it, e.g. posting a letter through the door, visiting Goldstein, delivering a parcel to the house, etc. The only motor skills he can use at any time to perceive and act are those that are relevant to his actual environment and current task, and so he only perceives those opportunities for action that relate to these. In contrast, a normal adult human would recognise the house, even if she is merely passing it on her way to somewhere else. Thus we can see that normal adult humans have access to more than just those motor skills that are made available by their actual environments and current tasks. To recognise Goldstein's house is to perceive an opportunity for action relative to the task of 'engaging' with the house in some way. So to recognise it when you pass it on the way to somewhere else is to see the house in the light of a potential task. It is to perceive the house as offering an opportunity to act in relation to the possible task of, for example, posting a letter through Goldstein's door. Thus the normal adult human can access more than just those motor skills that are made available by her actual environment and current task; she can also access motor skills that are relevant to merely possible projects she could undertake in her environment. The opportunities for action that correlate with her current task will be perceived as most urgent – and will therefore initiate action – but she will also perceive less urgent demands for action – those that relate to merely potential tasks.

We are now in a position to explain how, on Merleau-Ponty's account, the human agent is able to *decide* to take on a project, rather than simply having tasks imposed upon her by her physical nature. This is made possible by the ability to perceive more than just those opportunities for action that relate to one's current task. On Merleau-Ponty's view, an appreciation of the possibilities open to one is required for decision-making. The agent has to appreciate that she could be doing something other than what she is currently doing. She has to appreciate that she has taken one of two or more options, and she has to have a sense that the options in question are real possibilities – things she feels she could really do, rather than mere logical possibilities. The agent's appreciation of the live possibilities open to her gives her a sense of choice, and once the agent has a sense of choice, there is scope for the making of decisions. Merleau-Ponty claims that it is the power to reckon with the possible that furnishes humans with an appreciation of the options open to them. As we have seen, the power to reckon with the possible enables the agent to perceive more opportunities for action than just those that are relevant to the completion of her current task. Since the perception of an opportunity to behave in a particular way is the exercise of a motor skill that the agent possesses, she has the ability to engage in the behaviour that she perceives the world as demanding, so the perceived opportunity for action is presented as a real possibility for her, something that she can do. In this way, the power to reckon with the possible enables humans to *decide* to take on particular projects, rather than simply having tasks imposed upon them by their physical nature.

We are interested in Merleau-Ponty's account of how thought can generate action. An intention to do x can affect the agent's behaviour by shaping the agent's perceptions of her environment which in turn initiate and control her actions. However, as we saw above, there are cases where intention generates action but which cannot be explained along these lines, such as that of Juan.

Juan mimes a fight with an alien foe; his behaviour is generated by an intention. It seems that the skill Juan exercises when he mimes the fight is his skill
at fighting a real opponent. But since in this case there is no real opponent,
Juan's exercise of his fighting skill cannot be initiated and guided by his perception of an opportunity to exercise this skill. Consequently, his intention to
mime a fight with an alien adversary cannot be understood as bringing about
his behaviour in virtue of shaping his perceptual experience. Merleau-Ponty
explains cases like this one by again appealing to the human ability to access
one's motor skills in relation to merely possible tasks and environments. In
short, Juan 'interacts' with an imaginary opponent. He can thus be understood
as acting with respect to merely possible surroundings, rather than with respect
to his actual environment. Since his act of miming a fight with an alien foe
involves exercising his skill at fighting, to mime the fight, Juan must be able to
access his martial arts skills with respect to his imagined environment, which
contains an alien opponent.

Merleau-Ponty's analysis of cases where the agent acts with respect to a
merely possible environment has the same form as his account of absorbed
coping. It follows that to understand how action is brought about in these
cases, we need to re-describe his account of absorbed coping in more general
terms. Merleau-Ponty gives a very general statement of his account of human
behaviour in the following passage:

> [F]or the normal person every movement has a *background*, and the
> movement and its background are 'moments of a unique totality'. The
> background to the movement is not a representation associated or
> linked externally with the movement itself, but is immanent in the
> movement inspiring and sustaining it at every moment.
>
> (*PhP*, 110/127)

To uncover what he means here, let us consider the above passage with
respect to unreflective behaviour. In absorbed coping, the agent perceives
opportunities to act, which initiate and control her actions. What a subject
perceives depends on what she can do. Her perception of her environment is
also shaped by her current task or project, such that the most urgent demands
for action are those that relate to what she is currently doing. It follows that
one perceives one's surroundings primarily as a setting or backdrop for a particular sort of behaviour – activity that relates to one's current task. When
playing football, for example, the agent perceives the goal lines as real boundaries, members of the opposing team as adversaries to be avoided, spaces
between them as opportunities to progress towards goal, and so on. The player
perceives ways to interact with the world that are relevant to her task of
playing football, and so she perceives her environment primarily as a setting for
this project. It is the agent's immediate environment, perceived as a setting for
her current behaviour, that is the 'background' to action in cases of absorbed

coping. When Merleau-Ponty talks about the movement and its background as being 'moments of a totality', he is referring to the way in which there is an intimate correspondence between the behaviour, and the subject's environment perceived as a setting for it. The claim that the background to the behaviour is what 'inspires and sustains' it simply refers to the way in which the agent's unreflective behaviour is brought about and controlled by her perception of her environment as 'requiring' the behaviour in question.

The background to unreflective behaviour is the subject's environment, perceived as a setting for that behaviour. We have seen above that to perceive, on Merleau-Ponty's account, is to exercise one's motor skills. An essential part of being able to do x is the ability to recognise worldly settings that are appropriate for doing x, which is constituted by the capacity to perceive those settings as offering opportunities to do x. Perception on this account is an activity of the perceiver. When the agent perceives a demand for action, she is not passively receiving data from the world. Rather, she actively 'summons' the invitations to behave from the world; she 'projects' a situation around herself (PhP, 136/157); she invests her environment with a bodily significance. In perception, the projection of a situation around oneself that calls for a particular kind of behaviour is constrained by the nature of one's environment. When I perceive a space-to-park, for example, providing that nothing goes wrong with the perceptual process, my 'summoning up' of this demand for action is in line with what my environment is really like – I am confronted with a space that is indeed suitable for parking, and the fact that it is suitable for parking guides my summoning up of the invitation to park there.

Just as unreflective behaviour is initiated and controlled by its background, which is brought into being by the subject's ability to summon up demands for action from her environment, so too, behaviour such as that of Juan takes place against a background, which inspires and sustains it, and is again constituted by the subject's capacity to project a situation around herself that calls for a certain kind of activity. Merleau-Ponty holds that in a case such as that of Juan, where the agent 'interacts' with merely imagined surroundings, the agent represents those surroundings in thought. The agent then summons up the demands for action that this environment would make if it were real. Since the environment is not real, the demands for action that are summoned by the subject will not be perceived. Instead, they should be understood as imbuing his representation of the environment with a bodily significance. The representation thus exerts a pull on the subject; it demands a certain kind of activity, in a way that is analogous to, but not the same as, the manner in which the subject *perceives* his environment as demanding action. The representation, imbued with bodily significance, thus functions as the background to the action, pulling forth the agent's actions from him, and guiding his behaviour. The capacity to summon up demands for action from one's environment is conferred upon one by one's motor skills. When the agent perceives a rock-face as offering an opportunity to rock-climb, i.e. when she summons up an invitation to climb from the rock-face, she is exercising her skill at climbing. Likewise, when the subject summons up demands for action with respect to an environment that is represented in thought, she is exercising her motor skills. Thus it can be seen that the agent is able to imbue a possible, or imagined environment that she represents in thought with bodily significance because she is able to access her motor skills in relation to that represented environment – she is able to access those skills that she could use to perceive and act with respect to that environment if it were real.

Cases such as that of Juan are fairly unusual – miming is not a particularly commonplace activity. However, having analysed this case, we can see how the capacity involved is implicated in other cases that are more widespread. In the above case, the demands for action to which the agent responds by acting are not summoned up in line with the nature of the agent's environment. Instead, the agent summons up the demands with respect to a representation. Thus the agent does not perceive the demands for action; they imbue his representation with a bodily significance. Merleau-Ponty suggests that a similar analysis should be given of various other cases. It will further our understanding of how thought can generate action on Merleau-Ponty's account to consider another example: acting on the basis of a moral judgement (PhP, 112/129). Suppose, say, that I see some children kicking a hedgehog. It is the first time that I have been faced with such a situation. I judge that the morally correct thing to do would be to rescue the hedgehog, and on this basis, I take the hedgehog away to safety. In this case, my moral judgement – a thought which represents what I take to be the morally correct course of action – generates my action of rescuing the hedgehog. Although in this case the entity with which I interact – the hedgehog – is real rather than imagined, Merleau-Ponty nevertheless holds that the case involves the power to reckon with a possible environment and should be analysed in an analogous way to the case of Juan. Motor skills are acquired through practice. Since it is one's motor skills that enable one to perceive a demand for action, it follows that to perceive one's surroundings as demanding a certain form of behaviour, one must have behaved in that way in environments of the same kind, a sufficient number of times before. I have never before been faced with children kicking a hedgehog. Therefore I do not perceive the situation as requiring hedgehog-rescuing behaviour. The moral requirement to rescue the hedgehog is only represented in thought; I represent my surroundings as requiring hedgehog-rescuing behaviour. Through the power to reckon with the possible, I access those of my motor skills that are relevant to the way in which I represent my surroundings, and thus imbue my moral judgement with a bodily significance in the same way that Juan's imagined surroundings are imbued with bodily significance. My moral judgement, imbued with bodily significance, then functions as the background to the action, drawing forth my hedgehog-rescuing behaviour from me. Again, we can see how the power to reckon with the possible enables the agent to act on the basis of thought.

Conclusion

Dreyfus offers a reading of Merleau-Ponty's account of action according to which unreflective behaviour is immediately initiated and controlled by the agent's perceptions. The agent perceives opportunities to act, which draw forth her actions from her without the need for any intervening states that represent their performance. Dreyfus' interpretation runs into difficulties, however, when it comes to explaining how thought can generate action on Merleau-Ponty's model. He suggests that intention can initiate action when the flow of unreflective behaviour ceases. I have argued that this leaves us with an unsatisfactory account of how thought can generate action, since it means either thought can only generate action when the subject is asleep/unconscious, or the subject must wait for her perceptions to stop controlling behaviour before she can act on the basis of her decisions.

Dreyfus encounters problems when trying to explain how thought can bring about action on Merleau-Ponty's model because he does not address a capacity that Merleau-Ponty calls the power to reckon with the possible, and which he takes to be essential to the human ability to act. The content of perceptual experience on Merleau-Ponty's account is determined by the agent's actual environment, her current task, and her motor skills. Dreyfus conceives of this as the agent's actual environment and current task making certain of her motor skills available for her to use to perceive and act. I have suggested that the power to reckon with the possible should be understood as the capacity to access motor skills over and above those that are made available by one's actual environment and current task, so that the normal human agent can access motor skills in relation to merely possible environments and potential tasks. Thought affects behaviour in that humans can decide to take on tasks which then help shape the perceptions that bring about behaviour. However, a creature's physical nature imposes tasks upon it, and so one might wonder what makes it possible for humans to decide to engage in a project. On Merleau-Ponty's account this is explained by the power to reckon with the possible. One thing this power enables its possessor to do is see her current environment in the light of tasks in which she could be engaged. In other words, she can see more possibilities for action than just those that relate to her current project. He holds that this opens up the possibility of choice, and so humans can choose to take on tasks rather than simply having tasks imposed by their physical nature. However, there are some cases where we want to say that thought brings about behaviour, but which cannot be understood as cases where the agent's decision to take on a task affects the content of her perceptions. It is again the power to reckon with the possible that explains how action occurs in these cases – the power to access motor skills in relation to merely possible environments. To perceive, on Merleau-Ponty's account, is to exercise one's motor skills. The subject summons up demands for action, so projecting a situation around herself that calls for a certain form of behaviour. In perception, this process is constrained by the nature of the things the subject perceives. The power to reckon with the possible enables the agent to summon up demands for action independently of her environment. She is thus able to summon up demands for action in line with an environment that is merely represented in thought, thus imbuing the representation with a bodily significance, which can then initiate and guide action.

It has not been my aim in this paper to defend Merleau-Ponty's account of action, and there is much work yet to be done. However, I hope that I have shown that Merleau-Ponty's model does have the resources to explain how thought can bring about action, and is thus worthy of further investigation as an alternative to the orthodox view.

Notes

1 I will use 'action' to refer to any type of doing, but it should be noted that many theorists use 'action' in a more restricted sense.

2 Dreyfus talks about the agent having a sense that the current relationship between her body and the environment deviates from some optimal relationship between them. The deviation is experienced as tension, and the agent simply reacts to the tension, moving to reduce it. Although there are certain cases that can be described in this way – e.g. the example Dreyfus supplies of shuffling when entering a lift so as to stand the appropriate distance from each other, the appropriate distance being dictated, of course, by cultural norms (Dreyfus 2000, 300) – in other cases such as absentminded tea-making, there seems to be nothing describable as a sense of tension that I seek to reduce by putting on the kettle.

3 Dreyfus and Dreyfus 1999 offers a nice account of the different stages one passes through in acquiring a skill.

4

REPLY TO ROMDENH-ROMLUC

Hubert L. Dreyfus

Taking off from my account of absorbed skillful coping in Merleau-Ponty's *Phenomenology of Perception*, Komarine Romdenh-Romluc's paper raises two hard and important questions:

1 If our basic relation to the world is one of totally absorbed coping, how do we manage to switch from one task to another?
2 Given our basic way of being in the world is to be involved, how is detached reflection possible?

How can one be fully absorbed in one's current task and yet remain open to other tasks?

Aron Gurwitsch, who saw the similarity between gestalt psychology and Heidegger's phenomenology of everyday skillful coping, and who passed his insight on to Merleau-Ponty, gives an excellent description of our everyday absorbed coping:

> What is imposed on us to do is not determined by us as someone standing outside the situation simply looking on at it; what occurs and is imposed are rather prescribed by the situation and its own structure; and we do more and greater justice to it the more we let ourselves be guided by it, i.e., the less reserved we are in immersing ourselves in it and subordinating ourselves to it. We find ourselves in a situation and are interwoven with it, encompassed by it, indeed just 'absorbed' into it.
>
> (Gurwitsch 1979, 67)

But, Romdenh-Romluc asks, if we were so completely absorbed in our current task as Gurwitsch and Dreyfus claim, how could we shift from one task to another?

To see how Merleau-Ponty handles the phenomenon of task shifting, we need briefly to review Romdenh-Romluc's illuminating remarks on everyday coping. As she points out using Merleau-Ponty's example of the football player, when the player is totally absorbed in his task – in flow as an athlete might say – he sees the world as full of opportunities and threats that 'pull forth' appropriate responses from him, and he responds to these solicitations bodily, i.e. without any intervening reflection or sense of agency.[1]

Granted we need to be absorbed in our tasks in this way in order to have access to our skills, if, whenever we acted, we were fully in such an absorbed state, Romdenh-Romluc objects, we would be locked into each of our tasks like one of Kurt Goldstein's patients whom he calls 'Schneider'. If Schneider is absorbed in some errand other than to visit Goldstein, he cannot recognize Goldstein's house. If normal coping were so totally absorbing, we would lack the power to break free of our current task and become absorbed in anything else. So, to change tasks, Romdenh-Romluc contends, we must be able somehow to lessen our involvement.

Romdenh-Romluc thinks that I hold that there must be a *total lessening* – that one could only break out of one's current absorption if the task one was absorbed in became impossible. I never made such a claim, but rather, like Dewey, Heidegger, and Merleau-Ponty, I claim that, as long as one is succeeding in what one is absorbed in doing, one would have no motivation to interrupt one's activity. Normally, to stop the flow there would have to be some sort of disturbance.

To articulate how absorption can be *modified* without being *lessened*, it helps to borrow an example and some technical terms from Heidegger. While the absorbed carpenter is fully absorbed in her hammering, it can dawn on her that her hammer is too heavy. In Heidegger's terms, the mode of being of the hammer has changed from readiness-to-hand to unreadiness-to-hand. But it is important to see that to cope with this change the carpenter need not step out of, or even lessen, her absorption in her task. She can, as Heidegger points out, simply reach for a lighter hammer without stopping to reflect (Heidegger 1962, 102–3). Even in a more serious case of too-heaviness, when the hammer and the situation become conspicuous and lead the hammerer to shift her attention from the current task to a different task, say gluing the pieces of wood together, she can, nonetheless, remain fully engaged in the current situation, changing the with-which while retaining the towards-which, as Heidegger would say. In such cases, one doesn't need to step back, deliberate, and decide among alternative approaches. Rather, in simply letting oneself be drawn to attend to a marginal alternative, one has already made a 'choice'. That is how Heidegger, Merleau-Ponty and I would describe the way in which, in ordinary coping, a change of attention brings about a change in comportment without requiring the abandonment or even lessening of one's engagement in one's situation.

According to Heidegger, this involved shift in attention is to be sharply distinguished from what happens when there is neither a lighter hammer nor a glue pot in sight. When there is no task on the horizon that solicits attention and response, activity stops. As Romdenh-Romluc puts it, when perception is insufficient to bring about behavior, the ego emerges. Then, for example, instead of coping directly with the hammer-aspect, 'too heavy for this task', by switching tasks, I have to give up my task. I then observe the hammer as a present-at-hand object with certain detachable properties such as weight, and I can then deliberate and decide what to do. I can, for example, envisage other situations such as going out and buying a one-pound hammer to replace my three-pound one. My deliberation thus gives rise to a decision, which, in turn, brings about my action.[2] This is the kind of response to a breakdown I had in mind when I said coping stops.

For Heidegger and Merleau-Ponty, then, there are three ways of switching one's involved activity: sensing a disturbance and letting one's attention be drawn to another task, or, sensing some other situation and letting it lead me to become involved in it, or, in the face of a breakdown, detaching oneself from the current situation and entertaining possibilities that are not even on the horizon of one's current activity.

To adapt Romdenh-Romluc's driving example, if I'm tired of driving or the traffic is too dense, my sense of the difficulty makes me sensitive to new opportunities, and a parking space that I otherwise wouldn't have noticed may attract my attention and switch me to the task of parking, while I, nonetheless, stay fully engaged in the driving situation. Or I may be attracted by a situation on the margin of the current driving situation such as valet parking and seek it while still involved, or I may step back from the whole driving situation, envisage taking the metro and decide to abandon my car. In the first case, while one is involved in a task, a shift in attention allows a task on the horizon of the current task to solicit a response; in the second, one is attracted by and responds to a new situation on the horizon of the current one; while in the third case, the ego envisages a totally new possibility that was neither on the horizon of the current task nor of the current situation – a possibility that leads to a decision to become involved in a new task in a new situation.

But this brings us back to Romdenh-Romluc's objection. If skillful coping required being as totally absorbed in the current task as I claim, how could one ever escape the control of whatever task was guiding one's current activity so as to be open to alternatives? Romdenh-Romluc, therefore, quite reasonably attributes to Merleau-Ponty the view that either one is so completely absorbed in the concrete task that it completely 'controls' one's coping, as in the case of Schneider, or else one abstracts oneself from one's involvement and freely considers other situations. She quotes Merleau-Ponty as saying: 'The normal person *reckons with* the possible, which thus, without shifting from its position as a possibility, acquires a sort of actuality' (*PhP*, 109/125). Or, as Romdenh-Romluc puts it:

> It is the agent's actual environment and the project in which she is actually engaged ... which initiate and *control* absorbed coping. In absorbed coping there is thus a sense in which the agent contends or *reckons with* 'the actual': her actual environment and actual task.

Correlatively, *'the possible' with which the normal person has the power to reckon* can be understood as encompassing possible projects that the agent could undertake, and/or possible environments in which she could be located.

(Romdenh-Romluc, this volume, 51, my italics)

Thus Romdenh-Romluc suggests that Merleau-Ponty solves the problem of how normal people in flow can be totally involved in a task and yet, unlike Schneider, open to other tasks and other situations, the way Goldstein solves it. It's as if Schneider and animals, when coping with the actual task, are locked into what Goldstein calls the *concrete attitude* while normal people are saved from this fate because, at the same time they are coping, they are free to stand back from the situation, adopt an *abstract attitude,* and so summon up a new project.

But this is not Merleau-Ponty's view. In the passage Romdenh-Romluc is relying on that introduces summoning and projecting, Merleau-Ponty puts these terms in single quotes. Thus he says:

For a normal person his *projects* ... bring magically to view a host of signs which *guide* action. This function of *'projection'* or *'summoning'* (in the sense in which the medium summons an absent person and causes him to appear) is also what makes *abstract* movement possible.

(*PhP,* 112/129)

I will argue that Merleau-Ponty uses scare quotes because he is expounding Goldstein's distinction between concrete and abstract movement, rather than advancing his own account.

Merleau-Ponty and Goldstein agree on the phenomenology of everyday task absorption as parallel to that of perception. Schneider is directly summoned by his equipment to make the appropriate bodily responses:

The bench, scissors, pieces of leather offer themselves to the subject as poles of action; through their combined values they delimit a certain *situation,* a certain kind of work. The body is no more than an element in the system of the subject and his world, and the *task* to be performed elicits the necessary movements from him by a sort of remote attraction, as the phenomenal forces at work in my visual field elicit from me, without any calculation on my part, the motor reactions which establish the most effective balance between them.

(*PhP,* 106/122)

But Merleau-Ponty, contra Goldstein, holds that when something solicits me to shift my attention, I don't, like a medium, *summon up* a new task from outside the current situation; rather, in such a shift, an affordance on the horizon of my involved activity *summons my body* to a new task, or a different situation on the horizon of the current situation summons me directly into a new situation.

We should therefore distinguish between being *summoned*, while involved with one affordance or in one situation, to respond directly to an alternative affordance or situation, on the one hand, from projecting an abstract possibility, and deciding to act on it, on the other. When speaking of one's attention being drawn by an object, Merleau-Ponty uses the term *summons* (without scare quotes) to refer not to an action undertaken by me but to the influence on me of a perceptual object.

> To see an object is either to have it on the fringe of the visual field and be able to concentrate on it, or else respond to this *summons* by actually concentrating on it.
>
> (*PhP*, 67/78, my italics)[3]

Generalizing from perception to action, Merleau-Ponty speaks of 'something which is an anticipation of, or arrival at, the objective and is ensured by the body itself as a motor power, a "motor project" ... a "motor intentionality"' (*PhP*, 110/127).

Merleau-Ponty understands motor intentionality as the way the body tends toward an optimal grip on its object. As he puts it:

> For each object, as for each picture in an art gallery, there is an optimum distance from which it requires to be seen, a direction viewed from which it vouchsafes most of itself. ... The distance from me to the object is not [experienced as] a size which increases or decreases, but [as] a tension which fluctuates round a norm.
>
> (*PhP*, 302/352)

Objects, in other words, draw us to get an optimal grip on them, and we experience a tension whenever the body/world relation fails to achieve that optimum. For Merleau-Ponty, this tension is a fundamental aspect of our involvement. It explains such basic phenomena as our perception of size and shape constancy (see Kelly 2004).

Yet Merleau-Ponty says that Schneider 'lacks ... motor intentionality' (*PhP*, 110/127). This needs some explaining since it seems that Schneider is capable of switching tasks. When sewing is what is called for, he can presumably stop cutting and start sewing. Without some minimal form of motor intentionality Schneider would lack even the flexibility to make wallets. Indeed, without some tendency towards a maximum grip, Schneider couldn't even perceive objects having stable sizes and shapes.

It seems clear that Schneider can see objects and can switch tasks from cutting to sewing as he makes his wallets. What he presumably can't do is switch from a wallet-making situation to going home, or from a non-Goldstein related errand to a Goldstein-related one, unless explicitly told to do so. What Schneider lacks, then, is the ability to shift from absorption in one motor intentional *situation* to absorption in another.

This shows there must be a normal and a pathological version of motor intentionality.[4] But Goldstein, according to Merleau-Ponty, does not understand how to characterize it. He misses the crucial distinction between responding to an actual *summons* to change tasks *while staying involved*, and *projecting* a *mere possibility*, and so he mistakenly concludes that, if Schneider is locked into the concrete situation it must be because he lacks the abstract attitude. Thus Merleau-Ponty reads Gelb and Goldstein as groping towards the kind of adaptive intentionality missing in Schneider but never managing to grasp it. He notes:

> Gelb and Goldstein ... have done more than anyone to go beyond the traditional dualism of automatism and consciousness. But they have never named this third term between the psychic and the physiological, between the for itself and the in itself to which their analyses always led them and which we call existence.
>
> (*PhP*, 122 n1/140 n55)

Consequently, Merleau-Ponty expounds Gelb/Goldstein's analysis of Schneider's deficit in terms of the dichotomy between the concrete and abstract attitude sympathetically while, at the same time, claiming that it leads them to miss the basic phenomenon. No wonder Romdenh-Romluc attributes Gelb/Goldstein's view to Merleau-Ponty. But, according to Merleau-Ponty, seeing Schneider as controlled by the concrete situation and thus unfree, while people who can deal with pure possibilities are free, leaves out just that 'momentum of existence' which enables humans and animals alike to respond to situations on the horizon of their current situation neither as fully actual nor as merely possible, but as soliciting them to turn to them to get a better grip on their world.

Since Romdenh-Romluc fails to see that, thanks to motor intentionality, we shift tasks while staying absorbed, she devotes the early part of her paper to criticizing my version of Merleau-Ponty's account of involvement. She rejects my claim that, according to Merleau-Ponty, our motor intentional activity is always motivated by a tendency to decrease a felt bodily tension, and says that my example of the felt tension in an elevator that leads the bodies involved to move to an appropriate distance from each other, is a special case, and, as a good phenomenologist, she notes that there is no such sense of tension when things are going well. I grant that when things are going well, one does not feel drawn to change one's current bodily stance, but I feel sure that Merleau-Ponty would hold that this is a case of zero tension, where sensitivity to tension is still guiding one's coping. A pilot following a radio beacon doesn't hear a warning sound unless he gets off course, but the silence he experiences when he is on course doesn't mean the beacon isn't continually guiding him.

The important issue as to how to interpret Merleau-Ponty turns on the difference between sensing tasks and situations other than the one I'm actually engaging in right now as *potential* because they are *on the horizon summoning me right now,* as opposed to experiencing these alternative tasks as summoned up by me and so *merely possible.* This crucial difference can best be seen by comparing Gelb/Goldstein's and Romdenh-Romluc's mistaken account of the relation of actual and possible actions in terms of the dichotomy between concrete and abstract attitudes, to a parallel mistaken way of understanding how we experience the *backsides* of perceptual objects as present but concealed. In this case, the mistake is to claim that the front of an object is perceived as actual while the back, when concealed, is experienced merely as a *mere possibility* of perception. To state the two parallel mistakes in Husserl's terms, we can compare the way aspects of an object on its *inner horizon* are experienced as present even when I am not directly coping with them, with the way a task I am not currently absorbed in can be experienced as potentially absorbing because it is on the *outer horizon* of the current situation.

The intellectualist view of perception that Merleau-Ponty rejects is like that of C. I. Lewis, who held that perception has as conceptual content the contrafactual: 'If I do so and so, then I will have such and such an experience' (Lewis 1946, 18). Alva Noë has recently resurrected this view in more embodied terms as the enactivist view (Noë 2004, 18). He attributes to the body rather than the mind the understanding of the 'sensory-motor contingencies' involved in seeing an object, so that, for the hidden back to be experienced as present, I must have a bodily understanding that, were I to go behind the house, I would see its back. Romdenh-Romluc seems to adopt a view like Noë's when she says:

> Merleau-Ponty holds that the subject's surroundings and current task bring relevant motor skills 'online', making them *available for the subject to use* in perception and action.
>
> (Romdenh-Romluc, this volume, 52, my italics)

But, as Sean Kelly points out, (Kelly, forthcoming) merely being ready to walk around and see the back of an object is compatible with the back's coming into existence only when I actually go to look at it, and so doesn't solve the problem of the back's hidden presence. Something more is needed to account for the experienced presence of the back. On Merleau-Ponty's account, for the back to be experienced as already potentially present rather than as merely possible, it must somehow be already acting on me. But how is this possible? As we have already seen in discussing the tendency to obtain a maximal grip, Merleau-Ponty's answer is that, as one faces the front of a house, one's body is already being drawn (not just prepared) to go around the house to get a better look at its back.

We can now see how Merleau-Ponty's treatment of the *inner* horizon of the perceptual object, applies equally to the experience of the *outer* horizon of a task. As I cope, other tasks are right now present on the horizon as ways of attaining a better grasp on the current situation. These other affordances set up a tension through which a normal person is sensitive to these other opportunities as potentially (not just possibly) present in the current situation. For example, even when one is charging along in the grip of one's current errand, one has a sense of other objects and situations calling on one, so that, if he needs to make a phone call, he can turn his attention to the situation and respond to a familiar house as affording phoning and drawing him to enter it. Or, if someone calls his attention to a particular house and so interrupts the flow of his current task, he can recognize it as a familiar house that was already on the horizon of the current situation without resorting to detached reflection. Indeed, familiar houses remain on the horizon of one's experience, even if one is just standing around looking at things. One is still engaged in the situation of looking around, and so feels drawn to get the best possible view of the current scene.

Romdenh-Romluc comes close to making this very point but loses it as she proceeds because she believes Merleau-Ponty holds Goldstein's view that to switch situations one has to abandon one's involvement in the current situation and open a new space of possibilities. So her account passes from speaking of an opportunity, to a potential task, to a possible task, to a merely possible project, thereby blurring the point Merleau-Ponty is trying to make;

> To recognize Goldstein's house is to perceive an *opportunity for action* relative to the task of 'engaging' with the house in some way. So to recognize it when you pass it on the way to somewhere else is to see the house in the light of a *potential task*. It is to perceive the house as offering an opportunity to act in relation to the *possible task* of, for example, posting a letter through Goldstein's door. Thus the normal adult human can *access* more than just those motor skills that are made available by her actual environment and current task; she can also access motor skills that are relevant to *merely possible projects* she could undertake in her environment.
>
> (Romdenh-Romluc, this volume, 53, my italics)

Because she fails to see the distinction between those tasks on the horizon of the current situation that are experienced as *potential* because one is already resisting their attraction or giving it to it, as opposed to those merely possible situations whose relevant motor skills are merely *available* for use, she fails to see how new tasks can summon one directly from within one's absorption. That is, she thinks there is no way out of the sort of task absorption Gurwitsch describes, which she interprets as the control of the concrete, but to distance oneself from one's current environment in order to access or summon up motor skills for counterfactual tasks. There is no way out of the concrete attitude but the abstract attitude. This is presumably the mistake Merleau-Ponty criticizes

Goldstein for making, although, admittedly, Merleau-Ponty never says so as clearly as one would like.

How is detached reflection possible?

Merleau-Ponty as I read him has an answer to Romdenh-Romluc's first hard question: How do we shift tasks while staying fully involved? We do so by turning to a potential task already summoning us from the inner horizon of the current task in which we are absorbed, or else by turning from the current situation in which we are engaged to some other situation already summoning us from the current situation's outer horizon. But Romdenh-Romluc's even harder question is: If our coping activity normally stays embodied and involved, even when we switch tasks and situations, how, on Merleau-Ponty's and my view, could we ever step back from our absorbed and engaged coping and exercise disembodied, detached, decision making?

Romdenh-Romluc follows Gelb/Goldstein in holding that what makes it possible for us to detachedly deliberate is that normal people, unlike Schneider and animals, are never fully involved. They are always ready to respond to possible situations to which they are not yet responding. And so they are always already in a free space where they can reckon with the possible. As she puts it:

> Since the perception of *an opportunity to behave* in a particular way is the exercise of a motor skill that the agent possesses, she has the ability to engage in the behaviour that she perceives the world as demanding, so the perceived opportunity for action is presented as a *real possibility* for her, something she *can* do. In this way, *the power to reckon with the possible* enables humans to *decide* to take on particular projects, rather than simply having tasks imposed on them by their physical nature.
>
> (Romdenh-Romluc, this volume, 53, my italics)

But, as we have seen, we are normally so absorbed into our tasks that no 'I' is present to decide anything (see Sartre 1958). How then could we ever get out of our absorption in a specific task or in a specific situation? Moreover, if perception and action is always involved and holistic, how are we able to entertain propositional beliefs about isolable perceptual objects and their isolable properties and, more generally, how is thought able to make judgments on the basis of perceptual experience?

As far as I know, Merleau-Ponty had nothing to say on these subjects so we shouldn't fault Romdenh-Romluc for failing to find Merleau-Ponty's account of what makes abstract thought possible. Indeed, we should thank her for focusing attention on the problem of how to describe the transformed role of the body that allows us to stop our absorbed coping and reflect. The only philosopher I know of who has taken up this question is Samuel Todes. In his book *Body and World* (Todes 2001) he goes a step beyond Merleau-Ponty and offers a phenomenological description of how we can relax the tension drawing us towards an optimal grip on *actual* contextualized objects so as to open a space for the experience of context-free *possible* objects about which we can then deliberate.

We have, Todes claims, a skill for totally transforming our everyday coping skills. Todes discusses only the role of this skill in transforming perception, but a similar account could be given for its role in opening a space for reflection and deliberation. According to Todes, the transformation of *contextually determined perceptual objects* with *integrated aspects* into *decontextualized conceptual objects* with *isolable features* takes place as follows. To begin with, the *spectatorial attitude*, by deactivating one's bodily set to cope, transforms the integrated aspects of the perceptual object into a set of isolable qualities. To demonstrate that this transformation is possible, Todes points out that practical perception takes place in three stages:

1 In the first stage we prepare ourselves to perceive an object by getting into a proper position or attitude in respect to it.
2 Having prepared ourselves to perceive it, we next ready the object to be perceived.

This is done by 'getting at' the object in some essentially preliminary, tentative, and easily reversible way that allows us to test, with comparatively light consequences, the desirability of going on to fully perceive the object.

3 In the third stage we finally perceive the object.

When we reach stage three, Todes claims, we transform practical perception into observation and so become aware of *qualities* rather than things. Likewise, we can inhibit our involved tendency to get a maximal grip on the situation so as to reflect on the options available.

But how, then, does what Todes calls the spectatorial attitude differ from Gelb/Goldstein's abstract attitude? The answer is that, in the spectatorial attitude Todes is proposing to complete Merleau-Ponty's account, we, as embodied, are still involved in coping with the world even when we are thinking, only we are involved differently. In action we are fully absorbed in seeking a maximal grip in our task in our situation in the world. When we inhibit this *absorption* and take up the spectatorial attitude, we inhibit our tendency to get a maximal grip on *objects* and *tasks* and on the *current situation*, but as embodied we remain fully involved in the world. Only by reference to our tendency to get a general background grip *on* the world, as distinct from objects, tasks, and situations *in* the world, can we orient ourselves so that our thinking retains a sense of relevance and our decisions make sense and motivate us.

Conclusion

Systematizing Merleau-Ponty's terminology so as to adequately fit the phenomena, we can say that:

1 Embodied active beings (even Schneider) are absorbed in their tasks thanks to their minimum motor intentionality.
2 Normal people, higher animals, and infants (but not Schneider) are able to switch tasks while staying engaged in a situation that has other tasks on its horizon, thanks to the full motor intentionality Merleau-Ponty calls existence.
3 All normal active embodied beings are open to other situations on the horizon of the current one, because they are involved in the world.

Romdenh-Romluc is on the right track in thinking we must somehow be able to transform our absorption in the concrete situation without completely detaching ourselves from the world. But it is not that our involvement is lessened as Romdenh-Romluc thinks I hold, nor that it is eliminated as in the abstract attitude of Gelb/Goldstein. Happily, we needn't assume an abstract attitude that abandons completely our motor skills and our involvement in the world in order to think about merely *possible* situations, actions, and objects. Rather, we can skillfully inhibit our tendency to move towards a *maximal grip on specific objects*, while maintaining our *general grip on the world*. This general bodily grasp which is our *being-in-the world* allows us to be both fully absorbed in some specific task while remaining open to other tasks on the horizon of the current one, and to be fully engaged in a specific situation, while remaining open to other situations on the horizon of the world.

Notes

1 It helps here to introduce an idea that J. J. Gibson may have adapted from phenomenology – he told me once he was greatly influenced by Merleau-Ponty – and speaks of being solicited by affordances. So food affords eating, floors afford support, and parking spaces afford parking. When one needs any one of these goods, one is drawn to respond to the solicitations of that particular affordance.
2 This switch is not merely a switch from what John Searle would understand as one intention in action with its representation of its conditions of satisfaction to a new intention in action with its representation of new conditions of satisfaction. For Merleau-Ponty this would amount to a much more radical switch from motor intentionality to representational intentionality. He expresses his own view in the following passage: '[T]o move one's body is to aim at things through it; it is to allow oneself to respond to their call, which is made upon it independently of any representation' (*PhP*, 139/160–1). For further discussion, see Dreyfus 2000.
3 I admit that Merleau-Ponty does not always distinguish summoning and projecting in this way, nor, as far as I can see, in any systematic way.
4 Motor-intentionality is closely connected with what Merleau-Ponty calls the intentional arc. This is the ability to learn to see new affordances on the basis of past experience. Presumably even Schneider experiences an intentional arc, but Merleau-Ponty tells us that it has gone 'limp'. 'It is this intentional arc which brings about the unity of the senses, of intelligence, of sensibility and motility. And it is this which "goes limp" in illness' (*PhP*, 136/157). This is no doubt connected with Schneider's weakened motor intentionality.

5

THE PHENOMENOLOGY OF SOCIAL RULES[1]

Mark A. Wrathall

The role of social rules

The idea of a social rule plays a central role in the philosophy and science of language, jurisprudence and the philosophy of law, and all the various philosophies and sciences of man – political science, economics, anthropology and sociology, etc. Rules are also often appealed to in explaining the nature of cognition and even certain aspects of perception. One puzzling feature of the vast philosophical literature on rules, at least that portion of the vast literature with which I am familiar, is the near absence of careful reflection on what a rule is. Over and over again, theorists wheel out the mechanism of rules in order to explain this or that aspect of social behaviour, but without any careful effort to say what a rule is in the first place, and why it should be such a thing as to explain the behaviour in question. Another surprising oversight (I believe it is related to the first) is the near absence of any phenomenology of what it is actually like to follow a rule or be governed by a rule. This oversight leads, in my opinion, to a failure adequately to explain what it means for a rule to govern a social domain.

This latter question, that of the role rules play in ordering a domain, does attract a great deal of attention. So far as I can tell, each discipline that employs the idea of a social rule struggles with some version of the following problem: in what sense do social rules actually govern the social domain? Is the rule something that we intentionally follow – that is, is the rule internal to social action? Or is the rule something that obtains objectively – that is, is the rule something to be described from an external perspective? In each area concerned with social rules, this debate is repeated and results, characteristically, in a deadlock, with neither side able to muster determinative arguments against the other position. Indeed, a deadlock is inevitable since these alternatives for pursuing the issue – internal rule following versus external rule description – are both inadequate for the phenomena.

The whole debate, I suggest, arises from the failure to understand the way that rules actually figure in human experience. To correct this, we need a phenomenology of rules. This phenomenology will show that there is a way in which rules govern the social domain without being intentionally followed. But that does not mean that rules are a mere external description of regularities within the social domain. Rather, rules structure the social world and, as such, guide our everyday encounter with worldly things, events, and states of affairs. In the first part of the paper, I want to discuss a couple of characteristic ways in which the role of social rules becomes problematic. In the second part of the paper, I will explore the alternative way of thinking about rules.

The problem of rule-governed behaviour

Let me begin by briefly describing one example of the way that philosophers of the social domain appeal to rules. This example comes from the philosophy of law, where it has become customary to treat the law as consisting (at least in large part) of a system of rules. Following Hart's influential treatment in *A Concept of Law* (Hart 1961), it has become widely accepted in Anglo-American jurisprudence that unless we think of the law as a system of rules, it is impossible to distinguish the very different cases of (a) being obligated by the law to do or refrain from doing something, and (b) being coerced (perhaps by a criminal) to do or refrain from doing something. What distinguishes my relationship to a robber who orders me to do something from my relationship to a policeman or judge who order me to do something is that the judge's or policeman's order is legitimated by a system of rules.

At first glance, the thesis that being governed by the law is a matter of following rules seems quite plausible. There is no question, for example, that when we learn what the law is, we are usually learning rules. Much of the time in following the law, we *are* deliberately trying to follow the rules. When I fill out my federal tax forms every April, for example, I spend a lot of time figuring out what the rules are, and determining how they apply to me and what they require me to do. When a prosecutor decides to charge someone with a crime, or a judge makes a ruling on a case, when a corporation decides to sue for breach of contract, in each of these cases, there are deliberate efforts to determine what the rules are, and to follow those rules in one's own action. Moreover most of us, if called upon to do so, could articulate a great number of legal rules.

These observations are right so far as they go. But they only give a partial story. If much of the time we do know what legal rules govern us and our social institutions, we are also mistaken much of the time. And there are many instances in which people automatically do what the law requires them to do, without actually knowing what the legal rule is that they are following. Even if we do know what the rule is, there is, at least much of the time, no deliberate effort to follow the rules: when I am driving, for instance, I stop at the stop sign without ever thinking about the rule that one must stop at the stop sign, let alone deliberately trying to follow it. This is an important fact – one that we need to be able to explain because, in such instances, a rule governs my behaviour without my needing to try to follow it. In these respects, then, the law turns out to be much more ambiguous as an example of a domain in which rules are followed than we might have initially thought.

On the basis of such considerations, one can pose two very different questions about the role of rules in the legal domain. The first is the external question: to what extent do the laws as such actually succeed in describing our behaviour? That is, as a purely objective matter, we can be interested in discovering to what extent actual behaviour corresponds with the rules by which we take our legal actions and institutions to be governed. This is a question for social scientists; for a philosopher, the interesting question is the internal question: to what extent do our law-governed actions need to consist in intentionally following these rules?

There is, in addition, a further problem in understanding the nature of legal rules presented by the fact that so much of the law does consist in explicit rules. One of the rules of most modern legal systems is that something is a law (a rule) only if it complies with certain other rules. So if I announce that from now on the law requires everyone to pay their taxes to me, my announcement will not be a rule, and no one will be obligated to obey it. This is because one of the legal rules in the US is that something is a rule only if it has been legislated by Congress and signed by the president. Hart calls such rules 'secondary rules of recognition' – they are 'secondary rules' because they are rules about rules – rules governing what we can do with rules, whether it be to apply and enforce them, promulgate, extinguish, modify them, etc. Primary rules, by contrast, are rules which require us 'to do or abstain from certain actions' (Hart 1961, 81). They are rules of *recognition* because they tell us when something will be recognized as a binding rule.

The problem arises when we ask about the rules of recognition themselves – why, for instance, is something a law only if it is promulgated by Congress and signed by the president? The answer, of course, is that the American Constitution says so; but why is the American Constitution the ultimate rule of recognition? That is, what rule tells us that we must accept the Constitution as a valid rule? Eventually, the regress must stop, and we are seemingly confronted with the fact that it is just what legal actors do – they use the Constitution as a rule of recognition, but there is no deeper rule which they are following in doing so. This means that, at the deepest level, legal actors are not following a rule at all. While, as a rule, American legal actors recognize the Constitution as the ultimate source of law, they are not bound to do so by any rule. And so, it seems, the only sense in which their behaviour is ultimately law governed is that, from the external perspective, we can describe their action by means of a rule. But their intentions are irrelevant to this description – the rule describes them whether they intend to follow it, or even have any awareness of it, or not.

The example should have shown that there are serious limitations with an effort to explain the rule-governed nature of human behaviour using the model of deliberate, intentional rule following. First of all, much if not most of the time it is phenomenologically untrue that we are trying to follow a rule. We simply act in the appropriate way, in the vast majority of easy cases. But also in the deepest, most profound cases, we discover that the rules have to run out. We cannot have rules that tell us how to apply the rules, because we need to know how to apply those rules in turn. Rules are not self-applying. As phenomenologists like Dreyfus and Merleau-Ponty, and analytical philosophers like Wittgenstein and Searle have long pointed out, ultimately our ability to apply rules must be grounded in a background capacity that is not itself the product of rules. To posit that we are unconsciously following rules only defers, but does not solve, this problem. In addition, as we will see, the phenomenological contrast between applying rules and just behaving in a way that is rule governed suggests that the actions are ontologically distinct as well.[2]

But should we then give up on analysing social rules from the 'inside', as it were, and become linguists and social scientists? The problems with the external, objectivist perspective are well remarked. First is the fact that it cannot account for the *meaning* that the rules themselves hold for us. From the external perspective, all theories are acceptable which are equally extensionally adequate to describing the events under consideration. To a basketball, it makes no difference whether we describe it using the concepts and vocabulary of Newton or of Einstein; it bounces the same way regardless. The rules we identify in language, in law, and in other social institutions are not just useful ways to describe and predict what goes on in the social domain, but they themselves play a role in our social life *as* rules. And it makes a big difference to us how our actions and institutions are described. Extensional adequacy is not enough; we expect our theories to get it right in terms of the meaning that things hold for us from the 'inside'.

A second, but related, shortcoming is the fact that the external perspective cannot account for the *normative structure* of rules – the way that we find ourselves obligated by social rules. If there is a law that states that I must pay my taxes by 15 April, then I am obligated to do so. It does not capture my experience of these rules to treat them as external predictions of agent behaviour. As Hart has pointed out, if the rule – for example, that failure to pay taxes will be punished with a fine or imprisonment – is merely a means for describing or predicting social behaviour, then I would have no obligation to pay my taxes if there was no chance that I would be punished for it. But in fact, I am sorry to say, I do have an obligation to pay my taxes even if I know for certain that I can get away with not paying them.

Another way to see this normative dimension of rules is to note that the existence of a rule does not just explain behaviour, it also justifies it. We frequently take the existence of a rule not just as an explanation for what happens, but as the basis for critiquing what happens. But the external perspective cannot account for our *practices* of appealing to rules, deliberating about rules, arguing about rules, etc. We all act as if rules count for something, and we have developed what Habermas has called a 'culture of argumentation' within which we take rules seriously, not just as predictions about what will happen, but as determining what ought to happen (Habermas 1998).

Now, I do not pretend to have offered knock-down arguments against some version of either the internalist or externalist account of social rules. But I think I have offered some reasons to find these approaches deeply problematic. The examples we have examined have shown that both approaches fail to explain some important dimension of rule-governed behaviour. Rather than pursue these perspectives any further at this point, I would like to turn now to trying to develop a phenomenological account in some more detail. I think this will point us toward a way of thinking about social rules that is neither internalist nor externalist in orientation. But before going any further, we need to turn squarely to one of the questions I posed at the outset – namely, what is a rule anyway?

The nature of rules

As I have already noted, a striking feature of most discussions of rules is the absence of much systematic reflection on what a rule is in the first place. We have, to this point, followed this tradition. One might think this a serious oversight. Understanding what a rule *is* would seem to be a prerequisite to knowing whether things like language and the law can be modelled as a system of rules. Equally, knowing what a rule is would seem to be a prerequisite to understanding in what sense we follow rules in such domains. The problem is that, given the widespread scepticism over the idea that rule-following actually does govern the social domain, there is no agreement on what the paradigm instances of rule-following are. As a result, we have no such paradigm instance from which we can draw an uncontentious definition of what a rule is. So how are we to proceed?

We should begin with as broad and uncontroversial and formal a specification of rules as possible. What we can begin with, then, is a notion of rules that captures what is common to both those situations in which a rule is purportedly followed as well as those situations which are describable as falling under a rule. That is, we will look for necessary conditions of rulehood, anticipating that there will be some disagreement over whether these necessary conditions are also sufficient for the existence of a rule.

Whether we take the rule as being followed in action or merely describing behaviour, a rule encompasses two different kinds of functions. First, it *sorts* entities into types. Second, it *maps* those types onto one another. Take, for example, a simple rule like the chess rule that the bishop moves on the diagonal. This rule *sorts* pieces and it *sorts* moves – that is, it separates out the bishop pieces from other pieces, and it separates out movement along a diagonal from other kinds of movement (movement along a rank or file, moving two squares up and one square over, etc.). The rule then *maps* pieces onto moves – in particular, it maps the bishop pieces onto the movement along a diagonal.

Even rules that, on their face, consist of simple commands or prohibitions (for example, 'do not kill'), sort the world out into types, and then map those types onto one another in a particular fashion. Think of all the complex steps involved in following a rule like 'automobiles must be driven on the right hand side of the road'. It requires sorting out automobiles from all other things in the world (does it include toy cars? motorcycles?), as well as sorting out the right-hand side from the left-hand side of the road. It then requires 'mapping' auto-mobiles onto the right-hand side of the road – that is, when driving, each driver must (internal) or tends to (external) keep her automobile on the right-hand side.

All rules then, whether viewed from the internal or external perspective, involve sorting into types and mapping types onto types. In addition, some-thing is only rule governed if we can perform the mapping and sorting *reliably* and *projectibly*. In saying that it is reliable, I mean that it can be performed consistently in enough of the right sort of cases, although how many and how consistently is an open question. That is to say, if we cannot consistently tell which pieces are bishops and which are knights, then our use of the pieces cannot be governed by or described by the rules of chess. In saying that it is projectible, I mean that the rules can be applied even in circumstances we have not yet encountered. We should be able to tell how a piece will be able to move even in configurations on the board that we have never encountered before.

If consistently and projectibly sorting into types and mapping types onto types is essential to every rule, there are nevertheless quite different things to be accomplished through such mapping and sorting. Indeed, we can arrive at a rough taxonomy of rules in terms of the purpose played by the mapping and sorting.

Constitutive rules   These rules (purport to) *constitute* an entity as the entity it is by assigning to that entity a function that it does not have inherently. The rule that a bishop moves on the diagonal is such a constitutive rule; there are no chess bishops without the chess rules that sort pieces into types, create types of moves, and map those pieces onto moves. So sorting and mapping can stand in the service of constituting entities and practices to be performed with those entities.[3] The purpose of using sorting and mapping in this way is to make possible practices and activities (like playing chess, electing a president, etc.) which would not otherwise be possible.

Regulatory rules   These rules (purport to) *regulate or normalize* the behaviour of entities which exist independently of the rules. These can be either *obligatory* ('drive on the right side of the road'; 'a player must move the first piece tou-ched that can be moved') or *codificatory* ('one must not eat with both of one's elbows on the table') or *strategic* ('control the central four squares on the chess board'). Obligatory regulatory rules require a certain behaviour. They can, but

75

do not need to, accord with pre-existing practices. But they do require us to sort and map in a standard or normalized way – they obligate us. Codificatory regulatory rules must be based on a pre-existing practice – as the name implies, they codify in a canonical form regularities that already exists. Rules of language and etiquette are prominent examples of such rules. Once the regularities are codified, they can be taught as rules, and individuals can be criticized for breaking or praised for keeping them. Here again, mapping and sorting normalize situations and responses to promote the stability of societal expectations. Strategic regulatory rules *offer guidance* in the achievement of some particular purpose or end, and are only normative to the extent that we happen to want to achieve that end. They can be set aside if, in particular circumstances, the strategy embodied in the rule is less likely to produce the desired effect than some alternative. But if one sets them aside unwisely, one opens oneself to criticism.

In each of these cases, the purpose behind such mapping and sorting is to establish a normal response to recurring kinds of situations. Now, with this admittedly very general account of rules in mind, let us return to our inquiry into the role rules play in social life.

The phenomenology of social rules

What we want to know is: how do rules function in social life? By getting clearer about the sorting and mapping inherent in any view of rules, we can formulate the question somewhat more precisely: do the rules themselves play a direct role in mapping and sorting social facts, categories, institutions, actions, practices, etc.? Or are social facts, practices, etc., merely sorted and mapped in such a way that is describable by rules? The distinction between internal and external approaches to rules, in other words, is a distinction between the roles that the rules themselves play in the actor's actions. On the internal view, social actors intend to follow the rule as they deliberately sort and map. On the external view, no such intention is necessary.

I have been suggesting that traditional efforts to answer this question are hampered by the fact that they are working with an impoverished notion of the ways that actions can be produced. The only available alternatives are those of intentional action or physical causation. In the phenomenological tradition in philosophy, however, it has long been recognized that these alternatives are inadequate to explain much of human action and experience. Let us look briefly at a typical example of rule-governed behaviour to see why these alternatives are problematic.

Rule-following and rule-governed actions

As I sit down to play a game of chess, I find myself presented with an already meaningfully structured situation. The mapping and sorting, one might say, has already occurred. As the game begins, I do not apply the rules to the situation; the board lights up, as it were, as a situation that calls for particular kinds of response. As I look at the bishop, I see potential lines of attack, as well as sources of danger; I feel where it needs to be to best strengthen my defensive position, or prepare the attack, and I respond by moving it where it needs to be. There is never a need to reflect on the rules as such, nor do I need intentionally or deliberately to sort and map the board in terms of the rules. Moreover, it may be the case that I am actually unable to articulate the rule that has done the sorting and mapping. As I was preparing this paper, for example, I happened to look up the official rules of chess as promulgated by the World Chess Federation. It came as a surprise to me to learn the official statement of the rule that governs the movement of knights: 'the knight', the rule states, 'may move to one of the squares nearest to that on which it stands but not on the same rank, file or diagonal' (3.6). While I knew perfectly well how to move knights, it had never occurred to me to think of the rule in those terms, nor would I have been able to articulate the rule in that fashion, even if I had been asked to explicitly state the rule. I had always thought of it simply in terms of moving two squares in one direction, and one in another. It thus seems wrong, at least for a competent player of chess, to say that she is deliberately *following* the rules of chess when she plays.

My experience in playing a game of chess is, of course, very different to that of a beginner. When I teach my children to play chess, they first have to learn to sort the pieces into types, and the sorting is performed quite deliberately ('this one looks like a horse, so it must be a knight. This one looks like a castle, so it must be a rook', etc.). Having determined what the piece is, they then run through a kind of calculation of the possible moves – they map the piece, so to speak onto potential positions on the board. They then need, just as deliberately, to map out the opposing pieces' potential moves. Where I just naturally see danger zones and lines of attack, they need to step-wise connect pieces with squares to discover how to attack or how to defend their pieces.

One of the differences between the skilled chess player and the beginner, in other words, is that the skilled player simply sees the board as already shaped by the rules of chess. The beginner, on the other hand, must follow the rules; she must perform the act of sorting and mapping types onto types. It is precisely because the skilled player does not need to follow the rules intentionally that she can play so much better; the board arrays itself into threatening zones, weak zones, strong zones, lines of attack, impending moves, etc., and she can fluidly respond to whatever the game situation affords her.

The act of intentionally sorting, then, involves an experience of relating two (or more) types of things. When I sort things as automobiles, I must see the automobiles *as* something else, so that moving them into the class of automobiles involves a deliberate act. I might see them as complex machinery with wheels, for instance. To decide whether any particular complex machine is to be grouped with the automobiles, I examine it while running through the criteria for automobileness: 'can it move?'; 'can it carry passengers?'; 'can it be steered?', etc. Of course, most of the time, we do not perform any such sorting at all – we simply look and see the automobile as an automobile. The world comes to us as pre-sorted. But if someone has not yet acquired the skills for simply seeing automobiles as automobiles, or if there is a new device which differs from other automobiles in significant ways, then we might have to perform the sorting deliberately.

Similarly, mapping can be performed as an act, or the world can come to us already mapped. If we have acquired our skills for driving in Belgium or the United States (and most other countries in the world), we will automatically be drawn to the right-hand side of the road as we drive an automobile; there will be no experience of intending to follow the rule. But an English driver, for instance, might have to force herself quite self-consciously to drive on the right-hand side, at least at first. In her case, there is no need to *sort* deliberately; as an experienced driver, the world comes pre-sorted to her in terms of automobiles and right- and left-hand sides of the road. But she will need to *map* her driving onto the right-hand side of the road deliberately, because her skills make her tend to relate them in an unlawful way.

What we have seen, then, are two different ways that rules can regulate our actions. They can simply, transparently, and non-deliberately move us to act in a particular way, or we can deliberately apply them to relate things. In terms of realizing the content of the rule, the two ways that rules regulate are equivalent – we drive on the right-hand side of the road whether intentionally or automatically. But in terms of our experience of the rule and the world, these two ways are quite different. When the rule moves us to action without our having to perform any intentional sorting or mapping, I say that the action is *rule-governed*. When, in acting, we must also perform the sorting and/or mapping, I say that the action is *rule-following*. Finally, when, from the external perspective, the action is describable in terms of a rule, I say that it *accords with a rule*. Rule-governed action is free of any experience of sorting and mapping. Rule-following action involves an experience of sorting or mapping or both. In rule-governed action, we need have no intentional relationship to the rule at all, although the rule, one might say, is present in our experience in the way the world comes sorted and mapped. In rule-following action, we must represent the rule to ourselves as the basis on which we sort and map.

But despite all these differences, there is an important respect in which the rule-governed action and the rule-following action are, when successful, the same. If one recalls the chess example, the expert, rule-governed player moves her pieces in just the same way that the beginning, rule-following player does. Of course, the expert player makes different moves than the beginning player does. This is, in part, because the expert player has learned the limitations of the codificatory and strategic rules of chess. Most players will not sacrifice a queen to capture a bishop (this is a strategic rule of chess), but the expert player knows when it is appropriate to do so. This fact should not mislead us, however, into thinking that the constitutive and regulatory rules of chess are equally violable by the expert player. The expert player must abide by all the constitutive rules of chess on pain of no longer playing chess – that is, the expert player cannot decide, for instance, to move her bishop along a rank. The expert player must abide by the regulative rules of chess on pain of forfeiting the game.

If, at this point, we had to choose between reasons and causes to explain the action of the competent chess player, we have only two alternatives: (1) we can see the action as the result of an unconscious application of rules – the expert player does exactly the same thing that the beginner does, but at an unconscious level; or (2) we can see the action as not rule-governed at all, but simply produced by whatever causal forces give rise to the bodily movement. It might accord with a rule – that is, it might be describable with a rule, but the rule itself plays no role in the production of the action. Neither alternative, however, seems suitable for capturing the rule-governed behaviour.

The question we have been pursuing thus now becomes: how is rule-governed action possible? It is not produced by taking up an intentional stance toward the rule, as the phenomenological difference between rule-following and rule-governed action demonstrates. But nor does it seem right to say that the rule merely describes a causally induced pattern of behaviour. Like the rule-follower, the rule-governed actor responds to the rule itself. If someone points out that I have moved my knight incorrectly, I accept this as a criticism and hold myself accountable to the rule. The rule itself, in other words, *functions in* the chess game; it does not merely describe it.

The only philosopher that I am aware of who has tackled this problem head-on is John Searle (Searle 1995). Considerations like the ones I have articulated have led Searle to argue that we need a new kind of causation – one by means of which our background ability to cope with the world 'can be causally sensitive to the specific forms of the constitutive rules of the institutions without actually containing any beliefs or desires or representations of those rules' (Searle 1995, 141). The problem with Searle's account, however, is that it does not introduce a new kind of causation at all; rather, it holds that the old kind of brute causation can evolve in such a way that it produces behaviours that coincide with rule-following comportment.

The mechanism Searle offers to explain rule-governed action is the background that we have alluded to before. As I have shown elsewhere (Wrathall 2000), Searle has largely adopted Hubert Dreyfus' account of background practices with one important difference: he ultimately reduces the background to a neurophysiological structure that disposes us to be in an intentional state. What all background theorists accept is that the background is a non-intentional set of capacities that generate particular intentional states. That we have such a background is evidenced by our ability to understand determinately utterances that, at face value, are ambiguous. One of Searle's best examples is the English verb 'cut'. We understand what it means to cut the cake, cut the grass, or cut the paper, even though the action is very different in each instance. By the same token, we do not know what it would mean to cut the building or cut the mountain. The reason that we understand such utterances (when we do) is that we have background practices for cutting cakes, grass, and paper, but no background practices for cutting buildings or mountains. In other words, for our intentional states about cutting to have content – to determine conditions of satisfaction – Searle argues, we must have background practices for the relevant kinds of cutting (see Searle 1995, 130–1). But – and this is the important distinction between Searle and other background theorists like Dreyfus and Merleau-Ponty – this is not because the practices themselves determine the content; rather, the practices produce a neurophysiological state in the agent which then causes her intentional states to have the content that they do. 'It is important to see', Searle notes,

> that when we talk about the Background we are talking about a certain category of neurophysiological causation. Because we do not know how these structures function at a neurophysiological level, we are forced to describe them at a much higher level.
>
> (Searle 1995, 129)

Searle's background of capacities explains intentional states by showing how they can determine conditions of satisfaction without having to work through some sort of computation functioning at the intentional level. To understand language, for instance, we do not need to perform an act of interpretation; we instead have an 'immediate, normal, instantaneous understanding of utterances' (at least for languages in which we are fluent) (see Searle 1992, 192). Likewise, intentional action is generally not a matter of applying rules in order to do something, we just do it: 'for many institutions, particularly after I have become expert at operating within the institution, I just know what to do. I know what the appropriate behaviour is, without reference to the rules' (Searle 1995, 137).

Searle sees the background as something mental, by which he means that it could in principle be the way it is without any corresponding state of the world. Thus, where Dreyfus and Merleau-Ponty see much of our existence in the world as a kind of pre-intentional openness to affordances, Searle sees only a 'mind-brain', a mental or individualistic brain state.[4] The same holds true of his account of the role that rules play in producing non-intentional action that accords with rules. According to Searle, mastery of a set of rules produces in us a peculiar neurophysiological structure – one which disposes us to simply act just like we would if we were deliberately following the rules. Our practices, including our rule-following practices, produce in us a neurophysiological state, and it is the neurophysiological state against which intentional states determine their conditions of satisfaction. Thus, Searle argues, we can be disposed by our background to respond to the world in terms of rules without ever intending to follow rules. Our neurophysiological structure, having been shaped by rules, now produces in us rule-governed behaviour:

> Instead of saying that the person behaves the way he does because he is following the rules of the institution, we should just say, first (the causal level), the person behaves the way he does, because he has a structure that disposes him to behave that way; and second (the functional level), he has come to be disposed to behave that way, because that's the way that conforms to the rules of the institution.
>
> (Searle 1995, 144)

Of course, Searle is right that neurophysiological structures play a critical role in producing our rule-governed behaviour. But does the existence of a neurophysiological structure that has been shaped by rules succeed in explaining how rule-governed behaviour is possible? I think this account fails for two reasons.

First, causal structures cannot distinguish between rule-governed comportment and comportment that just happens to accord with a rule. Second, the existence of a causal structure cannot explain why the rule provides a norm for my behaviour. We can illustrate these two points with a simple example. I have a neurophysiological structure that disposes me to walk on my feet rather than my hands or my elbows or my knees. As a rule, I walk on my feet. But my walking on my feet is not rule-governed. Moreover, if I decide to walk on my elbows, I haven't done anything wrong. The point is straightforward – the existence of a neurophysiological structure that disposes me to act in a rule-like fashion is not the same thing as being rule-governed. I suspect that Searle was tempted to equate the two things because his focus was on actions governed by *constitutive* rules. In cases like voting for a president or playing chess – it is unlikely that anyone would act just like they were governed by a rule without the existence of the rule. With a good enough imagination, however, one could picture bizarre cultures that just happen to move pieces around a board or punch ballot cards on the third Tuesday of every fourth November without any notion of a game of chess or a presidential election. If there were such a culture, however, they would not be genuinely rule-governed, and they would not be under any kind of obligation to continue moving their bishops on the diagonal, etc. Nor could they be criticized if they moved the pieces in a new way.

With constitutive rules, it is generally the case that the rule itself plays a causal role (at least indirectly) in shaping the background disposition, so that it is unlikely that there could be comportment that just happens to accord with the rule. The case is different with other kinds of rules; it is possible if not plausible that actions exactly like those governed by codificatory or obligatory or strategic rules could arise without any kind of response to a rule. In such cases, we would want to distinguish between those individuals who are genuinely rule-governed, and those who merely act in accordance with a rule. And, in precisely those cases, we cannot make the distinction by alluding to a neuro-physiological structure which disposes the individuals to act in the way that they do since, presumably, at that level the structure is identical between the rule-governed individuals and the ones whose behaviour accords with a rule. Both are neurophysiologically disposed to do the same thing in the same circumstances.

To make the distinction, we need to locate the effect of rules at the place where the individuals are distinct – namely, in their experience of the world itself. The world that the rule-governed individual inhabits is a world that is already articulated according to rules, and her actions are thus themselves actions responding to the rules, even if she does not intentionally follow the rules.

The problem with Searle's account is, then, that, despite promising to deliver a new notion of background causality, his answer employs the traditional notion of brute causation. He merely tweaks this notion to allow for a brute causation that produces rule-like behaviour. To provide a genuine answer to the question how rule-governed behaviour is possible, we need to discover a different kind of moving force in the world. Following Merleau-Ponty, I call this moving force 'motivation'. Merleau-Ponty wrote that when motivations are operative,

> one phenomenon releases another, not by means of some objective efficient cause, like those which link together natural events, but by the meaning which it holds out – there is a *raison d'être* for a thing which guides the flow of phenomena without being explicitly laid down in any one of them, a sort of operative reason.
>
> (*PhP*, 49–50/57)

Motivations are not brute causes because they are responsive to meaningfully structured features of the world, rather than brute physical facts. But they link things by an 'operative reason', meaning that we do not intentionally connect things with each other, but are rather caught up in their connection, which operates below the level of intentional thought.

As we have seen, the key feature that we need to account for is the way that the rule itself (rather than a mental or physical representation of the rule) produces the action. Merleau-Ponty's account of motivation gives us the resources to do this because it shows how we can be responsive to meaningful features of the world without intentionally directing ourselves at them. Rule-governed action will therefore be possible only to the extent that the rules are themselves located in the world. Searle is right to see that the existence of the rules in the world can create in us a disposition to respond to the world in a rule-governed fashion. But the disposition cannot be reduced to a fact about the 'mind-brain'. Rather, the account must include the continued presence of the rule in the world as that which calls forth the action.

In fact, on reflection, we can see in some straightforward ways how this is the case. One reason I can drive on the right-hand side of the road in a rule-governed way is because cars and roads in the United States are themselves set up in accordance with the rule. Lines are painted on the road, and signs are oriented so that they can most easily be seen while driving on the right rather than on the left. The cars have the steering wheel on the left-hand side of the car in order to facilitate right-side driving, and all the other cars on the road are driving on the right-hand side. In such a world, it would be nearly impossible to drive on the left-hand side of the road in an easy, fluid, rule-governed manner. Instead, the world solicits me to drive on the right, and I only can stop driving deliberately when I am on the right-hand side of the road. The rule that one should drive on the right-hand side, we can say, is actually present in the world in a concrete form.

I believe that, in less obvious cases, the rule is actually present in the things themselves as well. When we see a chess piece like a bishop, we see it as having a field of force that surrounds it in exact conformity to the rules that govern its movement. But to explain this point, we need to look more closely at Merleau-Ponty's account of how motivation works.

Motivation

We have already discussed the phenomenological difference between intentional sorting and mapping on the one hand, and natural seeing of phenomena on the other. Natural seeing, on Merleau-Ponty's account, involves a motivational relationship in which our bodily set – our way of being prepared for action – polarizes the world and allows certain solicitations to appear while, at the same time, the condition of the surrounding environment draws us into a particular bodily set for responding. This complex interaction of our body and the surrounding environment is a motivational relationship – the body is moved by the world to comport itself in a particular way, and the bodily comportment in turn moves the world to reveal itself in a particular way. The reason that natural seeing is experienced differently than intentional sorting and mapping is that in natural seeing we are drawn or moved effortlessly to a state that resolves tensions, giving us the best possible practical grasp of the situation that we are in. This is in contrast to intentional action, which requires a discrete act of subsuming different things under an overarching category, with consequent conditions of satisfaction.

While I am not aware of Merleau-Ponty discussing the role of rules *per se*, he does discuss paradigmatically rule-governed situations. Consider the following description of a football game:

> For the player in action the football field is ... pervaded with lines of force (the 'yard lines'; those which demarcate the 'penalty area') and articulated in sectors (for example, the 'openings' between the

adversaries) which call for a certain mode of action and which initiate and guide the action as if the player were unaware of it. The field itself is not given to him, but present as the immanent term of his practical intentions; the player becomes one with it and feels the direction of the 'goal', for example, just as immediately as the vertical and the horizontal planes of his own body. . . . At this moment consciousness is nothing other than the dialectic of milieu and action. Each man-oeuvre undertaken by the player modifies the character of the field and establishes in it new lines of force in which the action in turn unfolds and is accomplished, again altering the phenomenal field.

(SB, 168–9)

This description helps us to see that what moves us is not rational or intentional in nature, because it is not directly available for thought. Because motives *move* us rather than necessarily giving us a reason for what they motivate, they cannot be reduced to a species of reason. Indeed, we are often motivated to have experiences or to act in ways for which we not only lack reasons, but have good reasons to reject, as when our bodily readiness impels us toward beliefs that we know are wrong. As examples of such a phenomenon, Merleau-Ponty discusses perceptual illusions like the way that the moon looks bigger when low on the horizon than when directly overhead, or Zöllner's illusion. Although we can demonstrate to ourselves that the moon is always the same size, still the 'various parts of the field interact and *motivate* this enormous moon on the horizon' (PhP, 31/36). Likewise, we can easily convince ourselves that the lines in Zöllner's illusion are in fact parallel, but the overall configuration of lines 'motivates the false judgement' by producing a bodily readiness that disposes us to the contrary beliefs (PhP, 35/41). Such examples show that our body is moved in a way that is independent of, and not necessarily a response to, reasons.

Of course, it is true that we can treat a motive as a reason. But in doing that, Merleau-Ponty notes, 'I crystallize an indefinite collection of motives' (PhP, 295/345). In other words, because motives are functioning on a bodily level, in ways of which we are sometimes only barely, if at all aware, any attempt to transform them into a reason ends up focusing on some narrow subset of a rich and complex set of motivational factors. In the process, it may end up treating the selected motive as more determinate and prominent than it actually was in our experience of it (Sartre's discussion of bad faith is a brilliant analysis of this fact).

But if motives do not function as reasons, could they function as causes? Merleau-Ponty offers a number of arguments to show that they could not, most of which turn on the fact that motivated experiences or events occur in virtue of a kind of bodily significance that the motive holds for us, given our current way of projecting ourselves into the world. This means that motivational rela-tionships aren't extensional in the way that causal relationships are – that is, they do not hold between entities solely in virtue of their physical properties, but only in virtue of their meaning. The illusions we discussed, for example, occur only because what we see has meaning for us as bodily beings who move through space. In vision, therefore, the scene struggles to resolve itself in the way that makes most sense for our bodily dealings with a spatially arrayed world.

To summarize this account of the relationship of motivation, we can say that the fundamental workings of motivations are found in the way that our environment and body work together to dispose us to respond to the possibilities the world affords. The world works by acting on our skilful bodily dispositions:

> we do not think the object, and we do not think ourselves thinking it, we are given over to the object and we merge into this body which is better informed than we are about the world, and about the motives we have and the means at our disposal for synthesizing it.
> (*PhP*, 238/277)

Thus, the different parts of the visual field act directly on my body in order to draw out of it the proper responses for coping with the situation. The arrangement of the visual field as a whole 'suggest[s] to the subject a possible anchorage' (*PhP*, 280/327) – that is, it helps me know what to fix on in making the most sense of the situation. Each part of the visual field can be seen, in this way, to motivate a certain significance for the rest, in the same way that each line in a perspective drawing motivates the way we see each of the others: 'the field itself ... is moving towards the most perfect possible symmetry ... the whole of the drawing strives towards its equilibrium' (*PhP*, 262/305–6). This equilibrium, I take it, consists in our having the proper disposition for fluidly responding to what the situation presents to us.

This is what the football player experiences when he is playing well: the ever-shifting situation on the field draws him to respond and his response, in turn, shifts the equilibrium, thus revealing new features (a new opportunity for passing the ball, say) and requiring new responses. But there are also some fixed features of the situation – the goal, the boundary lines, permissible and impermissible ways of handling the ball, in short, all the features of the game laid down by the rules. These rules play an intimate part in establishing the overall equilibrium of the field. And thus they govern the player's actions without his having to follow them: 'the rules of the game underlie each stroke of a tennis match' (*SNS*, 17).

With this the main problem I have tackled is solved. Rules can and do govern us without either causing us to act or being intentionally applied, because they feature in our overall motivated relationship to the world. This is more than our activity merely being describable by a rule, because we are actually responsive to the rule and, thus, responsible to it. But it is not a rule-following action, because we have no intentional states regarding the rule itself.

One consequence is that we can be governed by the rule even if we do not know the rule as such. If the world is organized by the rule in such a way that it embodies the rule, then we have an understanding of the rule whenever we are motivated by the rule to act in a rule-governed fashion. This is true even if we do not *know* what the rules are and therefore cannot deliberately follow the rule. A second consequence is that, ultimately, our ability to be governed by the rules is a non-rule-following skill. But that does not mean that we ever get below the rules to a world free of rules. The rules help make up the furniture of our world, and *our* world is always opened up partially in terms of the rules. (I will leave it as an open question whether there could be cultures which do not have such rules.)

Such conclusions should ease the worries we expressed at the outset that, at the deepest level, legal actors are not rule-followers. We can now see that the consequences are not what we might have thought. This is because one can be governed by a rule without being a rule-follower. As a consequence, the ultimate rule of recognition can govern the legal domain, and governs it as a rule, without the need for another, more fundamental rule to direct us to follow the ultimate rule of recognition. We can see this as soon as we recognize that rule-governed activity does not require that the actor be intending to follow a rule.

Notes

1 This is a slightly modified version of a paper which initially appeared in *Tijdschrift voor Filosofie* 67 (2005): 123–47. Earlier versions of this paper were presented at the Center for Ethics, Social and Political Philosophy, Catholic University of Leuven, Belgium, 10 May 2004; at the Political Science Department at Brigham Young University, Provo, Utah, USA, 23 June 2004; at the Utah Valley State College Philosophy Colloquium, Orem, Utah, USA, 27 October 2004; and Chengchi University, Taipei, Taiwan, 12 November 2005. I would like to thank all those present on those occasions for their helpful comments on this paper. Particularly deserving of gratitude in this regard is Brett Scharffs, both for his careful responses to the paper, and his invitation to discuss the paper in his philosophy of law seminar. I am also indebted to Hubert Dreyfus, not just for his tutelage in phenomenology in general, but in addition for his provocative and helpful comments on this paper in particular.

2 One of the clearest and most persuasive arguments along these lines remains Dreyfus 1972.

3 Searle has argued, probably correctly, that all constitutive rules have the logical form: 'X counts as Y in C'. Following such rules as rules requires that we be able to sort entities in types X and Y, and map them onto one another in the appropriate contexts. As Dreyfus has shown, however, we rarely, if ever, have an experience of mapping onto brute facts. See Dreyfus 1999.

4 'What I have been calling the Background is indeed derived from the entire congeries of relations which each biological-social being has to the world around itself. Without my biological constitution, and without the set of social relations in which I am embedded, I could not have the Background that I have. *But all of these relations, biological, social, physical, all this embeddedness, is only relevant to the production of the Background because of the effects that it has on me, specifically the effects that it has on my mind-brain.*' (Searle 1983, 154, emphasis added)

6

SPEAKING AND SPOKEN SPEECH

Thomas Baldwin

One the most striking chapters of Merleau-Ponty's *Phenomenology of Perception* (*PhP*) is that on speech – 'The Body as Expression, and Speech'. It occurs right at the end of his discussion of 'The body', as a climax to his discussion of the body's central role in our lives. We have learnt from previous chapters, especially the discussion of motility, that there is a basic bodily intentionality, an imposition of meaning, which is antecedent to judgment and inherent in our capacity for spontaneous creative bodily movement. In the chapter on speech Merleau-Ponty develops his line of argument in such a way that our capacity for judgment is itself seen to be an extension of this bodily intentionality: we learn here of the intentionality of gesture and voice through which we point and speak, and thereby express meanings of a much richer kind than would otherwise be available. In this way Merleau-Ponty prepares the ground for the remarkable thesis with which he ends this part of the book, that 'my body is as it were a "natural" subject, a provisional sketch of my total being' (*PhP*, 198/ 231). For central to this conception of the body is the account of meaningful speech as a fundamental type of bodily action. This point is then central to his subsequent argument, in particular to the discussion of self-consciousness in the chapter on 'The Cogito'. It is because thought is accomplished only through speech, even if it is often silent speech, that a thinker is necessarily a speaker and thus an agent whose life is an essentially embodied being-in-the-world.

Merleau-Ponty says at the start of his discussion of speech that in coming to understand this phenomenon 'we shall have the opportunity to leave behind us, once and for all, the traditional subject-object dichotomy' (*PhP*, 174/202). It is easy to see what he has in mind here: for he proceeds to reject both a rationalist intellectualism which supposes that speech is just the clothing for pure thoughts and an empiricist reductionism which seeks to construct meaningful speech from a causal account of linguistic behaviour. His objection to the first is, I think, essentially Aristotelian: thought is the way in which some 'matter' is informed so that it says or means something. Hence there cannot be a pure thought with no matter, and it is primarily the capacity for speech which provides the bodily matter of thought. So speech does not 'clothe' a bare, naked, thought that does not depend on it; instead it 'accomplishes' it (*PhP*, 178/207). His objection to the second, reductionist position, is that there is an unbridgeable gap between causal explanations of changes which take place in the human body and a human subject intentionally saying something. In his essay 'The Indirect Language', which was written c.1950 and is included in *The Prose of the World* (*PW*), he uses an idiom reminiscent of Wilfrid Sellars' discussion of knowledge to describe the gap here:

> We have moved from the realm of causes to the realm of reasons and from a temporality that accumulates changes to a temporality which understands them.
>
> (*PW*, 105)[1]

There is much that might be said about the relationship between these two realms, between brute causes and normative reasons, but I shall not pursue this matter here.[2] Instead I want to concentrate on Merleau-Ponty's positive account of language. For I want to argue that although he leaves behind the traditional dichotomy of the rational subject and the causal object, it turns out that as he elaborates his position in his *Phenomenology of Perception* he reinserts a different subject-object dichotomy back into it.

Speech as bodily gesture

The starting point for this argument is Merleau-Ponty's conception of expressive speech as an 'originating realm' (*PhP*, 174/202);

> We must recognise as an ultimate fact this open and indefinite power of giving significance – that is, both of apprehending and conveying a meaning – by which man transcends himself towards a new form of behaviour, or towards other people, or towards his own thought, through his body and his speech.
>
> (*PhP*, 194/226)

This is, therefore, a distinctive aspect of our bodily being. Merleau-Ponty's account of it rests on his conception of the role of bodily gestures, such as speech and sign language, as ways of expressing and articulating feelings and thoughts in such a way that others can grasp and respond to them:

> Our view of man will remain superficial so long as we fail to find, beneath the chatter of words, the primordial silence, and as long as we do not describe the action which breaks this silence. The spoken word is a gesture, and its meaning, a world.
>
> (*PhP*, 184/214)

Merleau-Ponty's account of this vocal gesture and its meaning is strongly reminiscent of Paul Grice's famous 1957 account of meaning.[3] Merleau-Ponty writes:

> The communication or comprehension of gestures comes about through the reciprocity of my intentions and the gestures of others, of my gestures and intentions discernible in the conduct of other people.
>
> (PhP, 185/215)

There is then a question here that is familiar from discussions of Grice's account, that, as Merleau-Ponty acknowledges, 'the whole difficulty is to conceive this act clearly without confusing it with a cognitive operation' (PhP, 185/215). For the comprehension of simple gestural meanings is supposed to be prior to the conceptual meanings inherent in cognitive operations since these latter meanings are to be dependent upon the former. So the thesis has to be that human beings have a capacity to begin to make and interpret simple meaningful gestures without relying on antecedent rules about the intentions and beliefs of those who make and witness these gestures. My own view on this matter is taken from Jonathan Bennett, who some years ago provided a rational reconstruction of a plausible route to the development of this capacity, starting only from simple forms of cooperative activity and moderate intelligence and showing how with recursive elaborations the development of communicative conventions can be motivated without assuming sophisticated cognitive abilities.[4] Hence what Merleau-Ponty asserts to be an 'ultimate fact' is, I think, accessible to the kind of non-reductive dialectical explanation that he generally favours. But it is certainly a capacity of fundamental importance to us, and what matters here is the description that Merleau-Ponty gives of this capacity and of the ways in which speakers make use of it.

Authentic speech vs second-hand speech

No sooner has Merleau-Ponty begun his description than he qualifies it with the following footnote:

> There is, of course, every reason to distinguish between an authentic speech, which formulates for the first time, and second-order[5] expression, speech about speech, which makes up the general run of empirical language. Only the first is identical with thought.
>
> (PhP, 178 n1/207 n4)

And only a few lines later there appears another footnote:

> Again, what we say here applies only to first-hand speech – that of the child uttering its first word, of the lover revealing his feelings, of the

'first man who spoke', or of the writer and philosopher who reawaken primordial experience anterior to all traditions.

(PhP, 179/208 n5)

Merleau-Ponty is here introducing a distinction which thereafter runs through all his discussions of language. His terminology is varied, but, as in the notes just quoted, it is clear that he thinks of himself as characterising one and the same distinction in different ways. His favoured description of it comes towards the end of the chapter on speech, as a distinction between 'speaking speech' (*parole parlante*) and 'spoken speech' (*parole parlée*), and I will take these as labels for the two clusters of opposed terms. So 'speaking' speech is, as we see in the passages quoted above, 'authentic' and 'first-hand'; it is later described in the *Phenomenology of Perception* as 'transcendental' (*PhP*, 390/454), and in the essay 'Science and the Experience of Expression' (in *The Prose of the World*) Merleau-Ponty writes of it also as 'operative' (*operant*) and 'constituting' (*constituant*) (*PW*, 14; see p. 10 for explicit use of the 'speaking'/'spoken' distinction, applied now to language [*langage*] and not speech, to introduce this discussion). By contrast 'spoken' speech is, as we see above, 'second-hand'[6] and 'empirical'. It is characteristic of speech as an 'institution' in which we make only 'commonplace utterances' with 'ready-made meanings' (*PhP*, 184/214): so it is 'constituted speech' (*PhP*, 184/214).

It is clear from the way in which this distinction is introduced and developed that the account of gestural meaning set out above applies to speaking speech; but it is equally clear that Merleau-Ponty does not intend to restrict speaking speech to 'the child uttering its first word' and 'the first man who spoke'. Instead it applies also to the intimate dialogue of 'the lover revealing his feelings' and equally to those writers and philosophers who are able to 'reawaken primordial experience'.[7] Thus his intention in identifying 'speaking speech' seems to be to capture the creative use of language, its use to say something new. The obvious case of this will be where new idioms are introduced; but it is clearly not restricted to this. When lovers first reveal their feelings, they do not need to create new idioms, but only to express themselves in ways that are new to their relationship. Hence, although poetry is a paradigmatic case of speaking speech, and Merleau-Ponty thinks of this creativity as characteristic of works of literature, he does not restrict speaking speech to literature. Despite the fact that our 'commonplace utterances' are merely spoken speech, he remarks that:

> The same transcendence which we found in the literary uses of speech can also be found in everyday language. This transcendence arises the moment I refuse to content myself with the established language, which is in effect a way of silencing me, and as soon as I truly speak to someone.

(PW, 20)

Thus when I find for myself the words to say something new, instead of falling back on established modes of expression, my speech is 'speaking speech' even if my statement belongs to some familiar genre such as that of a lawyer where most speech is necessarily spoken speech.

Merleau-Ponty sometimes suggests that scientific language is inherently 'spoken', and it can appear that his speaking/spoken distinction is in part a revised version of the stale old argument between the arts and the sciences. But in fact this is not right. For in his paper 'The Algorithm and the Mystery of Language' (in *The Prose of the World*) he discusses at length a mathematical case of speaking speech, namely the formulation by Gauss of the algorithm for determining the sum of the first *n* natural numbers as follows:

$$\sum_{i=0}^{n} i = (n+1).n/2$$

According to Merleau-Ponty, what is creative here is the use of *n* as both a cardinal number (in '*n* + 1') and an ordinal number (in '*n*/2'). This double use captures the intuitive *gestalt* about the organisation of the number sequence which Gauss' formula expresses. Merleau-Ponty provides no similar discussion of the creative uses of language in the natural sciences, but in the same paper there are brief references to Galileo's work (*PW*, 105) and to the development of non-Euclidean geometry (*PW*, 128) which imply that these are further examples of speaking language. And once one thinks about it there is no end of further cases which might be legitimately drawn from the history of science, wherever a radically new approach, or 'paradigm', in Kuhn's idiom, is proposed.[8]

What now of 'spoken speech'? The initial description of it as 'speech about speech', picked up in the translation of *seconde* as 'second-order' (see note 5 above), is, I think, misleading: it makes it appear that some move to a metalanguage is involved. But this conflicts with what he goes on to say, namely that spoken speech 'makes up the general run of empirical language'. So I take it that spoken speech is 'second' only in the sense that it is second-hand, dependent upon other more creative uses of the language which establish an idiom or practice that is here just taken over and followed. When describing this use of language Merleau-Ponty often writes that its use gives rise only to thoughts which are merely 'ready-made' – simply taken over without any fresh consideration by the thinker of the issues involved. Hence the picture we are offered is one of a use of language that is thought of as following established rules, and thereby not saying anything essentially new, even if it does capture new truths. This, for Merleau-Ponty, is by and large our ordinary, everyday, use of language; but it is also, he thinks, the way scientific language is generally supposed to work – which is why it can appear that he holds that it is only in literary uses of language that there is genuinely speaking speech.

This last point merits some further attention. In his paper 'Science and the Experience of Expression' (in *The Prose of the World*) Merleau-Ponty sets out a conception of language as a self-effacing representation of some state of affairs: in understanding it, we have no problem conceiving of the state of affairs which it purports to record, so much so that our attention passes directly through language to the world itself. Hence this kind of language seems transparent – a 'pure language', as Merleau-Ponty puts it in his paper 'The Spectre of a Pure Language':

> It is language which propels us towards the things it signifies. In the way it works, language hides itself from us.
>
> (*PW*, 10)

Merleau-Ponty characterises this 'pure' language as an ideal familiar to us from reflection on scientific language from the time of Descartes and Leibniz to the twentieth century. Having set up this ideal, however, and without disputing that there is some point to it, he goes on to argue that it can be only a derivative phenomenon. For it is a use of language which draws on established meanings to express thoughts which, precisely because they are ready-made for us, do not attract our attention and permit us to pass effortlessly from established senses to questions of reference that are dependent only on the state of the world. Thus, for statements of this kind, truth seems to involve no more than correspondence. And yet, Merleau-Ponty argues, this use of language is essentially dependent on the other use, on speaking speech, which is altogether different in kind. For here, precisely because the use of language is novel, there are no ready-made thoughts, and the audience needs to attend to the words actually used in order to grasp the speaker's meaning. So there can be no transparency of language here; instead, as Merleau-Ponty puts it, playing on the word 'sous-*entendre*' ('*under*standing' – i.e. incomplete understanding), 'in any such language there is nothing but *under*standings; the very ideas of a complete expression and of a signifier that would exactly cover the signified are both inconsistent' (*PW*, 29).

This dependence of 'spoken' scientific language on a 'speaking' language supports the suggestion made earlier, that Merleau-Ponty must allow that the speaking/spoken distinction applies within science itself; for it is not as though the ready-made idioms of an established scientific language can be borrowed from non-scientific discourse. Thus his critique of the ideal of a pure language of science is implicitly an internal critique, from within science itself. Again, a comparison with Kuhn is suggestive; Merleau-Ponty's account of the supposed ideal language of science is similar to Kuhn's account of 'normal science', scientific work which takes for granted some established paradigm and its language, and then seeks to extend its application by fitting more phenomena within it. Within normal science, because the established concepts of the paradigm are not called into question, truth appears to be essentially a matter of correspondence with the facts and the progressive ideal of natural science as the accumulation of empirical truths is confirmed. But, for Kuhn, this ideal is only part of the story: paradigms wear out, and then a different kind of science, 'revolutionary science', has to be practised in which the aim is not to accumulate truths but to find a better language for capturing truth in the first place. Here, therefore, the scientist is precisely engaged in the kind of creative investigation which Merleau-Ponty describes as speaking speech.

Reintroducing the subject

It is this distinction between speaking and spoken speech that I had in mind when I said earlier that having used the phenomenon of speech to finally expel the traditional subject/object dualism from philosophical psychology, he reintroduces a new version of it in his description of this phenomenon. For, surely, speaking speech is the creative activity of a subject, an activity which constitutes the agent as a thinking subject; whereas spoken speech is the established product of this activity, a product which makes possible objective truth. But what is difficult is both to characterise this point accurately and to appraise it fairly, and what is especially critical here is the issue of the dependence or not of these two kinds of speech upon each other.

In one direction, the dependence seems straightforward: spoken speech depends upon speaking speech, for that which is 'spoken' must have once involved 'speaking'. In more detail, the dependence here involves the notion of 'sedimentation' which Merleau-Ponty takes over from Husserl. This describes the process whereby a new type of movement or activity, once repeated, becomes habitual; applied to language, therefore, it describes the way in which a new linguistic gesture – a new idiom or just a new way of expressing one's feelings – becomes routine through repetition, and thereby losing the spontaneity of its first use, but gaining the unthinking transparency of a familiar phrase. Jonathan Bennett's account of the evolution of linguistic meaning to which I alluded earlier can be invoked to develop this thought: for it is the silent transformation of a simple regularity between gesture and communicative intention into a convention that sets up the interlocking beliefs and intentions that constitute Gricean non-natural meaning.[9]

What is more difficult, however, is the question as to whether there is also a dependence in the other direction, of speaking speech upon spoken speech. In one way Merleau-Ponty does indeed maintain that there is such a dependence. For he holds that the creative writer proceeds precisely by taking apart the established idioms of spoken speech, with their ready-made thoughts, in order to express something new which transcends those thoughts:

> The author who is not content to carry on in the language he inherited or to repeat what has already been said still does not want ... to replace it with an idiom which is self-sufficient and closed within its

own signification. He wants to fulfil language and destroy it at the same time.

('The Indirect Language', *PW*, 99)

This point does indeed set up a kind of interdependence between speaking and spoken speech. But it is very far from being a partnership between equals: on the contrary, spoken speech is presented either as the sediment formed from the transformation of a creative speaking gesture into an established rule or as material to be 'destroyed' in the course of some new creative transcendence. This way of thinking of the relationship is inherent in much of the language Merleau-Ponty uses to characterise it: speaking speech is 'transcendental', 'constitutive', 'first-hand', etc.; spoken speech is 'empirical', 'constituted', 'second-hand'.

Speaking speech is also said to be 'authentic'; by implication, therefore, spoken speech is 'inauthentic'. Although, to the best of my knowledge, Merleau-Ponty never in fact uses this latter idiom, the implication cannot but remind one of Heidegger's discussion in *Being and Time* of discourse (*Rede*) and 'idle talk' (*Gerede*), with the further implication that the relationship between speaking and spoken speech is one of 'falling' (*Verfallen*). This is surely not a happy way to think about the matter; for it implies that there is something inherently second-rate, and not just second-hand, about spoken speech, which does not fit well with the conception of it as, for example, the language in which objective truths are expressed. Of course there are lazy, derivative, habits of speech in which speakers just repeat current attitudes without thinking about the implications of what they are saying. But the careful use of language in which one seeks to make oneself understood by sticking closely to established meanings in order to draw out their implications in the light of new discoveries or to construct an internal critique by means of a careful *reductio ad absurdum* argument is very removed from that kind of 'idle talk'. Yet writing of this kind is also different from that in which one constructs a striking new idiom that sets people thinking in a new way, and thus from Merleau-Ponty's 'speaking' language.

It appears, therefore, that Merleau-Ponty's characterisation of the relationship between speaking and spoken speech has two aspects. There is a functional distinction between creative and established uses of language; but attached to this is a value-judgment, to the effect that it is only the first of these uses which is 'authentic'. This judgment is, I think, a residue within his *Phenomenology of Perception* of the existential subjectivism which is manifest in the emphasis here on the role of the embodied subject, but of which he is also sometimes critical, most notably in his discussion of freedom in the final chapter of the book. His great insight there is that creative freedom is impossible without a background of motivations that are not freely chosen in a Sartrean original choice of ourselves, so that 'we exist in both ways *at once*' ('*à la fois*', M-P's emphasis; *PhP*, 453/527). Applied to language, the moral of that thesis would be that speaking speech is impossible without spoken speech, so that, understood properly, language is both speaking and spoken *at once* (*à la fois*). I shall show how, in his later writings, Merleau-Ponty does indeed move to this position. But first I want to discuss how far in his *Phenomenology of Perception* Merleau-Ponty connects his account of language to his discussion of perception, in particular whether he employs here a distinction comparable to that between speaking and spoken speech, since it would seem odd that such a fundamental aspect of his account of speech and its intentionality should not be prefigured in his discussion of perception and its intentionality.

The phenomenal and the objective body

When discussing the phenomenon of 'double sensation' which arises when one touches one's right hand with one's left hand in the chapter on 'The Experience of the Body' Merleau-Ponty writes of 'an ambiguous set-up in which both hands can alternate the roles of "touching" [*touchante*] and being "touched" [*touchée*]' (*PhP*, 93/106). Merleau-Ponty's idiom here (*touchante/touchée*) is exactly similar to that which he employs with respect to speech (*parlante/parlée*); so a first thought might be that the phenomena involved are indeed similar. But on second thoughts it is clear that this is not entirely right. For there is no suggestion in the discussion of speech that we have here 'an ambiguous set-up' in which speech can 'alternate the roles' between speaking and spoken; indeed, unlike the *touchante/touchée* distinction, the speaking/spoken distinction is not a distinction of roles, but one between two types of speech, original and second-hand speech. Nonetheless there is something to the comparison: for just as it is speaking speech which opens up new meanings, the touching hand is never 'completely constituted' as an object since it is that by which there are tangible objects for us (*PhP*, 92/105); and by contrast the hand that is touched is felt to be an object, 'a system of bones, muscles and flesh fixed in a point of space' (*PhP*, 92/105), just as spoken speech is speech that follows established rules which enable it to capture objective truths.

The way to take this comparison further is to consider Merleau-Ponty's generalisation of the *touchante/touchée* distinction, namely his distinction between the phenomenal and the objective body (*PhP*, 105–6/121). His conception of the phenomenal body is the conception of our embodiment, our bodily being-in-the-world, and thus like the 'touching hand' not a conception of an object at all; whereas the conception of the objective body is the 'impoverished image' (*PhP*, 431/501) of our embodiment which we obtain when we experience it as we experience the 'touched hand', i.e. as a physical object in space. So can we say that speaking speech is, so to speak, 'phenomenal speech', whereas spoken speech is 'objective speech'? I think this suggestion does capture Merleau-Ponty's basic presumption. But there are complications here which are exemplified by his discussion of the former German soldier, Schneider, whose varied symptoms following a brain injury received during the First

World War had been closely described by the psychologists A. Gelb and K. Goldstein in works of which Merleau-Ponty famously makes extensive use in his *Phenomenology of Perception*.

Merleau-Ponty in fact introduces the distinction between the phenomenal and the objective body when discussing Schneider. In this context he is discussing Schneider's inability to perform 'abstract' movements such as pointing to his nose despite his ability to hold down a job as a leatherworker by using scissors, needles, etc. For Merleau-Ponty, this incapacity shows that while Schneider retains the practical knowledge which comes with his embodiment, his phenomenal body, because of his brain injury he has lost a sense of his objective body:

> The patient is conscious of his bodily space as the matrix of his habitual action, but not as an objective setting; his body is at his disposal as a means of ingress into a familiar surrounding, but not as the means of expression of a gratuitous and free spatial thought.
>
> (*PhP*, 104/119)

> It is never our objective body that we move, but our phenomenal body, and there is no mystery in that, since our body, as the potentiality of this or that part of the world, surges towards objects to be grasped and perceives them.
>
> (*PhP*, 106/121)

So far, then, the implication would seem to be that Schneider's injury has left him with his phenomenal body but destroyed his capacity to make sense of his objective body. If we now associate the phenomenal with speaking speech and the objective with spoken speech, the implication would seem to be that Schneider should have some capacity for speaking speech, but little or none for spoken speech. But when we turn to what Merleau-Ponty says about Schneider's capacity for speech, this is exactly the wrong way round (*PhP*, 196/228). For, as described by Merleau-Ponty, the symptoms of his injury include an inability to engage in creative speaking speech even though he can manage the ordinary 'ready-made' idioms of spoken speech. Thus there is a complete misfit here and, as a result, a difficulty in assimilating the speaking/spoken distinction to the phenomenal/objective one.

Since Merleau-Ponty's description of Schneider's limited capacity for speech seems entirely sensible, it is necessary to rethink the way in which Schneider's problem fits onto the phenomenal/objective distinction. I suggested above that, for Merleau-Ponty, Schneider's situation is that of someone who has been left with his phenomenal body but deprived of a conception of his objective body. But this is too simple. Schneider's fundamental problem is that he lacks the ability to 'reckon with the possible' (*PhP*, 109/125), and this explains why he lacks the capacity to perform abstract movements. So although of course he retains a phenomenal body, his inability is itself rooted in his bodily being-in-the-world, in his phenomenal body itself.

This is not the place to discuss this matter is detail, but in order to deal with the problem identified above it is necessary to pursue a bit further Merleau-Ponty's characterisation of the basis of Schneider's inability. The following passages are, I think, characteristic:

> The essence of consciousness is to provide itself with one or several worlds, to bring into being its own thoughts *before* itself, as if they were things. ... The world-structure, with its two stages of sedimentation and spontaneity, is at the core of consciousness, and it is in the light of a levelling-down of the 'world' that we shall succeed in understanding Schneider's intellectual, perceptual and motor disturbances.
>
> (*PhP*, 130/150)

> Let us therefore say ... that the life of consciousness – cognitive life, the life of desire or perceptual life – is subtended by an 'intentional arc' which projects round about us our past, our future, our human setting, our physical, ideological and moral situation, or rather which results in our being situated in all these respects. It is this intentional arc which brings about the unity of the senses, of intelligence, of sensibility and motility. And it is this which goes limp in illness.
>
> (*PhP*, 136/157)

> Bodily experience forces us to acknowledge an imposition of meaning which is not the work of a universal constituting consciousness, a meaning which clings to certain contents. My body is that meaningful core which behaves like a general function, and which nonetheless exists, and is susceptible to disease.
>
> (*PhP*, 147/170)

Thus Schneider's symptoms are to be attributed to a loss of the capacity for a bodily 'imposition of meaning', or 'intentional arc', which would situate him in a variety of worlds, future and possible, as well as present and actual. His habitual routines show that he has a capacity for sedimentation; but unlike a normal person he cannot see the possibilities inherent in his situation and use them to detach himself from his current situation. Schneider's incapacity, therefore, belongs firmly 'within' his phenomenal body. It has the consequence that he cannot take an detached, objective, view of himself; but that is only an implication of his disability, not a fundamental characterisation of it, which adverts instead to his inability to engage in spontaneous actions which engage with the possible as opposed to the habitual routines that are appropriate to his current actual situation.

Returning now to the case of language and the speaking/spoken distinction, it is now easy to see how Schneider's incapacity for speaking speech fits with this characterisation of his condition. For Merleau-Ponty, as we have seen, speech is a fundamental aspect of our bodily being-in-the-world. So precisely because of his deep-seated inability to engage in spontaneous action, it is not surprising that when it comes to speech Schneider is restricted to the habitual routines of spoken speech and cannot see the point of speaking speech. Thus the explanation for the speaking/spoken distinction lies within the phenomenal body, in the distinction between spontaneity and sedimentation. Nonetheless it remains an implication of Merleau-Ponty's distinction that whereas speaking speech manifests the spontaneity of an embodied subject who has the capacity to create new possibilities, spoken speech is in two ways more closely tied to the objective. First, because it follows established rules, it admits of objective characterisation; so far from being 'second-order', speech about speech, it can be an *object*-language captured within a (metalinguistic) syntax and semantics. Second, precisely because it follows established rules shared by speakers of the language, it is especially suitable as a way of expressing objective truths. Hence my earlier suggestion that with his distinction between speaking and spoken speech Merleau-Ponty brings a subject/object distinction back into his account of language is not in the end subverted by the rather complex and indirect way in which it connects with his distinction in the *Phenomenology of Perception* between the phenomenal and the objective body.

The interdependence thesis

Why does all this matter? Because it helps to provide a context for the thesis which I want to propose as an alternative to the account of the relationship between speaking and spoken speech in Merleau-Ponty's *Phenomenology of Perception*, namely the thesis that there is here an interdependence of equals: speaking speech depends on the possibility of being spoken, i.e. establishing a rule, just as much as spoken speech depends on speaking, i.e. the possibility of initiating new practices.

Let us go back to touch and the distinction between hands that are touching and being touched. In the *Phenomenology of Perception* Merleau-Ponty notes that our hands can exchange these roles (*PhP*, 93/105), but he makes nothing of it. In *The Visible and the Invisible*, by contrast, this 'reversibility' of roles, as he now calls it, is 'the ultimate truth' (*VI*, 145). For, he argues, it shows that the subject/object distinction, as exemplified by the touching/touched distinction, is only a distinction between two roles of equal importance which the one and the same body can play; touching no longer has any priority over being touched. Hence, generalising and thereby going back a bit on the position he had advanced in the *Phenomenology of Perception*, the distinction between the phenomenal and the objective body is equally just a distinction between two roles the body can occupy since 'my body is at once phenomenal body and objective body' (VI, 136):[10]

> We say therefore that our body is a being of two leaves, from one side a thing among things and otherwise what sees them and touches them; we say, because it is evident, that it unites these two properties within itself, and its double belongingness to the order of the 'object' and to the order of the 'subject' reveals to us quite unexpected relations between the two orders. It cannot be by incomprehensible accident that the body has this double reference; it teaches us that each calls for the other.
>
> (VI, 137)

What lies behind this change is, I think, Merleau-Ponty's explicit repudiation in this late work of the existential subjectivism of the *Phenomenology of Perception* which is only mitigated there by the more balanced discussion of freedom to which I alluded above, and its replacement by a complex thesis in which equal emphasis is placed on subject and object, which are conceived as the poles of a primary field in which things come to have meaning only through the way in which they relate to both poles. So he writes here:

> The appeal to the originating [*originaire*] goes in several directions: the originating breaks up [*éclate*], and philosophy must accompany this break-up, this non-coincidence, this differentiation [*différentiation*].
>
> (VI, 124)

Thus if what is fundamental is inherently 'differentiated' then it cannot be thought of as essentially a subject; instead, assuming, as before, that it is the body that is fundamental, the body must be essentially something differentiated, 'a being of two leaves'. So, in place of the central thesis of his *Phenomenology of Perception* from which I started, that 'my body is as it were a "natural" subject, a provisional sketch of my total being' (*PhP*, 198/231), we have instead its 'double belongingness to the order of the "object" and to the order of the "subject"'.

For the moment let us just accept this position without seeking to clarify or question it (I shall come back to it briefly at the end). What strikes me is that if, despite all the complexities and qualifications explored in the previous section, we can bring the speaking/spoken distinction under the scope of the old phenomenal/objective distinction, then this new move implies that, instead of privileging speaking speech as before, we should instead find a way of thinking about speech, or language, such that it too is recognisable as a 'being of two leaves', one the speaking role, the other that whereby it is spoken, but such that 'each calls for the other' so that just as 'my body is at once phenomenal body and objective body' language is 'at once' speaking speech and spoken speech. Merleau-Ponty does indeed assert at one or two points in *The Visible and the Invisible* that he takes this view: for example, towards the end of the chapter 'The Intertwining – The Chiasm', he writes of 'the same fundamental phenomenon of reversibility which sustains both mute perception and speech' (*VI*, 155). But he does not provide any argument for this new position.

How might one argue for it? It seems to me that one key premise is to be found implicit in Merleau-Ponty's discussion of speech in the *Phenomenology of Perception* itself, when he says that what is distinctive about language is the fact that 'speech is able to settle into a sediment' (*PhP*, 190/220) and connects this, albeit only rather indirectly, with the thought that 'speech implants the idea of truth in us as the presumptive limit of its effort'. For what this suggests is that insofar as we aim, even in speaking speech, to speak the truth, what we say must be such that it can settle as a sediment, i.e. become merely spoken. This is still enigmatic, but there is a way of developing the thought here via the familiar point that if we are to speak the truth it must also be possible for us to make a mistake. For that possibility arises only if our speech invokes general concepts governed by rules with criteria of application that are independent of the case in hand. But this is pretty much what Merleau-Ponty seems to envisage as spoken speech, insofar as it involves following rules. So speaking speech, insofar as it aims at truth, depends upon the possibility of becoming spoken speech.

The opposite dependence, of the spoken upon the speaking, seemed before to be immediate within Merleau-Ponty's account. Yet there is a further refinement to be added. Merleau-Ponty's account of spoken speech, with its ready-made thoughts, is deliberately dismissive; he treats it as if it were almost a mechanical procedure, and what he thereby fails to see is that since it inescapably involves the application of rules to new cases, the exercise of judgment concerning the particular case in hand is always involved. So where we think of speaking speech not as requiring new idioms but as involving new judgments, then spoken speech turns out to depend on speaking speech. Hence we can find here a vindication with respect to speech, or language, of the strong interdependence thesis that is hinted at, but not argued for, in *The Visible and the Invisible*. And in this way, finally, we can rebalance the slightly lop-sided approach to language that we find in the *Phenomenology of Perception*.

Writing and spoken speech

This argument for the interdependence of speaking and spoken speech is essentially taken from Wittgenstein, from the famous 'rule-following' considerations advanced in his *Philosophical Investigations*. I make no apologies for this, since I take the view that Wittgenstein managed to capture here an absolutely fundamental tension that is fundamental to meaningful activity: on the one hand, because mistakes must always be possible if there is to be meaning at all, the activity must be thought of as informed by rules whose application is independent of the use of them on any given occasion; so a speaker's speech-act must be conceived as satisfying rules and in this respect as a case of 'spoken speech'. But, on the other hand, since no statement of the rules can fix how they are to be applied to a new case, the speech-act must also be creative and in this respect equally a case of 'speaking speech'. There is then more to be said about the way in which the tension between these two perspectives is to be resolved. For Wittgenstein the resolution famously involves the thesis that speech belongs within language-games that are essentially public, and although it is notoriously disputed just what this thesis involves, it seems to me that it employs a strategy which would in principle be entirely congenial to Merleau-Ponty, who was, after all, the philosopher of the 'inter-monde' (*PhP*, 357/415).[11]

But there is, finally, another name to be mentioned briefly here – Jacques Derrida. It is, I think, entirely legitimate to associate the thesis I have taken from Merleau-Ponty's late writings, that 'the appeal to the originating [*originaire*]' leads to a recognition of a fundamental 'differentiation [*différentiation*]' (*VI*, 124) with Derrida's thesis that insofar as it makes sense to speak of anything at all as originating (*originaire*) it is 'differance' (Derrida 1974: 23). In both cases there is a post-structuralist appropriation of Saussure's emphasis upon language as a system of 'difference'. This is not the place, however, to explore what Derrida means by 'differance'; nonetheless there is one easy way to connect Derrida's approach to language with that of Merleau-Ponty. In his early writings Derrida contrasts two ways in which we encounter language, speech (*voix*) and writing (*écriture*).[12] Although, for obvious reasons speech has always been given priority over writing in accounts of language and has been taken to be the basic vehicle of thought, Derrida argues that once one takes into account two fundamental aspects of language, the holistic inter-dependence of the distinctions, 'differences', it captures and the fact that its use on any one occasion has 'deferential' implications concerning the way in which it should be used on other occasions,[13] one will see that in some respects we get a better idea of language when we think of what writing requires than when we simply imagine ourselves giving voice spontaneously to a passing thought or feeling.

> I would rather suggest that the alleged derivativeness of writing, however real and massive, was possible only on one condition: that the 'original', 'natural' etc. language had never existed, never been intact and untouched by writing, that it had itself always been a writing. An 'arche-writing' whose necessity and new concept I wish to indicate and outline here; and which I continue to call writing only because it essentially communicates with the vulgar concept of writing.
>
> (Derrida 1974, 56)

In putting forward this thesis, Derrida is not seeking, absurdly, to reverse the traditional priority of speech over writing and give priority to writing over speech; instead his thought is that language involves the free expression of thought and feeling in speech ('presence') which can take place only within a systematic network of signs that have application in other contexts ('absence'). So language conceived as differance is 'the play of presence and absence' (Derrida 1974: 244); it is *at once* expressive, as speech is, and systematic, as writing is.

The comparison with Merleau-Ponty will now be obvious. The priority of speaking speech over spoken speech which we find in the *Phenomenology of Perception* is another instance, for Derrida, of the traditional priority of speech over writing. Merleau-Ponty's characterisation of the distinction between speaking and spoken speech exactly matches Derrida's distinction between speech and writing. Merleau-Ponty, however, did not need to wait for Derrida's critique of this distinction. For, as we have seen, in his late writings he precisely anticipates Derrida's critique by rejecting the priority of the subject over the object and, by implication, of the speaking over the spoken, replacing this with the thesis that our body, and thus our language, is that strange being in which subjective and objective, speaking and spoken speech, are essentially 'intertwined'.

Notes

1 Cf. W. Sellars, 'Empiricism and the Philosophy of Mind':

> The essential point is that in characterizing an episode or a state as that of *knowing*, we are not giving an empirical description of that episode or state; we are placing it in the logical space of reasons, of justifying and being able to justify what one says.
>
> (Sellars 1963, 169)

2 The comparison with Sellars indicates some of the issues here, for despite the similarity in idioms there are major differences between Sellars' conception of the status of the 'logical space of reasons' and Merleau-Ponty's conception of the 'realm of reasons'. Sellars combines a thorough-going scientific realism with a functionalist theory of mind such that 'the "relationship" of the logical to the real order is, in the last analysis, a matter of certain items in the real order playing certain roles' (Sellars 1963, 57). Merleau-Ponty unequivocally rejects any such scientific realism: so for him the realm of reasons is a domain within his dialectical idealism.

3 According to Grice, by his act (e.g. an utterance) a speaker means in the 'non-natural way' that *p* (e.g. that it is raining) if the speaker intends by his act both that his audience should recognise that he intends that they should come to believe that *p*, and that their recognition of this intention should be a reason for them to form that belief (Grice 1989, 219f.). But see note 9 below for a qualification of the comparison suggested here between Merleau-Ponty and Grice.

4 See Bennett 1976, 179–80. Bennett here relies on the account of conventions developed by David Lewis in *Convention* (Lewis 1969).

5 This translation is problematic; the French is just 'seconde', and despite the phrase 'speech about speech' ('une parole sur des paroles') I think it would be better here to

think of 'second-hand' speech; notice that in the next footnote (*PhP*, 179 n1/208 n5) the contrasting kind of speech, speaking speech, is said to be 'first-hand' ('originaire').

6 See note 5 above.

7 As he explains in the 'Preface' to his *Phenomenology of Perception*, for Merleau-Ponty this is precisely the aim of phenomenology; and he certainly took it that Husserl had successfully accomplished this aim, especially in *Ideas* II which he studied at Louvain before writing his *Phenomenology of Perception*. We might well say the same about Merleau-Ponty's *Phenomenology of Perception* itself.

8 See T. Kuhn, *The Structure of Scientific Revolutions* (Kuhn 1962).

9 This way of coming at the matter slightly rearranges the relationship between Merleau-Ponty's gestural meaning and Grice's non-natural meaning. In my previous discussion above I suggested that the similarity was close enough to think of them as the same phenomenon. What I am now suggesting is that we only get to full non-natural meaning where we have an established convention and thus, for Merleau-Ponty, spoken speech; in which case speaking speech has to start from the kind of simpler coordination of beliefs and intentions that is the input into the evolution of conventions.

10 It is worth emphasising the sharp change here from the position advanced in the *Phenomenology of Perception*, according to which the objective body is only an 'impoverished image' of the phenomenal body, which is 'the true version of the body we live by' (*PhP*, 431/501).

11 I discuss Wittgenstein's later philosophy of language, including the rule-following considerations, in 'Philosophy of Language in the Twentieth Century', in *The Oxford Companion to Language* (Lepore and Smith 2006, section 3.7).

12 See Derrida 1973.

13 The term 'differance' is coined to express these two fundamental aspects of language, its 'differential/deferential' structure.

7

THE GENIUS OF MAN

Simon Glendinning

I

The vast bulk of the fairly vast bulk that is *Phenomenology of Perception* (*PhP*) is devoted to an elucidation of the various ways in which one's own body and that of others is disclosed prior to scientific theorizing. However, as is obvious to even the most cursory glance at its pages, one of the most unusual features of this elucidation, unusual at least for most philosophers, is that it is developed through the close examination of case studies in empirical psychology. For readers used to philosophy that is at best 'science lite', Merleau-Ponty's keenness to acknowledge that one should not pursue philosophy of psychology 'without psychology' is profoundly refreshing (*PhP*, 63/73).[1]

It would be a mistake, however, to regard this interest in empirical inquiries as a surreptitious re-introduction of the scientific realism or reductive naturalism he is always and everywhere at such pains to resist. Indeed, it is ultimately the implicit philosophy within such empirical psychology that he engages with – and often takes issue with – and his efforts to achieve a clarification of the facticity of existence is not itself pursued as an empirical investigation. Thus, even if he disapproves of the idea of pursuing a philosophy of psychology 'without psychology', he is equally clear that such an inquiry cannot be conducted 'with psychology alone' (*PhP*, 63/73).

An exemplary case of this complex mode of inquiry is found in his attempt to shed light on the fundamental relation *having a body* through an analysis of bodily expression and the crucially connected and widely empirically studied phenomenon of *having a language*.[2] In what follows, I will present Merleau-Ponty's basic line of argument and will suggest that, in principle, his approach outlines just the kind of non-reductive naturalism that a philosophically satisfactory phenomenology should aim at. However, I will also raise the worry that there is an aspect of his conception of the facticity of a distinctively *human* existence (an existence which is everywhere run through or caught up with having a language) which involves it in a step beyond that kind of naturalism into a problematic a priori anthropology. Within that anthropology, our idea of the distinctive difference between human beings and animals and the significance we attach to that idea is conceived as something that can be *justified* by features of reality; the difference is 'an object of observation' rather than, say, 'of contemplation', to use the language of Cora Diamond (see Diamond 1995). While that *cognitivism* about the human/animal difference can seem compelling, I hope to show that it leaves Merleau-Ponty with a profound difficulty concerning the 'origin of man'.

II

First, however, I want to look at his account of having a language. As a preliminary to his inquiry, Merleau-Ponty identifies a grammatical difference between two uses of the relation 'having' that we need to keep in view throughout. In ordinary life we speak indifferently of someone, for example, 'having an idea' or 'having a dog' or 'having a desire' or 'having a hat' or 'having a pain' or 'having a house' or 'having a bad temper'. Despite the uniformity of this way of talking, the use of these expressions is not, Merleau-Ponty suggests, everywhere the same. On the one hand, there are cases in which the term 'having' designates a simple proprietary or ownership relationship of a given subject to an independently given object. At issue here is an external relation between two distinct items in the world. On the other hand, however, there are cases where the subject and object are not merely externally related but, as Merleau-Ponty puts it, the subject 'projects itself' into the possessed term: the 'possession' or 'belonging to me' involved here expresses an *existential involvement* of myself with or in something (*PhP*, 174 n1/202 n1).

Borrowing (and in fact reversing) a distinction introduced by his existentialist contemporary Gabriel Marcel, Merleau-Ponty attempts, as he puts it, to 'take account' of an aspect of the 'usage' of the term 'being' to help mark out these two senses of possession (*PhP*, 174 n1/202 n1). The recommendation is that in the first (simply proprietary) kind of case we should replace the relation 'having' with what he calls 'the weak sense' of being as existence or predication. So instead of using the expression 'I have a hat' we will use instead 'The hat is mine'. Nothing prevents us from using this way of speaking in the second, projective kind of case too (it is not pure nonsense), however, in those cases that replacement tends to conceal the internal or existential relation involved by presenting it on the model of external or ontic relations obtaining between existents in the world (*PhP*, 174/202). So wherever one does *not* want to say that the case of possession concerns two specifiable items that independently are or exist then one should retain 'having'. Hence, taking the examples above, one should form the following lists:

1 'I have an idea', 'I have a pain', 'I have a desire', 'I have a bad temper'.
2 'The hat is mine', 'The house is mine', 'The dog is mine'.

If the first list is formulated in the grammar of the second we do not produce nonsense but a set of reifying objectifications which are, Merleau-Ponty supposes, more likely to produce misunderstandings:

1 'The idea is mine', 'The pain is mine', 'The desire is mine', 'The bad temper is mine'.

'The hat is mine' will thus go along with the list: 'The hat is brown', 'The hat is old', 'The hat is unfashionable', 'The hat is smelly', and so on. What is asserted with the expression 'I have an idea' can also be formed in predicative terms, and belongs to a similar list: 'The idea is mine', 'The idea is old', 'The idea is stolen', 'The idea is good', 'The idea is unfashionable', and so on. Again, Merleau-Ponty's claim is not that there is something wrong with the sentence 'The idea is mine' but that it will help us avoid mistaking it for a hat if we remember that its truth condition is that I was the first to *have* it.[3]

Emphasizing Merleau-Ponty's distinction between being and having also helps us avoid the idea that his philosophy of the body aims to affirm the identity claim that 'I am my body'.[4] This is an attractive but impoverished reading of Merleau-Ponty's view. Indeed, one of the reasons that he explores the sense of possession involved in 'having a body' through an analysis of bodily expression and 'having a language' is that the identification of the subject with the body produces just the kind of tempting objectification he wants to resist. That is, it is precisely because he wants reflectively to accept the Cartesian idea that I am not related to my body 'as a pilot to his ship' that he recommends we *retain* the ordinary expression 'I have a body' (SB, 208–11). What commentators who assert an identity of the subject and the body are rightly recognizing, then, is that it is misleading to think that, 'having a body' designates a proprietary relationship. However, what the identification they replace it with fails to acknowledge is that a (different) sense of possession is, nevertheless, still in play: a sense of possession (Merleau-Ponty's 'having') which indicates an internal and not a merely external relation. It is a central aspect of this internal relation, the relation captured most precisely with the idea of the body as '*the visible expression of a concrete Ego*' (PhP, 55/64; italics mine), that Merleau-Ponty aims to make explicit through an investigation of someone's 'having a language'.[5]

III

Turning then to studies of language possession in empirical psychology, Merleau-Ponty first notes that the standard interpretation of that idea is drawn in exclusively naturalistic and objective terms: in terms of the real presence in the body of a stock of verbal images (it is of no special significance whether these are understood as physical or psychic traces); images which would be mechanically produced as speech through neurological mechanisms or psychological associations in virtue of which 'a flow of words' would occur (*PhP*, 175/203). Merleau-Ponty's initial observation is that while such a mechanistic view might seem able to make sense of the fact that speaking is going on, it is far less clear that it leaves room for *a speaking subject*. For on this understanding of speech the emission of sounds is not an intentional action by some 'who' who has something to say, and whose various sayings are thus also pointedly telling with regard to who they are. Thus, according to Merleau-Ponty, an empiricist psychology committed to scientific realism does not really put the subject back into the world (as it often likes to think it does), but simply abolishes it: 'there is no speaker … speech occurs in a circuit of third person phenomena … man can speak as the electric lamp can become incandescent' (*PhP*, 175/203).

Efforts to give fully or baldly naturalistic explanations of speech need not feel unduly threatened by these conceptual worries, however. For example, one could imagine a theoretical scientist urging us to resist 'the myth of the speaker'. But things become more difficult for such a view when it has to face empirical research that speaks against it. And in addition to the conceptual objection, Merleau-Ponty appeals to cases where patients do not simply lose the power of articulate speech (*anarthria*) – a phenomenon which could obviously be explained in terms of a loss of verbal images from the previously possessed 'stock' – but lose it only in certain contexts (*aphasia*).

Interestingly, under pressure from such research, psychological theory has tended to flip over or recoil from naturalistic, empiricist explanations to intellectualist ones. The fact that a patient cannot identify certain colour samples in certain contexts, for example, is interpreted as a genuinely intellectual and not merely functional or mechanistic disorder. The cases at issue are ones where the patient may still have a sense of an immediate resemblance, and so can identify coloured objects with reference to given colour samples, but can no longer classify the colour samples when taken on their own. The intellectualist suggestion then looks very plausible: the problem is 'not that he has lost the verbal image of the words red or blue, but that he has lost the general ability to subsume a sensory given under a category' (*PhP*, 176/204).

As Merleau-Ponty notes, this alternative theory appears to be the antithesis of the naturalistic account 'since language now appears as conditioned by thought', and hence there is at least a return to a subject here. However, it is important to recognize that this subject does not utter intrinsically meaningful words but rather has intrinsically meaningful thoughts. And so while we have a subject here alright, it is fundamentally 'a thinking subject, not a speaking one' (*PhP*, 177/205).

The situation, then, is that neither empiricism nor intellectualism can make sense of the idea of the living human being as itself a speaking subject. In what should be seen as a classic gesture on Merleau-Ponty's part, he identifies the fundamental kinship in the two standard positions in a way that will enable him to dismount the see-saw and move towards a genuinely distinctive phenomenological conception. The two traditional views are 'at one', he notes, 'in holding that the word *has* no significance' (*PhP*, 176/205; italics in original). His reasoning in the first case (that of mechanistic psychology) runs as follows:

> In the first case this is obvious since the word is not summoned up through the medium of any concept, and since the given stimuli or 'states of mind' call it up in accordance with the laws of neurological mechanics or those of association, and thus that the word is not the bearer of its own meaning, has no inner power, and is merely a psychic, physiological or even physical phenomenon set alongside others, and thrown up by the working of an objective causality.
>
> (*PhP*, 176/205)

The second case, the intellectualist psychology of categorial operations of thought, fares no better:

> The word is still bereft of any effectiveness of its own, this time because it is only the external sign of an internal recognition which could take place without it, and to which it makes no contribution. It is not without meaning, since behind it there is a categorial operation, but this meaning is something which it does not *have*, does not possess, since it is thought which has a meaning, the word remaining an empty container. It is merely a phenomenon of articulation, of sound, or the consciousness of such a phenomenon, but in any case language is but an external accompaniment of thought.
>
> (*PhP*, 176-7/205; italics in original)

He then lays out the absurdity of the two cases' failure to come to terms with the idea of a speaking subject, pointing out the shared objective conception of the human body and its behaviour. Merleau-Ponty concludes with an affirmation that aims to refute both cases at once:

> In the first case, we are on this side of the word as meaningful; in the second we are beyond it. In the first there is nobody to speak; in the second, there is certainly a subject, but a thinking one, not a speaking one. As far as speech is concerned, intellectualism is hardly any different from empiricism, and is no better able than the latter to dispense with an explanation in terms of involuntary action. Once the categorial operation is performed, the appearance of the word which completes the process still has to be explained, and this will still be done by recourse to a physiological or psychic mechanism, since the word is a passive shell. Thus we refute both intellectualism and empiricism by simply saying that *the word has a meaning*.
>
> (*PhP*, 177/205–6)

So at the heart of Merleau-Ponty's attempt to develop a satisfactory conception of the speaking subject, is an effort to avoid conceiving speech as a
natural event which is in itself insignificant. Against such a view Merleau-
Ponty affirms a very suggestive and elegant alternative: my possession of language is not a matter of the presence in my body of a store of verbal images but
is a matter of me having under my belt the 'articulatory style' of each word as
'one of the possible uses of my body' (*PhP*, 180/210). In this way, Merleau-
Ponty's analysis makes viable an analysis of speech which situates it within a
general field of intrinsically significant *bodily expression*, and thus opens up the
possibility for a coherent conception of the living human being as a speaking
subject.

IV

Merleau-Ponty's counter-proposal is that the use of language in speech, though
distinctive in many respects, is itself, essentially, a form of *gesture*: 'The spoken
word is a genuine gesture, and it contains its meaning in the same way as
the gesture contains its' (*PhP*, 183/213). Before exploring this further, it is
worth noting that this line of thought fundamentally challenges the distinction
between expression and indication that launches Husserl's phenomenology.
Husserl famously begins the first Logical Investigation with the stipulation
that there are cases of what we call 'signs' which, he acknowledges, we ordinarily call 'expressions' but that he will *not* count as such: namely, facial
expressions and bodily gestures (smiles, frowns, winking, gesticulated obscen-
ities and waving for example). Such signs serve, Husserl insists, only to 'indicate' something and do not themselves 'express' anything (see Husserl 1973a,
275). In *Speech and Phenomena*, Derrida makes clear the implicit connection
between Merleau-Ponty's conception and Husserl's when he asserts that a
rehabilitation of the indicative sign allows us to see that 'the spoken word,
whatever dignity or originality we still accord it, is but a form of gesture'
(Derrida 1973, 21).[6]

On this view, the work of words we produce or fabricate when we utter a
novel sentence is neither a mere 'flow of words' nor just the external 'clothing'
of an original thought (*PhP*, 182/211), but, for anyone who possesses – that is
has – the vocabulary and syntax of the language in question, a 'new gesture'
comes into being (*PhP*, 183/213). And when I 'grasp the meaning' of gestures
formed by others this is not due to the fact that the signs they use arouse
associated representations in me, or lead me to form meaningful thoughts in
myself. On the contrary, what is made manifest to me is 'the presence of that
thought in the phenomenal world' (*PhP*, 182/211). Or, again, 'speech in the
speaker does not translate ready-made thought, but accomplishes it' (*PhP*, 178/
207). There is here, therefore, a '*thought in speech* the existence of which is
unsuspected by intellectualism', and which is utterly foreign to empiricism
(*PhP*, 179/209).

V

While Merleau-Ponty is, in general, more sympathetic to intellectualism than bald naturalism, he insists nevertheless, that 'the thinking subject must have its basis in the subject incarnate' (PhP, 193/225). Hence, for Merleau-Ponty, the other who I am talking to is not just there for me as some 'exterior' bodily surface which supplies the indicating 'data' for his or her hidden thoughts and feelings. On the contrary, the other is manifest precisely as he or she is: as the visible presence of 'a speaking subject' (PhP, 183/213). As John McDowell might put it, the scene here is not a meeting of external surfaces but a genuine meeting of minds. Or as Merleau-Ponty puts it, when I 'read' their 'gestures' (PhP, 24/27) 'the mental life of others becomes an immediate object, a whole charged with immanent meaning' (PhP, 58/67).

To avoid an empiricist misunderstanding of this we should note that the 'immediate object' in view here is not something simply given for just anyone you please. For Merleau-Ponty, as we shall see, culture informs human existence and human perception from its roots. Thus, for example, when I see a particular gesture as 'angry' or 'threatening' this is not perceived by me 'as the colour of the carpet' is, and the unfamiliar gestures of people from different cultures shows how people with the same anatomical apparatus can learn to 'use their bodies' differently and with different 'expressive meaning' (PhP, 189/220). Here, then, we have available a notion of the intrinsic visibility of the other unavailable to objective thought. Towards the end of the book, Merleau-Ponty summarises his position with great clarity:

> We must learn to distinguish the body from the objective body as set forth in works of physiology. This is not the body which is capable of being inhabited by consciousness. We must grasp again on visible bodies those forms of behaviour which are outlined there and which appear on them, but are not really contained in them.
>
> (PhP, 351/409)

This conception outlines a powerful and compelling response to the traditional objectifying construals of the body, construals that lead inexorably to scepticism and solipsism. However, in doing so a new difficulty might devolve to it. In overcoming objective thought it risks presenting the other as in some way *too* present to me, too much part of the visible world as it is given to me. This is, in fact, the flip-side of the misreading of Merleau-Ponty which would have him affirming that 'I am my body'. For if the other too *is* his or her body we seem committed to a totally unsatisfactory behaviourism. This concern is at the heart of Levinas' response to Merleau-Ponty in *Totality and Infinity*. Merleau-Ponty is referred to by Levinas as having offered an account of 'the solidarity of thought with speech' that is 'better than others' (Levinas 1969, 206). But he (Levinas) still questions whether language, 'the system of signs', is really necessary for thought, and, equally, whether the 'corporeal operation' really gets to the heart of the relation with the other that belongs to the essence of language (Levinas 1969, 206). Levinas is sympathetic to Merleau-Ponty's effort to avoid the idealism of a 'transcendental consciousness constituting objects' but thinks that the 'corporeal operation' with words that Merleau-Ponty puts in its place 'presupposes' the revelation of the other *as a face* (Levinas 1969, 206). That is, it presupposes the revelation of the face of the other *not* as a visible (as it were facial) feature of the world but as infinitely exceeding any idea or 'plastic image' I may form of him or her. Levinas' non-perceptual conception is not without its own problems, of course. However, it seems to me that Merleau-Ponty is not himself totally closed-off to the worry Levinas raises, and one should attend to his discussion of 'the truth in solipsism' in the same chapter of *Phenomenology of Perception* as his affirmation of our apprehension of the other in the behavioural forms manifest in 'visible bodies'.[7] Merleau-Ponty does not place the kind of stress on interiority and the first person that one finds in Levinas, but he is not a behaviourist either. He no more affirms the idea that the other is his or her body than he does that I am mine.

VI

Nevertheless, in virtue of its distinctive emphasis on the body and the incarnate subject it seems plausible to characterize Merleau-Ponty's philosophy of psychology as having a fundamentally *naturalistic* orientation.[8] However, if we do want to apply this label we need to recognize that it is not a naturalism of even a 'weakly scientistic' form: it is not just a matter of admitting (against 'strongly scientistic' views) that some non-scientific modes of investigation have cognitive value.[9] On the contrary, the naturalism in question is rather of the kind often associated with the later Wittgenstein: what I want to call a fundamentally *privative* naturalism which implies a steady resistance to non-natural or supernatural explanations but without itself speculatively anticipating or indeed uncritically embracing the results of empirical inquiries.[10]

My own view is that this is just the kind of naturalism that phenomenology should aim at. Phenomenology will then be a distinctively descriptive inquiry that is both capable of working with scientific studies and also free of any assumption that scientific status and method protects such studies against confusions and prejudices which careful reflection may show up.

On the whole, I think that Merleau-Ponty pursues this wonderfully well. However, there is an aspect of his own discussion of the expressive human body which seems to me to involve it in a step beyond the merely privative naturalism appropriate to a purely descriptive phenomenology: namely, its implicit adherence to a basic *cognitivism* concerning the idea of the difference of the human (what Merleau-Ponty generally calls 'man') from every animal. Thus, for example, although this is clearly not one example among others, despite offering an analysis of having a language that invites comparisons with the gestural traits of animals, Merleau-Ponty affirms the rather more traditional idea that the possession of language involves 'man' in a form of life that is utterly unique, fundamentally different from that of a mere (pure) animal. Language, he no doubt correctly notes, is something that we 'ordinarily' take to be 'in a peculiar category' (*PhP*, 190/220). However, Merleau-Ponty appeals to this not in order to acknowledge the significance we attach to the concept of the difference between human beings and animals but as marking an objective feature of human life that would (as it were from sideways on) *justify* it: it marks that the life of 'man' lies radically apart from the life of a merely animal being.

I do not suppose and am not suggesting at all that Merleau-Ponty follows the Cartesian tradition and regards non-human animals as automata. Indeed, he does not altogether disregard what we might equally well call 'the view that we ordinarily take': namely, that expressive behaviour is manifest in the lives of a great many living things, and not only in human life. Animal life is, he suggests, 'poor in expressive means' but not utterly non-expressive (*PhP*, 151/174). Similarly, he acknowledges that 'animals lead their lives' in what he calls 'a sort of *ek-stase*' (*PhP*, 87/100), so that 'the mere presence of a living being transforms the physical world, bringing to view here "food", there a "hiding place", and giving to "stimuli" a sense which they have not hitherto possessed' (*PhP*, 189/220). Nevertheless, there is no suggestion whatsoever that what is called history or culture might belong to what he, I think far too blithely, calls 'the simplicity of animal life' (*PhP*, 189/220). Indeed, at this point we might bring Merleau-Ponty against himself to affirm that philosophical anthropology would benefit from a deeper engagement with empirical studies of the lives of non-human animals, with ethology. However, we know too that such studies are swarming with philosophy and so, again, there is no question of going on here with ethology alone.

VII

In the absence of such supporting work, and despite his attractive privative naturalism, it seems to me that Merleau-Ponty holds fast to a more or less traditional 'humanistic' prejudice, a basic and uncritical *cognitivism* about the human difference: a conception of the lives of animals as, on the one hand, 'pre-ordained' by nature and a fundamentally contrasting view of the life of 'man', on the other, as a natural life radically or fundamentally transformed. In other words, he endorses the distinction, familiar in the work of Heidegger, Gadamer and McDowell, between animal inhabitation of an 'environment' or 'setting' (*Umwelt*) and 'man' living in a 'world' (*Welt*). It is, I think, typical of Merleau-Ponty's usual resistance to philosophy's traditional binary oppositions, and his sensitivity to ambiguity, that he actually states that 'man' is said to have '*not only* a setting, *but also* a world' (*PhP*, 87/100). Nevertheless, 'man' can, he speculatively suggests, be defined by 'a genius for ambiguity' which confers on human life and human behaviour a status that, while never purely cultural, is nevertheless radically unlike that of any animal: it is not purely natural, not natural through and through. 'Man' is unique, the nature of human beings alone is touched by culture, by spirit:

> It is impossible to superimpose on man a lower layer of behaviour which one chooses to call natural, followed by a manufactured cultural or spiritual world. Everything is both manufactured and natural in man, as it were, in the sense that there is not a word, not a form of behaviour which does not owe something to purely biological being – and which at the same time does not elude the simplicity of animal life, and causes forms of vital behaviour to deviate from their pre-ordained direction, through a sort of *leakage* and through a genius for ambiguity which might serve to define man.
>
> (*PhP*, 189/220)

Thus, as he puts it, human inhabitation in a culture results in the fact that, for humans alone 'behaviour creates meanings which are transcendent in rela-tion to the anatomical apparatus, and yet immanent to the behaviour as such' (*PhP*, 189/220). Later in the book Merleau-Ponty illustrates this idea with a nice – if, in this context, rare – example from scientific literature: Darwin's thought-provoking suggestion of a cultural adaptation of the natural behaviour of knitting the brows. Such behaviour, which serves naturally simply to protect the eyes from the sun, is transformed by 'man's genius for ambiguity' into a visible part of 'the human act of meditation' (*PhP*, 194/225).

VIII

There is a good deal to admire here. However, and despite its advances over more inflexible dualistic views, I think this conception is still highly proble-matic. I will try to bring this out by looking at how adherence to the idea of a rigorous and fundamental distinction (in the nature of things) between nature and culture, even one which is in the special case of 'man' radically undiffer-entiated,[11] gives Merleau-Ponty's analysis a profound difficulty concerning what must in some way be, on his own terms, the *naturally impossible* event of 'the origin of man'.[12]

In certain respects my claim here poses something of a challenge to Tom Baldwin's suggestion that the absence of 'any reference to evolutionary theory' in Merleau-Ponty's account is due simply to its 'familiarity'.[13] Holding to one side what Merleau-Ponty might have wanted to affirm here, my point is that *however* he thinks 'man' comes into being, he regards what comes about with this coming into being as a state of affairs in which we have, on the one hand, merely natural life and on the other hand something which is essentially more than merely natural. And my worry is that this state of affairs is not something that could have come about merely naturally.

The basic difficulty here can be seen as a generalization of the 'insistent problem' that Merleau-Ponty himself acknowledges regarding the origin of language (PhP, 186/216). In the case of language (again not one case among others in this context), he knows, for example, that when he looks to 'culture' to supply 'what nature does not provide' this merely pushes the problem 'one stage further back' (PhP, 186/217). And at this stage further back, with the question of the origin of culture, he cannot not, I am suggesting, encounter the 'insistent problem' (for his analysis) of 'the origin of man'.

Merleau-Ponty is not without a response. In an effort to resolve the paradox that the linguistic expressions of the 'first' speaker can function as such only if they communicate already available meanings from 'former acts of expression' (PhP, 186/216), Merleau-Ponty appeals to what he calls an 'emotional essence' that is retained in language and which links it to 'an earlier means of communication' (PhP, 187/217). Such content he suggests makes the wonderful and distinctive sonorousness of different so-called 'natural languages' amount to 'so many ways of "singing" the world', ways in which a people express in sound the experienced 'emotional essence' of things: 'ways for the body to sing the world's praises' (PhP, 187/218).

It is not clear, however, that this (perhaps rather more typically German than French) proposal resolves the paradox rather than simply pushes it one stage further back again. Indeed, his totally anti-naturalistic insistence that 'there is here *nothing* resembling the famous naturalistic conceptions which equate the artificial sign with the natural one, and try to reduce language to emotional expression' only serves to heighten the problem (PhP, 188/219): for if world-praising emotional contents *too* are no more natural in man than they are cultural, then it will already be a 'man' who is the subject of the 'acts of expression' which the first 'singing' words presuppose.

The basic difficulty, then, is this: as long as one sticks to the idea that there is in the nature of things a fundamental difference or split between animal life and human life, then anything one appeals to in order to explain how 'man' became not-merely-an-animal is a priori inadequate to the task and destined to offend the idea of phenomenology as a privative naturalism: *either* the explanation will involve exclusively *natural* structures, in which case it is not clear how or why it could do more than put an animal on a new 'pre-ordained' natural path (rather than be the origin of a creature without one) *or* the explanation will appeal to something that is already *not-merely-natural*, in which case it only pushes the problem one step further back by presupposing what it is meant to explain – or would have to involve an implicit appeal to the kind of *non-natural* or *supernatural* explanation (the Genius of God as it were) that a consistent (even if only privative) naturalism aims to eschew. It seems, then, that as long as he interprets what he surely rightly calls 'the ordinary view' of the 'peculiarity' of language in terms which presume that one being, called 'man', has achieved some kind of radical break from the rest of animal nature (resulting, for example, in a definite and unique 'surplus of our existence over natural being' – *PhP*, 197/229) such theoretical embarrassment over *the necessity and impossibility* of finding an 'origin of man' will prevail.

IX

I do not have space here to do more than sketch the outlines of an alternative, but its principle would seem to me fairly clear, and even open to (contestable because at least partly imaginatively framed) ethological investigation: namely, that many non-human animals are not simply or purely creatures *without* culture. And, indeed, I do not regard it as at all implausible to suppose that there are symbolic cultures within non-human animal lives too, that many non-human animals need it too. With the movement from the non-human to the human there is, to be sure, *a transition within this field of culture* sufficiently radical that one might want to call it 'a transition from quantity to quality'. So rejecting Merleau-Ponty's dualism does not imply that one winds up affirming an asinine biologism or continuuism. On the other hand, acknowledging the existence of genuinely objective differences within the continuity of the field does not imply either that one could specify something like an 'origin of man' that would mark a fundamental or radical rupture with all animal nature. At issue is what Stephen Mulhall calls the 'discontinuous continuity' and the 'uncannily intimate distance', between the lives of human beings and the lives of non-human animals (Mulhall 2005, 68). On this view one can embrace the hypothesis that a form of life with genuinely *sui generis* traits can emerge from a prior state by a process of small and incremental quantitative changes because this transition involves a development *within* a certain field (a field of culture) and not a radical break in kind of being. Thus, as Merleau-Ponty acknowledges, there is already 'gesture' in animals, and I want now to add, there is already culture and history too. There is a transition with intermediate cases, but the process leads to a situation in which, looking back, it seems that there must have been an event that is a changeover or break in kind of Being. But there is no such event. In short, therefore, while there is no radical origin of the new condition, what emerges can effect a transition (over the very long evolutionary run) from quantity to quality sufficient to justify talk of objective differences and structural breaks, and not just a simple continuum.

X

But that is certainly not the end of the story. The account just outlined is, it seems, blind to the significance we attach to the human difference. There is, one might accept, a 'structural break' between many animals, between a blind-worm and a dolphin, to take David Wiggins' example (Wiggins 1998, 124). But isn't there a different difference between blind-worms and dolphins on one side and humans on the other?

It would be crazy, I think, to deny the force of this point. Nevertheless, that does not make it in every way acceptable. Remember that, all along, the complaint against Merleau-Ponty's view was against its *cognitivism*, not the general acuteness of his phenomenology. What is at issue is our idea of the difference between human beings and animals and the significance we attach to that idea. As should be clear, nothing I have said should imply that we need to give up on the idea that 'the differences between higher and lower forms of life' are real, or that we should accept that they are simply fictitious. On the contrary, we can accept that 'they are even objective' (Wiggins 1998, 124). However, we can rejoin Merleau-Ponty by insisting that these objective differences are not *decisive*. As Wiggins puts it, 'such differences may be important to us. But they depend for their significance upon a framework that is a free construct, not upon something fashioned in a manner that is answerable to how anything really is' (Wiggins 1998, 124).

The possibility that human life has special significance or (as the basic Greco-Judeo-Christian thematization of this special significance has it) *that every human life has an incomparable uniqueness*, never was something that we as a species ever found or discovered. A fortiori it is not an error to be corrected by a better empirical theory of nature either. Indeed, what is at issue here (the developing significance to us of the human difference) is the result of processes of a kind that Darwin himself regarded as *contrasting* markedly with the kinds of forces which produce objective differences in nature: namely, 'unconstrained inventive processes' (Wiggins 1998, 124). Of course, unlike the splendidly deliberate work of men that fascinated Darwin and which gave rise to numerous new pigeon varieties, the inventive processes which have given rise to the construction upon which depends the significance we attach to the human difference were, as Wiggins puts it, 'gradual, unconscious and communal' (Wiggins 1998, 124). What is gradually constructed here is precisely a construct of our history – indeed, in a deep sense it *is* our history. But, and this is surely a profoundly phenomenological conclusion, it is not something that can be justified (as it were from sideways on) by features of reality.

Notes

1 A comparable point can be made with regard to the philosophy of language. Indeed, at a conference entitled 'La Philosophie Analytique' held at Royaumont in 1958, Merleau-Ponty raised this point with Gilbert Ryle (whose *Concept of Mind* Merleau-Ponty stated he knew and had 'worked with'). In discussion Merleau-Ponty broached the question whether philosophical investigations of language should not 'have recourse ... to an immanent study of linguistic phenomena for which certain parts of linguistic science might be the rough sketch' (*T&D*, 66–7). At the end of this essay I will make a Merleau-Pontian point of this kind concerning philosophical anthropology or ethology *against* Merleau-Ponty.
2 This is the topic of chapter 6 of part I of *Phenomenology of Perception*.
3 A personal experience of mine shows something of the general importance of this distinction. I was once pointedly rebuked for what now seems to me to be a conflation

of these uses. I was at a conference dinner with, among others, the German philosopher Eike von Savigny, and I cheekily criticized him for saying 'My wife will have the steak'. Well, maybe he could have let her order for herself. But Eike was ordering for everyone on this occasion. And he picked me up for my cheek. He pointed out that the sense of 'my' in this case ('My wife') indicated a relation not a possession. So he was not suggesting proprietary ownership of something (as he might, say, with his hat) but publicly presenting (celebrating) his relation to someone (his wife). Merleau-Ponty's schema would mark this distinction, and help one avoid mistaking a wife for a hat, by rendering the sense of 'my' involved in 'my wife' with the sentence 'I have a wife' and not the sentence 'The wife is mine'. What, however, should one say of a pet dog? My comments on Merleau-Ponty's humanism at the end of this paper may shed light on his response to this question.

4 See, for example, Primozic 2001, 17; Wild 1963, xv.

5 Anyone who thinks it is needlessly refined to deny that persons are bodies should read Glock and Hyman (1994).

6 I interpret Derrida's conception of language with some further help from Merleau-Ponty in Glendinning 1998, ch. 8.

7 *Phenomenology of Perception*, part II, ch. 4, 'Other Selves and the Human World'.

8 See Moran 2000, 403. It is worth noting that Merleau-Ponty's first major work, *The Structure of Behaviour*, comes to its conclusion with a section called 'Is There Not a Truth of Naturalism?'.

9 For these contrasts, see, J. P. Moreland's (wonderfully entitled) essay 'Should a Naturalist be a Supervenient Physicalist':

> Contemporary naturalists embrace either weak or strong scientism. According to the former, non-scientific fields are not worthless nor do they offer no intellectual results, but they are vastly inferior to science in their epistemic standing and do not merit full credence. According to the latter, unqualified cognitive value resides in science and in nothing else.
>
> (Moreland 1998, 37)

10 I am indebted to conversations with Matthew Bell for this idea.

11 So the binary distinction 'in the world' for Merleau-Ponty is not so much between nature and culture as it is between a purely natural life and a natural life everywhere informed by culture.

12 I am indebted to Daniel Whiting for discussion of this issue as it arises in Merleau-Ponty.

13 Baldwin 2004, 9.

8

CONSCIOUSNESS, SELF-CONSCIOUSNESS AND COMMUNICATION

Naomi Eilan

Introduction

Merleau-Ponty's target in his essay 'The Child's Relations with Others'[1] is what he takes to be the assumption that governs 'psychology of the classical period', namely that 'the psyche, or psychic, is what is given to only one person ... what constitutes the psyche in me or in others is something incommunicable' (*PofP*, 114). The way he develops his opposition to this idea brings together two kinds of debate that tend to get treated in complete independence of each other in current philosophy. One is the question of how we should characterise both the development and constitutive nature of mental concepts, and how such characterisations relate to problems of our knowledge of our own and other minds. The second is the question of how we should characterise the phenomenal properties of conscious experience, those properties in virtue of which there is something it is like to be in states with them.

Not only does he bring these together, but he does so in way that contains the materials for a very radical theory. The radical story promised here is one in which both consciousness and self-consciousness need to be explained by appeal to dually owned, pre-communicative experiences of a kind which, it is claimed, we find in early infancy. This idea can be developed in ways that make it as radical a challenge to individualism regarding the nature of both conscious experience and self-consciousness as it is possible to find.

Merleau-Ponty is emphatic that he intends such a challenge. Crudely put, I will be suggesting that while Merleau-Ponty almost delivers on the idea that there are experiences in early infancy that can, and perhaps should be char-acterised as dually owned, he fails to exploit this in a way that would make good the claim that we need to appeal to such experiences to explain self-consciousness and consciousness in general. The fact of failure, though, is far

118

less interesting both than the promise itself and at least some of the reasons for failing to deliver on it.

In many ways Merleau-Ponty's concerns and claims anticipate very recent interdisciplinary discussions among philosophers and developmental psychologists who want to give social interaction, and, in particular, communication, a stronger role in explaining the nature and emergence of mental concepts than is given by those who think that our grasp of mental concepts is to be explained, solely, by appeal to our growing capacity to theorise about the observed behaviour of others. One reason for his own failure to deliver on the promise lies in idiosyncratic appeals to the empirical literature of the time. Empirical and theoretical progress in developmental psychology allows us to take the issues a great deal further, and I will be drawing on some recent work to sharpen up some of Merleau-Ponty's claims. But many of the more interesting reasons for failure turn on the difficulty in formulating, let alone justifying, a thesis that could provide a serious communication-theoretic account of the nature of self-consciousness; and the ambiguities revealed in trying to formulate one are equally present in the current literature.

And here Merleau-Ponty adds something lacking in recent debates, which can be formulated as a challenge to 'communication-theoretic' aspirations, and used to sharpen the kinds of claim a communication theorist should be making. The challenge, at its sharpest, is that we can only get a real communication-theoretic account of mental concepts off the ground if we also adopt a seriously social account of the nature of human consciousness. More specifically: justifying a real alternative to the 'theory theory' of mental concepts requires adopting a radical social externalism, of a particular kind, about the nature of phenomenal consciousness.

Although I find this idea extremely attractive and interesting, my aim will be not so much to argue for it as to draw out some of the key claims, ideas and lines of reasoning underpinning it, further development of which is needed for making good the challenge. This may be a challenge one has good reason to resist trying to meet; and there may well be ways of meeting it that do not require adopting the full fledged social theory I will be articulating on Merleau-Ponty's behalf. But at least part of the interest in articulating it lies in the kind of sharpening it forces on us both with respect to the debate between communication-theoretic and 'theory theory' accounts of mental concepts, and the kinds of issues about consciousness that it brings to the fore, issues that tend not to get so much as raised in the current consciousness literature.

Merleau-Ponty on the 'theoretical issues'

In the first section of the paper, entitled 'The Problem of the Child's Perception of Others: The Theoretical Problem', Merleau-Ponty sets out the main lines of the picture he is opposing and of the one he wants to replace it with.

The questions he is concerned with here are: 'How and under what conditions does the child come into contact with others? What is the nature of the child's relations with others? How are such relations possible from the day of birth on?' (*PofP*, 113). As he sees it,

> [c]lassical psychology approached the problem only with great diffi-culty. One might say that it was among the stumbling blocks of clas-sical psychology because it is admittedly incapable of being solved if one confines oneself to the theoretical ideas that were elaborated by academic psychology. Given the presuppositions with which that psy-chology works, given the prejudices it adopted from the start without any kind of criticism, the relation with others becomes incomprehen-sible for it.
>
> (*PofP*, 113)

What were these presuppositions, and why did they render our access to other minds 'incomprehensible'? The presupposition is the 'tacit agreement' mentioned at the outset that

> the psyche, or the psychic, is what is given to only one person ... what constitutes the psyche in me or in others is something incom-municable. I alone am able to grasp my psyche. A consequence of this idea is that the psyche of another appears to me to be radically inac-cessible to me ... since I cannot have direct access to the psyche of another, for the reason just given, I must seize the other's psyche only indirectly, mediated by bodily appearances.
>
> (*PofP*, 114)

As Merleau-Ponty develops the consequences of this picture, the only way a subject could begin to have access to others' mental states is by analogical reasoning using four terms:

> (1) myself, my 'psyche'; (2) the image I have of my body by means of the sense of touch or coenaesthesia, which to be brief we shall call the 'introceptive image of my own body'; (3) the body of the other as seen by me which we shall call the 'visual body'; (4) a fourth (hypothe-tical) term which I must reconstitute and guess at – the 'psyche' of the other, the other's feeling of his own existence – to the extent that I can imagine or suppose it across the appearances of the other through his visual body.
>
> (*PofP*, 115)

One kind of argument against this is an echo of Wittgenstein's argument against the analogy making so much as making sense. In addition, and here too we find analogues in Wittgenstein, Merleau-Ponty points to the conceptual sophistication required for thinking in this way, and the incompatibility of this what he takes to be an obvious fact, of the 'relative precociousness of the perception of others' (*PofP*, 115):

At a very early age children are sensitive to facial expressions. How could this be possible if, in order to arrive at an understanding of the global meaning of the smile, and to learn that a smile is a fair indication of benevolent feeling the child had to perform the complicated task I have just mentioned (i.e. the analogical reasoning).

(*PofP*, 115)

The solution he advocates, though, is far more radical than anything we find Wittgenstein suggesting. The way out, he says, is to adopt the following picture of the origin and consequently the nature of our mental concepts:

Psychogenesis begins in a state where the child is unaware of himself or the other as different beings. We cannot say that in such a state the child has genuine communication with others. In order for there to be genuine communication there must be a sharp distinction between the one who communicates and the one with whom one communicates. But there is initially a state of pre-communication (Max Scheler), in which there is not one individual set over and against another but rather an anonymous collectivity, an undifferentiated group life, wherein the other's intentions somehow play across my body while my intentions play across his.
[...]
Next on the basis of this initial community, both by objectification of one's own body and the constitution of the other in his difference, there occurs segregation, a distinction of individuals, (a process which, as we shall see, is never completely finished).

(*PofP*, 119)

The idea of self-consciousness emerging, together with consciousness of others, from an initial state of community is, Merleau-Ponty notes, 'a conception common to many trends in contemporary psychology. One finds it Guillame and Wallon; it occurs in Gestalt theories, phenomenologists and psychoanalysts alike' (*PofP*, 119). The message to be extracted from all of these is that we should

neither treat the origin of consciousness as though it were conscious, in an explicit way, of itself nor treat it as though it were completely closed on itself.

(*PofP*, 119)

121

At first the me is both entirely unaware of itself and of the other ...
the adult me, on the contrary, knows its own limits yet possesses the
power to cross them by genuine sympathy that is at least *relatively*
distinct from the initial form of sympathy. The initial sympathy rests
on the ignorance of oneself rather than on the perception of others,
while adult sympathy occurs between 'other' and 'other'; it does not
abolish the differences between myself and other.

(*PofP*, 120)

The radical reading of the theory

There is clearly a great deal going on here, many dimensions along which one
might contrast the 'classical theory' with the picture he opposes to it. Many of
these figure, if only fleetingly, in Merleau-Ponty's own discussion. However,
there is a set of ideas it is possible to extract from the above statement of his
theory that I want to focus on, and which can be summarised as follows.

1 There are early experiences in the child's life that we can only get right,
   phenomenologically speaking, if we think of these experiences as constitutively (a) pre-communicative, and (b) dually owned. This is a claim
   about the ontology of some early experiences; they have more than one
   subject. Call this the 'Phenomenological Thesis'.
2 Our capacity to single out others and ourselves as particular subjects, and to
   ascribe mental states to others and ourselves depends, constitutively, on
   these early phenomena. This is a claim about the development and nature
   of our mental concepts, including our capacity to think 'I' thoughts. Call
   this the 'Conceptual Thesis'.
3 Because of the dependence of self-consciousness on early dually owned
   experiences, a correct account of phenomenal properties in general must
   give dually owned experiences a constitutive role in explaining the nature
   of human consciousness. Call this the 'Consciousness Thesis'.

Merleau-Ponty almost delivers on the first set of phenomenological claims.
Drawing largely on Henri Wallon, the phenomenon he points to in their support is one that is currently labelled 'mutual affect regulation'. Things begin to
get shakier with respect to the Conceptual Thesis, and for this reason the
Consciousness Thesis never really gets off the ground.

There are many reasons for this failure, some more interesting than others. I
distinguish among some of these as we begin to unpack the Conceptual Thesis,
and come back to what I take to be the deepest at the very end. Before that I
want to have in place a sketch of the kind of account of mutual affect regulation which we need in order to begin to make good the Phenomenological
Thesis.

122

Mutual affect regulation and the Phenomenological Thesis

In early stages of mutual affect regulation we find processes such as the child smiling, the adult responding with a related expression of an emotion to which the child again responds with another expression of a related emotion and so until one of them gets bored or distracted. It is this reciprocal structure that has also led developmentalists to describe such exchanges as 'proto-conversations' (Reddy 2005).

One aspect of this phenomenon stressed by Merleau-Ponty and also by current theories, is that the state of mind, the emotion, is expressed directly by the face, where this enables direct perception of the emotion, without the need for any inferential or analogical mediation. This is a claim many have made but, on its own, it does not warrant describing such events as consisting in the occurrence of multiple-, or at the very least, dually owned experiences. There is a second aspect of mutual affect regulation, though, that would begin to do the trick, and which is mentioned only fleetingly by Merleau-Ponty, and certainly not developed. This is the fact that the detection of this state by the other is naturally, irresistibly, accompanied by the production of an expression of emotion (which can again be responded to immediately by the child, and so forth). One way of theorising about this aspect of mutual affect regulation, which begins to yield the kind of claim we are looking for, is to be found in Peter Hobson's account of these kinds of exchanges. On his account, the right way to think of them is that in these cases 'to detect and to respond with a new or related emotion come to the same thing'. What he means, at least, is that we should treat each felt emotion in such exchanges as, essentially, a response to the other's (Hobson 2005).

If we treat this as a claim about what it is like for the subject, a claim about phenomenology, which we must if it is to have any interest, then what we have here is the potential material for externalism about other minds in accounting for the nature of each subject's experience. There are two ways one might develop such an externalism. One is to say that the other enters into the phenomenology of the experience as an *object* experienced. The second is to say that the other enters into the nature of the experience as a *joint subject* of the experience. Each is possible. Which should we prefer in this particular case?

For an object to be an object for the subject, and hence integral to the phenomenology of the experience, it is not enough that it cause the experience. It must be present to the subject as an object. In the case of emotions it must be the kind of object that is the bearer of mental states, that is, a subject. Now there are theories of mutual affect regulation that maintain that we should ascribe to infants in these early bouts the capacity to take the other as a subject of experience. This would not be Merleau-Ponty's own account; he rejects, rightly in my view, the idea that there is enough structure and conceptual sophistication in these early exchanges to warrant such a claim. He is adamant that in such exchanges there is no separation, by the infant at least, of herself from the adult.

The second option, of bringing in the other as a joint subject, does not meet such objections. It is a familiar point in accounts of the way in which subjects enter into a characterisation of individual experiences that they do so as a 'point of origin', where this is a metaphor for the idea that they do so in a way that does not involve the representations of themselves as objects. If this is true of one subject, it would be equally true of two. So if it is right to bring in more than one subject in characterising the phenomenology of early reciprocal exchanges of emotion, the dual ownership model has a better chance of getting off the ground in characterising such early experiences, prior to the onset of the kind of conceptual sophistication needed for self-consciousness.

The best way of understanding this kind of move is by analogy with relational theories of perceptual experience. On a relational account of the nature of perceptual experiences, experiences are relations between subjects and portions of the world, and the phenomenal properties of the experience are properties of the perceptual relation between the subject and the world. Correlatively, the claim here is that in cases of mutual affect regulation the experience consists in a particular relation between two subjects, and the phenomenal properties of the experience are properties of that relation. (I come to this analogy and substantive use of it to justify the Conceptual Thesis later on.)

Suppose it is right to say that there are early emotional experiences which should be correctly described as shared, in the strong sense that they are dually owned. To a great extent the interest of such a claim lies in the theoretical use to which it is put. First, we want to know to what use these descriptions are being put in explaining the developmental trajectory of infants. What kinds of achievement are they heralding, and what role do they play in making these later achievements possible? Second, we want to know exactly how claims about development relate to constitutive claims about mature human conceptual capacities. The same applies to Merleau-Ponty's (and developmentalists') descriptions of such these events as 'pre-communicative'. Again, this is a possible description, but here too, for this to be more than a suggestive metaphor we need to know to what theoretical use they are being put. This is where the Conceptual Thesis comes in, and to which we must now turn.

From the Phenomenological to the Conceptual Thesis

If we adopt the Conceptual Thesis, we will say that the experiences, described as dually owned and pre-communicative, play a critical role in the emergence of both consciousnesses of oneself and of others. The very least this suggests is, first, that the emergence of self-consciousness is to be accounted for by explaining the transition from pre- to genuine communication. Call this the 'Communication Claim' about self-consciousness. Second, it suggests that early shared, dually owned affective experiences play a role in making this possible. Call the latter the 'Shared Experience Claim'.

Making good the Communication Claim requires a phenomenon that can plausibly be said to exhibit the emergence together of communication, self-consciousness and consciousness of others. Correlatively, making good the Shared Experience Claim requires showing that we need to appeal to shared experience in explaining the nature of the emergence of such communication. The central phenomenon that has the potential to fit the bill is the emergence of a particular kind of pointing behaviour, labelled 'declarative pointing', viewed by many developmentalists as a precursor to full blown verbal communication.

In the next section I lay out the basic Communication Claim about self-consciousness that can be found in one attempt to explain the significance and nature of declarative pointing. Before that, though, a brief comment about what Merleau-Ponty himself says, and here, it must be admitted, Merleau-Ponty falls at the first hurdle, so to speak. When he turns from the elaboration of 'theoretical issues' to drawing on contemporary empirical work about the actual development of infants (*PofP*, 125–41), instead of referring to the development of communicative abilities, and the behaviours that manifest them, he talks about children's growing capacity play with mirrors and understand them as self-reflections. But it is important to distinguish between two different ways he appeals to mirrors here.

First, drawing on somewhat anecdotal work by Wallon, he suggests that it is the actual playing with mirrors that in fact gives the child the capacity to think of himself objectively, as one object among others. That is, appeal to mirror manipulation replaces the kind of appeal I will be making to pointing. This immediately debars him from being a communication theorist, at least in empirical terms. However, the idea that playing with mirrors is what gives a child the capacity for self-conscious thoughts is anyway not one that one can take seriously; and from now on I simply ignore this aspect of his thought, though it does explain why some of his ideas did not get developed in the way they might have.

Second, Merleau-Ponty appeals to mirrors to explain what subjects have to achieve if they are to achieve self-consciousness. And here, somewhat confusingly, he switches to a purely metaphorical appeal of mirrors, of the kind we find in psychoanalysis and, in particular in Lacan. This is the idea that the kind of objectification of oneself and others involved in self-consciousness and consciousness of others rests constitutively on the capacity to see one's own states, in particular one's emotional states 'mirrored in the Other's gaze'. At least one ingredient in this metaphor can be expressed as follows: self-consciousness involves, essentially, a kind of reflective counterpart to the kind of reciprocity we find in early bouts of mutual affect regulation.

The idea that an understanding of oneself as a subject depends constitutively on a reflective counterpart to the kind of reciprocity we find in mutual affect regulation is one, if not the only, way of making good the Communication

Claim and, on some accounts the Shared Experience Claim. Or so I will be suggesting. This is what warrants ascribing to Merleau-Ponty at least the aim of developing a communication-theoretic approach to self-consciousness, despite his failing to focus on the right empirical phenomenon when explaining and justifying it.

Declarative pointing, joint attention and the Communication Claim

The actual gesture of pointing emerges spontaneously as early as three months. (See Franco 2005 for a discussion of the gesture and its pattern of emergence, and Woodward 2005 for the later emergence of its perceptual detection). However, most psychologists agree that it is only at about the age of twelve months that it begins to be used with what appears to be some kind of deliberative intent. In a pioneering paper, Bates et al. (1976) distinguished between two kinds of pointing that emerge at roughly this age, proto-imperative and proto-declarative. The first was interpreted as a request for an object (the baby appears satisfied when he gets the object). The interpretation of the second is more controversial – but described maximally neutrally, it is a form of pointing the aim of which appears to be simply to get the adult to engage with the baby's attention to the object (the baby seems satisfied when this has occurred).

Declarative pointings are not produced by chimpanzees (Gomez 2005), nor, usually, by autistic children (Hobson 2005). The fact that they are not produced by chimpanzees provides one impetus for the idea that there is a kind of capacity for objectification, coupled with a kind of self-consciousness, that is absent in chimpanzees but which is essential for verbal communication about the world to get going. The fact that they are not produced usually by autistic children has been taken as an indication of their requiring a kind of mutual awareness which, again, is essential for the development of full blown communication but which is lacking in autistic children. Both these capacities, for objectivity and mutual awareness, have in turn been thought to be manifest in the kind of joint attention that underpins the capacity for declarative pointing only. The issues we are interested in get going on the back of interpretation of joint attention, so let me begin with a brief description of the phenomenon.

The term 'joint attention' refers to a form of attentional activity that infants begin to engage in at about the age of twelve months. Prior to that age they direct attention either to their carers or to objects in their environment. At about the age of twelve months they begin to 'triangulate', mutually attend with their carers to a 'third object'. By the age of eighteen months, on most accounts, they are engaging in full blown episodes of joint attention.

The importance of joint attention for the development of early pre-verbal and verbal communications is hard to overestimate. As Bruner, who coined the term, puts it, joint attention 'sets the deictic limits that govern joint reference, determines the need for referential taxonomy, establishes the need for signalling intent, and eventually provides a context for the development of explicit pre-dication' (Bruner 1977, 287).

From the perspective of making good the Conceptual Thesis, there are two aspects of joint attention that are of particular interest. The first says that genuine joint attention introduces the capacity for a kind of objective take on the world, coupled with self-consciousness, conceptual capacities not mani-fested in earlier dyadic interactions. The second says it involves mutual or shared awareness by both participants that they are attending to the same thing. Explanations of the first yield a version of the Communication Claim; explanations of the second, a version of the Shared Experience Claim. I say something about the former in this section and the next, and then turn to the latter.

According to Werner and Kaplan (1963), Gestaltist contemporaries of Merleau-Ponty, the triangulations we find in joint attention are the first mani-festations of the child's adoption of a 'contemplative stance', where this is contrasted with a purely practical stance. As they put it:

> Thus the act of reference emerges not as an individual act, but as a
> social one: by exchanging things with the Other, by touching things
> and looking at them with the Other. Eventually a special gestural
> device is formed, *pointing* at an object, by which the infant invites the
> Other to contemplate an object as he does himself.
>
> (Werner and Kaplan 1963, 43)

The central metaphor they use to describe the role of triangulation under-pinning pointing is the familiar Gestalt metaphor of polarisation or distancing. Prior to triangulation, objects exist as 'things of action'. The transformation that begins to take place when joint attention sets in transforms objects from 'ego-bound things of action to ego-distant things of contemplation'. A correla-tive distancing of the infant from the adult takes place, though they are less explicit about what exactly this involves.

This distinction has informed many attempts to characterise the distinction between proto-imperative and proto-declarative pointing (see Franco 2005), where the idea was that a correct account of the distinction would lend support to the picture. The main picture behind this metaphor is, I think, something like the following. Prior to triangulation the child is engaged in two kinds of dyadic relations – perception of objects and mutual affect regulation with per-sons. When the child shows the object to another, successful showing requires taking into account the other's perspective, taking into account what she sees, and so forth. This yields a distancing of child from the object for the child to succeed, in that the object cannot be treated by her purely as an affordance for her own actions. But having to show it to someone else also requires more than mere mutual affect regulation. When all we have in play is the latter, the adult need be treated as nothing more than an affective affordance. Introducing a

127

third element requires treating her as someone who can have a take on the world, can have a perspective on it – where the differentiation comes in the more the child needs to take into account the difference of perspective. Taking the latter into account simultaneously strengthens the grip on the idea of a mind-independent world. Awareness of others as having a different perspective and awareness of the world as being as it is independently of one's own perspective, come together.

Although the idea that declarative pointing is a manifestation of an emerging contemplative stance is by no means uncontroversial, for our immediate purposes I want to take it as read. For our concerns begin with the way we interpret it. The problems here echo problems John Campbell has raised for Donald Davidson's communication theoretic claim about what gives us the idea of an objective world. On Davidson's account, we arrive at the idea of world by triangulating our own and others' responses to the world; the world is the common cause of both sets of reactions to it (Davidson 2001). The challenge raised by the opposing 'thought-theoretical' claim is that while communicative triangulations may indeed be correctly said to *suffice* for grasping the idea of an objective world, they cannot be necessary, and cannot explain what it actually consists in, on pain of ending up with an anti-realist account of objectivity (on which the world out there just is the world we triangulate on). On the alternative thought-theoretical account developed by Campbell (1986), what gives the subject the idea of an objective world is his use of spatial concepts within the framework of a primitive theory of perception. The idea here is that a full explanation of what this involves will itself require ascribing to the subject a grasp of the idea of different perspectives on the same world; we do not need to appeal to triangulations to introduce the very notion of other perspectives on the same world.

Campbell's interest is in explanations of objectivity. Suppose we shift attention specifically to self-consciousness. A challenge similar in structure might be formulated here. Suppose we agree that engaging in declarative pointing suffices for a basic grip on the difference between one's own and another's perspective on the world. In what sense can it be the capacity to produce such pointing which actually gives the subject this grip? Isn't it rather presupposed in the very ability to engage in declarative pointing?

The key both to formulating the challenge in a sharper way, and to attempting to meet it, lies in how we explain the *dyadic relation between the two subjects* when communication about the world, the third object, begins to take place. When two people communicate they think of each other in the second person, and of themselves in the first. The suggestion I want to pursue in the next section is that the kind of communication theoretic approach to self-consciousness needed for supporting the Communication Claim says that use of the first person emerges, essentially, with the emergence of the *second* person, and depends constitutively on this link. As I will be interpreting it, to say this is to say, among other things, that we can and should give an account of the first/second person distinction that makes it not wholly derivative on the account we give of the way mental concepts are used in third-person mental ascriptions, and on independently explained first person ascriptions. Where we find such derivativeness the thought-theoretical challenge is not met.

I should say in advance that what follows is very far from a full account of what second person thought consists in. What I will be trying to do, rather, is give an indication of the kinds of claim about what the first person/second person distinction involves, and how it emerges, the making good of which would begin to give substance to the Communication Claim.

Mutual awareness and the Communication Claim

As developmental psychologists (usually) use the term, for joint attention to be in play, it is not sufficient that the infant and the adult are in fact attending to the same object, nor that the one's attention cause the other's. The latter can and does happen much earlier, whenever the adult follows the baby's gaze and homes in on the same object as the baby is attending to; or, from the age of six months, when babies begin to follow the gaze of an adult. We have the relevant sense of joint attention in play only when the fact that both child and adult are attending to the same object is, to use Sperber and Wilson's (1986) phrase, 'mutually manifest'. Psychologists sometimes speak of such jointness as a case of attention being 'shared' by infant and adult, or of a 'meeting of minds' between infant and adult, all phrases intended to capture the idea that when joint attention occurs everything about the fact that both subjects are attending to the same object is out in the open, manifest to both participants.

What we have here is an epistemological characterisation of the dyadic relation that holds between two subjects when joint attention, and the communication based on it, are achieved. Let us say that such openness is one essential ingredient that goes into two people thinking of each other, in the course of a single exchange about the immediate environment, in the second person. One important way of bringing out what is needed for establishing the Communication Claim turns on how such openness is explained. There are at present two main models for explaining such openness in the developmental literature, the 'primitive Gricean theory' and the 'intersubjectivity theory'. As we shall see, the kind of account of openness in the first is too weak to support the Communication Claim. I then turn to an alternative, which has at least, the potential to do so.

The primitive Gricean theory

According to Tomasello (1995, 104f.), between the ages of nine and eighteen months the child undergoes a cognitive revolution akin in significance and structure to the revolution it undergoes between the ages of three and four. During the latter, the child progresses from understanding 'other persons in terms of their thoughts and beliefs' to understanding 'that others have thoughts and beliefs that may differ from their own', and eventually to understanding 'that others have thoughts and beliefs that may not match the current state of affairs (false beliefs)'. During their second year of life children have an analogous, agency-based understanding of persons that develops along similar lines. That is, they progress from understanding 'other persons in terms of their intentions' to understanding 'that others may have intentions that may differ from their own', and to understanding 'that others have intentions that may not match with the current state of affairs (accidents and unfulfilled intentions)'.

The first step of the agency-based revolution occurs at about nine months when children achieve their own newly formed capacity for mean-ends reasoning, and hence for a distinction between goals and the means to achieve them. They apply this understanding to their own actions, and by simulation to the perceived activities of others. They also apply this to their own and others' looking behaviour, conceived of as a kind of object-directed action. This is how they think of attention.

At around twelve months they begin to manifest a grip on the possibility of manipulating others' attentive behaviour by pointing and then by uttering their first words – both vehicles for such manipulation, first to objects, and then, when predication sets in, to properties or aspects of objects. These manipulations performed and responded to constitute an implementation of and comprehension of a primitive form of communicative intention. What makes it primitive is that it employs agency-related notions only, that is, does not use the concept of belief. But they have the same kind of embedded structure, as do Gricean communicative intentions. So the child producing a point will have intentions relative to the other's intentional states (attendings), and will realise when she responds to an adult's pointings that the adult has intentions relative to her intentional lookings. More specifically, the intention infants need to recognise when responding to a point is 'You intend for [me to share attention to (X)]' (Tomasello 1999, 102). Naturally the question arises, what do children mean by 'share'? Tomasello's answer is that it will involve at the very least the child thinking of her own response to an adult's pointing as a case of looking because this is what the adult wants her to do, and the correlative understanding of what the adult is intended to do when she, the child points, namely look because the child wants her to. Presumably this is how she will think of the adult's and her own lookings when she takes the intentions to have been satisfied. This is the first stepping stone in the Gricean analysis: communication occurs only when the audience responds to the speaker's intention for the reason that the speaker wants her to.

For Davidson, the kind of triangulation that yields objectivity requires ascribing to each speaker an intention to get her audience to form a belief about her, the speaker's, beliefs. That is the speaker's primary intention. Her secondary intention is to produce an utterance that has features that will provide the audience with evidence about the contents of her belief. Her third intention is that that her primary intention be recognised by the audience, and serve as the audience's reason for acquiring a belief about the speaker's belief. What Tomasello gives us, then, is exactly the same kind of account we find in Davidson of how openness is established in communication, scaled down to accommodate evidence to the effect that children do not yet possess the concept of belief.

From our perspective, the first most striking feature of this kind of account, which makes both versions of Gricean theory vulnerable to thought-theoretic objections, is that the basic input to each subject's thought about the other subject's mental states is the other's perception of an object. The basic input to each subject's thought about herself is her own intentions and perceptions. The second, consequent striking feature is that the mutual awareness that is required for joint attention is established by each subject's capacity to entertain independently-accounted-for first and third person thoughts. Or, to put it in earlier terms: to the extent that mutual awareness is a key ingredient in the capacity to entertain second person thoughts, then on this account, the capacity to entertain second person thoughts is derivative on the capacity to entertain first and third person thoughts.

If this is the correct account of mutual awareness then there is nothing that communication *adds* to self-consciousness, unless one is prepared to say implausibly that the capacity for the formulation of iterative intentions is constitutive of self-consciousness. Communication presupposes rather than contributes to self-consciousness.

The intersubjectivity theory

Establishing the Communication Claim, and thereby the Conceptual Thesis, requires something different. This is one way to understand the force of the contrasting intersubjectivity theory of mutual awareness to be found in the developmental literature, though its main motivation is not formulated in precisely these terms. It takes its point of departure from Bates *et al.*'s original way of drawing the distinction between imperative and declarative pointing (Bates *et al.* 1976). Their distinction is fitted by them into a distinction between two stages in means-ends reasoning – (a) the use of adults as a means to obtaining an object (person to object); and (b) the use of objects to obtain affective engagement with adults (objects to person). Proto-imperatives were seen as an exemplification of the first; proto-declaratives as a form of the second. The theories I will be collecting under the intersubjectivity heading can all be seen as attempting to put flesh on the ideas we have been sketching by explaining joint attention in the terms Bates *et al.* use for the motivational structure and aims of declarative pointing. They can all be seen as attempts to articulate the idea that affective engagement is in some sense the engine of the child's beginning to adopt the contemplative stance.

Two of the central ideas underpinning this approach are that (a) the kind of mutual awareness we find in joint attention should be seen as a reflective counterpart of the kind of reciprocity we find in early mutual affect regulation, and that (b) this reflective ability is made possible, in part, by the way in which early dyadic relations now 'expand to include' a third object, the world. For purposes of a comparison with the primitive Gricean theory, I will make do with a few brief comments about the way to begin to unpack each claim.

Recall the reciprocal structure we described in early events of mutual affect regulation. Suppose now, as the second year progresses, we begin to equip the child with the conceptual wherewithal to understand what is going on in such cases and allow these concepts to imbue her experiences. She will now see smiles of delight, say, *as* responses to her own smiles of delight, where this perception of the other's emotion is still accompanied by the immediate response on her own part, now conceptualised as a response to the other's smile, which triggers more smiling from the adult and so forth, till for whatever reason the process comes to a halt. Note there is a mimicking over time over the iterations we find in Gricean definitions of mutuality – but what we have here is just a temporal causal chain. At any one time all that is required for full reflective reciprocal openness is that each participant is aware of the perceived expression of delight, say, as a response to her own; and her own as a response to the other's.

The basic idea behind the intersubjectivity approach is that this is all we need to explain the kind of openness achieved in joint attention, except that now the emotions reciprocated 'include' objects, that is, the shared emotions are now gurgles of delight or expression of alarm directed at objects. The first thing to note is that it is a consequence of this explanation of openness that the intentions we need to ascribe to the infant when she points to the object need not have the complicated, and developmentally implausible, iterative structure they have in Tomasello's theory, where according to the latter theory, openness is established in virtue of the content of the iterated intentions. All we need ascribe to the infant is a pointing with the intention that the adult look to the object. Openness is explained separately, as sketched above.

From our perspective, though, the most important ingredient in this picture lies in the insistence that self-consciousness, the use of the first person, emerges, essentially, through a process of beginning to conceptualise dyadic *reciprocated* psychological relations. Explaining the emergence of self-consciousness is a matter of explaining what this involves and requires.

The communication theorist is someone who says that that there is something that communication gives us with respect to self-consciousness that is essential to self-consciousness. One way of beginning to articulate what this comes to, I suggested, was to have the communication theorist claim that that there is a sense in which the first/second person distinction is not derivative on the first/third person distinction. We can now give a slightly fuller account of what this sense is. To say that it is not derivative is to say that the basic rela-tion, reflective grasp of which yields grasp of the first/second person distinction, is the dyadic relation of reciprocated psychological relations.

Earlier on, when discussing the Phenomenological Thesis, I distinguished between two ways the other might be said to enter into the characterisation of the phenomenology of experience in cases of mutual affect regulation, as a joint subject or as an object. As I noted, Merleau-Ponty, rightly in my view, rejects the idea that the very young infant has the conceptual wherewithal to think of the other as an object, and correlatively of herself as one. One way of putting the basic idea underlying the intersubjectivity approach is that the task of theorists explaining the nature and emergence of self-consciousness is to explain how such dual objectification, of oneself and the other, emerges in the context of conceptualising the reciprocal relations we find in mutual affect regulation.

This is the picture Merleau-Ponty wants to borrow from the psychoanalysis. It is to his great credit that, unlike Lacan, he realises that we need an account of how objectification of the self and others in fact gets going, an account of the cognitive mechanism that makes possible conceptualised reciprocity. This is where he appeals to playing with mirrors, where this is supposed to give the child a grip on herself from the outside, as one object among others in space. Apart from its empirical implausibility, this loses the connection with the reciprocated relations as input. This is where the Werner and Kaplan theory steps in as a communication theoretic alternative. In principle. In fact getting the details clear here is a major task, but let me make two comments on how this might work.

The route to unravelling the details turns on how we explain what it means to say that when joint attention sets in emotions begin to 'include' objects, and that it is this inclusion that provides simultaneously for the conceptual wherewithal for a grip on the idea of an objective world and of oneself as one object among others in it. The key here turns on how we explain two features in the development of declarative pointing noted by Franco and Butterworth. A study of particular interest with respect to the first feature is one conducted by Butterworth and Franco (1993), who found that the pattern of gaze check-ing changed over this year from looking at the adult after the pointing, to during the pointing and after it, and finally, at the age of eighteen months, we find the beginning of what they call anticipatory looks, gazes at the adult before the child embarks on pointing. This is suggestive of an increased sensi-tivity to the fact that the adult may not be attending to what engrosses the child. This is strengthened when combined with findings that it is about at the age of eighteen months that children begin to display sensitivity to whether or not the adult can see the object that they themselves can see. For example, if the object is placed behind the adult we find, initially, far more pointing and vocalisation than if both adult and child can see it. Moreover, pointing decreases markedly if the interesting event is a sound emanating from an object invisible to both adult and child, and becomes pretty random if a paper bag is placed over the adult's head.

From our perspective the most striking feature of the child's behaviour is the way it makes vivid the idea that the kind of spatial understanding needed for manifesting a grip on the idea of an objective world, a world which is there independently of perception, gets going by a progressive capacity to *distinguish* her own perspective from that of the adult's. She begins, as it were, with an assumption of shared perception. Her concept of perception takes hold as she learns to distinguish her own from others, which in turn relies on a progressively objective use of spatial concepts. This is one way to give substance to the notion that self-consciousness emerges though a process of separation.

So far, though, there has been no mention of the capacity for shared emotions, no role given to it. This comes in when we note that the mere fact of sensitivity to spatial considerations when engaged in some form of interaction with another does not suffice to show that these sensitivities are inputs to the idea of a world out there independently of one, inputs to the idea of an objective world. As Call and Tomasello (2005) show, apes display remarkable spatial sensitivities to where the other is looking when their interest is obtaining food, without this giving rise to any temptation that they are displaying the kind of objective take on the world manifested in declarative pointing. On one view, this is precisely the role we should give emotions here. This is where a second feature of declarative pointing makes an entrance.

Franco claims that infants' first expressions of delight, fear and so forth that accompany declarative pointing should be seen as the beginning of 'commentary' on the world. Johannes Roessler (2005) has suggested that this is the key to unpacking what is meant by talk of emotions beginning to 'include' objects, and that it is in unpacking this that we get to the role that conceptualising emotions plays in providing the infant with a grip on the idea of an objective world. On his account, what makes it true to say that the child (in contrast to the ape) is using spatial concepts in a way that manifests a grip on the idea of a world out there, is precisely this primitive use of emotions in *evaluating* the perceived object – this is what makes such expressions of emotion primitive predications. For it to be true that this is what the child is doing, as Roessler points out, there must be some sense in which this use of affective responses is imbued by some sense of getting it right in some respect. Things are scary or not, funny or not. The suggestion is that this primitive sense of right and wrong begins to be manifested as social referencing sets in where the appropriateness or not of the responses is precisely what the child is seeking reassurance about. One way of putting this is that affect regulation becomes, at this stage, regulation of the *appropriateness* of the response to the world.

From the perspective of the Conceptual Thesis, the importance of this picture is that it yields the beginning of a framework for making sense of the idea that it is by distinguishing her own emotions from those of others that the child simultaneously begins to manifest a grip on the idea of her own identity as distinct from the other's, where this is linked intrinsically to a primitive grip on the idea of a world being such as to *warrant* her own and the other's response.

The Shared Experience Claim

It goes, I take it, without saying that this is only the first glimmer of the way the intersubjectivity theory would have to be developed to make good the Communication Claim. But, suppose we grant that the intersubjectivity approach to mutual awareness in joint attention does begin to provide materials for articulating the Communication Claim. The particular form it takes might also seem, at the same time, to secure the Shared Experience Claim, and thereby give us everything we need for making good the Conceptual Thesis. But even if this is true, more needs to be said to get there.

It is true that the particular intersubjectivity theory we have considered does appeal to mutual affect regulation to explain openness in joint attention. It is also true that there is a good sense, as we noted earlier, in which we might want to say that the correct explanation of the phenomenology of experiences in mutual affect regulation will treat such experiences as having, essentially, two subjects. Combining these two claims, we might say that what we have here is a blueprint for making good Merleau-Ponty's claim that we should think of self-consciousness and consciousness of the other as emerging from dually owned experiences. That is, we might think that we have here what we need for making good the Conceptual Thesis. But the fact is that there is nothing we have said so far about the openness we find in joint attention that explicitly exploits the claim that we should treat the emotions in joint attention as themselves dually owned.

To get to that we need to come back to one of the central problems that motivate Merleau-Ponty – the question of how we can explain the unity of concepts we apply to others and ourselves. Tomasello needs to appeal to simulation. At some point infants need to be credited with the capacity, brute as it were, to entertain the idea that others are in the same kind of state as one is oneself, which in turn motivates simulations of particular states they ascribe to others (see Roessler 2005 for discussion). If there is here a solution to the epistemological problem of other minds, it is by denying there is an epistemological basis at all for the ascription of mental states to others; what gets it going is a brute disposition to simulate. One of the most powerful points in favour of the Shared Experience Claim is that it provides an extremely attractive alternative. If the phenomenal properties about which subjects are thinking are emotions that are in fact shared, then getting right the predicate in one's own case is *ipso facto* to get it right for the other. There is no epistemological gap to be bridged, either by reasoning or brute simulation, because there is no ontological gap to be bridged. Rather, what is needed, and this is where conceptual sophistication and epistemology set in, is the capacity to begin to *distinguish* (rather then draw together) one's own states from those of others.

This is the picture Merleau-Ponty seems to pushing in the section on theoretical issues. For the Conceptual Thesis to be made good we need to justify appeal to this epistemological picture in explaining how self-consciousness gets going. Here is a brief sketch of the way this might go.

The first move is to note the following *analogy* between a particular kind of 'solution' to the problem of our knowledge of other minds and our knowledge of the external world. A key feature in relational theories of perceptual consciousness is that the phenomenal properties of the experience, the properties of the relation, are conceived of as being determined by the properties of the world perceived. One of the main motivations for adopting such a theory of perceptual consciousness is the idea that this is what is needed for explaining the intuition that consciousness makes knowledge of the external world possible. The idea is that knowledge involves conceptualising basic experiential input, and if the basic input is world-independent sensational properties then the concepts we then have at our disposal for theorising about the input are inadequate to the task of making sense of the idea of an external world. The very idea of a mind-independent external world cannot get off the ground on the basis of thinking about wholly world-independent sensations.

One ingredient in the line of thinking needed for supporting the Shared Experience Claim would involve an analogous claim. Consciousness is what makes our knowledge of other minds possible. The only way this would be possible is to think of conscious experiences as individuated by other subjects and the phenomenal properties as properties of the relations between subjects. Unless we think of experiences in this way, then the concepts available to a subject when she begins to express knowledge about her own mental states would be inadequate to the task of expressing knowledge about others. The second ingredient in the line of reasoning needed for justifying the Shared Experience Claim is the following unpacking of the Communication Claim. Knowledge of the external world involves the conceptualisation of experiential input *as* input about an objective world. What makes this possible in our case is the kind of triangulation we find in joint attention. The third step is to say that the sense in which such objectifications can count as expressions of knowledge, is only as good as the sense in which the ascriptions of mental states to oneself and others in cases of joint attention can count as expressions of knowledge, and this rests on adopting the Shared Experience Claim.

One way of summing up this line of reasoning is with the claim that perceptual consciousness yields knowledge of the external world only for creatures that can share experiences, in the strong sense, with other creatures.

From the Conceptual to the Consciousness Thesis

To buy into the picture or set of claims just sketched is, *ipso facto*, to endorse the Consciousness Thesis. The Consciousness Thesis, recall, was the idea that we need to think of consciousness in general, in the human case as having an essentially social character. Suppose the Shared Experience Claim is right. Then we do not have the basic structure of self-consciousness and objectivity in place unless we conceive of at least some experiences as dually owned. If we think that at least part of what is distinctive of human consciousness is that it does provide for precisely such capacities, then we have in place the main route into the Consciousness Thesis.

This particular way of thinking about consciousness runs counter to far too many prevailing assumptions in the current mainstream consciousness literature to begin to list, let alone engage with. To put it crudely, either they or the Conceptual Thesis must go, as the latter seems to entail the Consciousness Thesis. But there is one very general, quasi-methodological aspect of the kind of argument I have been sketching for the Conceptual Thesis that I do want to highlight, as it runs not merely counter to many current prevailing theses but also shows up an ambivalence in Merleau-Ponty's own approach to consciousness, and which helps explain why he doesn't in the end deliver the Conceptual Thesis.

As I have presented it, the main motivation for ascribing to Merleau-Ponty a version of the Shared Experience Claim is epistemological – he thought treating experiences as dually owned was the only, or at least the best way of explaining how knowledge of other minds is possible. For this kind of reasoning to carry weight, though, we must accept a more general thesis to the effect that it is a constraint on accounts of at least human consciousness in general that we explain how consciousness makes knowledge possible. We would also have to be willing to apply this, for example, to accounts of the nature of perceptual consciousness. Indeed, the sketch of an argument I gave for the Conceptual Thesis relied on this extension. In effect the claim on behalf of the thesis was that giving consciousness a knowledge-yielding role in the perceptual case requires giving it a role in making knowledge of other minds possible too.

Now it has to be said that this approach to perceptual consciousness specifically is nowhere to be found in Merleau-Ponty, and in this sense he is close to many current approaches to perceptual consciousness, many of which actually appeal to Merleau-Ponty on this subject. Crudely put, he held that the chief constraint on explanations of perceptual consciousness was to be found in answers to the question: how must we think of such consciousness if we take it that consciousness is what makes *action* (rather than knowledge) possible; and he built links with action into his account of the phenomenal properties of perceptual experiences. This is as evident in this paper as it is in others, where much attention is devoted to explaining how such links are established in early infancy. Perhaps the deepest reason for Merleau-Ponty not delivering on the Conceptual Thesis lies here. It is fair to suggest that even had he been aware of it, and for all I know he may have been, he would not have appealed to Werner and Kaplan's basic insight in order to make good what I have labelled the Conceptual Thesis. On their view we should treat the development of language as the development of a 'tool of knowing'; their main target was the

137

Vygotskyan idea that language is primarily a 'tool for doing'. This is why they emphasised the role of triangulation in providing for objectivity, where declarative pointing was the first manifestation of a 'theoretical', objective take on the world. It is the first expression of the kind of attitude to the world required for knowledge. It is the role of shared experiences in providing for the possibility of such knowledge that I have put at centre stage in sketching out an argument for the Conceptual Thesis. To my knowledge there is nothing to suggest that Merleau-Ponty would have been remotely sympathetic to this line of thought (objective thought, for him, came in only with science and had no internal links with the phenomenology of perceptual consciousness). Indeed, had he thought about joint attention he may well have favoured a Tomasello-like approach, which puts agency at centre stage at the expense of objectivity. In my view, one of the great virtues of the paper we have been discussing is that it throws into relief the idea that we need the link with knowledge for establishing the Conceptual Thesis, and, more generally, the problem of whether and how we should treat epistemological concerns as a constitutive constraint on explanations of consciousness.

Note

1 This essay was originally published by itself in 1958 as 'Les Relations avec autrui chez l'enfant: Introduction', Paris: Centre de documentation universitaire. The English translation occurs in *The Primacy of Perception and Other Essays* (*PofP*).

9

FREEDOM, PERCEPTION AND RADICAL REFLECTION

Eran Dorfman

I

The *Phenomenology of Perception* closes with a quasi-Wittgensteinian gesture, admitting the limits of philosophy and announcing its silence:

> But what is here required is silence, for only the hero lives out his relation to men and the world, and it is not fitting that another speaks in his name.
>
> (*PhP*, 456/530)

It is the hero, rather than the philosopher, who fully assumes his or her being in the world, so that the philosophical treatise seems to do nothing but illustrate or conceptualise the domain in which this heroic life takes place. However, unlike Wittgenstein's *Tractatus*, it is not with silence itself that the book ends, but with *another* speech, precisely that of the hero, evoked by Merleau-Ponty under the figure of the pilot in Saint-Exupéry's novel *Flight to Arras*:

> Your son is caught in the fire: you will save him. ... If there is an obstacle, you would be ready to give your shoulder to get help. You dwell in your act itself. Your act is you. ... You exchange yourself against something else. ... Your meaning shows itself, effulgent. It is your duty, your hatred, your love, your loyalty, your invention.
>
> (*PhP*, 456/530, translation modified)[1]

It is thus a matter of fully appropriating life, of coinciding *doing* and *being*. In this way the personal meaning of both this doing and this being can appear: you are your duty, your hatred, your love, your loyalty, but also, surprisingly, your *invention*. What is exactly invented?[2] Is it the meaning of the act? Is it possible, then, that at the moment this meaning appears to be the most truthful, at the moment it appears simply to be there, effulgent, it proves to be nothing but a fiction?

Perhaps this tension can explain why the last chapter of the *Phenomenology of Perception*, entitled 'Freedom', closes with an *imposed* situation, an urgent one, where there is no time for reflection or deliberation, the son being in danger. Freedom can thus be characterised as the appearance of the meaning of the act and the self, or more exactly as the *invention* of that meaning. But this invention seems to take place and this meaning seems to appear only in a situation of extreme danger. Should one then await such a dreadful event in order to liberate oneself? What freedom do we have outside such a heroic situation?[3] Yet we must bear in mind that this situation is evoked by Merleau-Ponty as a *fiction*, a story, a citation of Saint-Exupéry's novel. It is thus the *evocation* of the situation rather than the situation itself which matters, as is proved by the following celebrated passage from the *Phenomenology of Perception*'s preface:

> True philosophy consists in relearning to look at the world, and in this sense a story's being told [*une histoire racontée*] can give meaning to the world quite as 'deeply' as a philosophical treatise. We take our fate in our hands, we become responsible for our history through reflection, but equally by a decision on which we stake our life, and in both cases what is involved is a violent act which is validated by being performed.
>
> (*PhP*, xx/xxiii, translation modified)[4]

It is on the one hand the story, for instance that of *Flight to Arras*, and on the other hand the philosophical treatise, for instance that of the *Phenomenology of Perception*, which both give the meaning of the world and teach us how better to look at it. This perceptual (re)learning is at the same time a free act, an appropriation of our life, of our fate, of our history. Philosophical reflection is thus no longer considered as a detached vision, since it becomes a violent act *in* the world, an act which has the same stakes as a personal decision committed in 'real' life. Could the *Phenomenology of Perception* itself then be this violent act? Could the philosophical treatise help us not only to *understand* what freedom is, but also to *acquire* freedom concretely? And what would such a freedom be like?

II

Let us first try to understand the nature of radical reflection that philosophy should become, and how it is different from an intellectualist or a Cartesian reflection. Whereas the latter conceives itself as all-powerful, as capable of constituting the world on its own, radical reflection recognises on the contrary what lies *beneath* it, that is, the enormous carnal zone which is characterised by Merleau-Ponty as 'pre-objective' or 'unreflective':

> When I begin to reflect, my reflection bears upon an unreflective experience; my reflection cannot be unaware of itself as an event, and

so it appears to itself as a truly creative act, as a change in the structure of consciousness, and yet it has to recognize, beneath [*en deçà*] its own operations, the world which is given to the subject because the subject is given to itself. The real has to be described, not constructed or constituted.

(*PhP*, x/xi, translation modified)

This passage contains a striking contradiction: the real has to be described, and yet, when this is done, we have at least the appearance of a *change* in the structure of the real, so that it no longer seems simply, neutrally and theoretically described, but rather created and invented. How can this tension be resolved? Does phenomenology *describe* phenomena as they are or does it *create* them?

It is only by understanding radical reflection as freedom, as an invention and appropriation of meaning, that we are able to resolve the contradiction and find again the force of phenomenology where it seemed to show its weakness. Let us look at this passage from the 1946 lecture 'The Primacy of Perception':

It is true that we discover the unreflected. But the unreflected we go back to is not that which is prior to philosophy or prior to reflection. It is the unreflected which is understood and conquered by reflection. Left to itself, perception forgets itself and is ignorant of its own accomplishments. Far from thinking that philosophy is a useless repetition of life, I think, on the contrary, that it is the agency without which life would probably dissipate itself in ignorance of itself or in chaos. But this does not mean that reflection should be carried away with itself or pretend to be ignorant of its origins. By fleeing difficulties philosophy would only fail in its task.

(*PofP* 16, translation modified)

Philosophy as radical reflection has thus the task of reminding perception of that which it tends to forget, namely its own accomplishments. Perception omits that the objective world is not independent of it but constantly created by it. This is the reason why perception needs reflection, yet it is not a detached reflection, posterior to perception, but rather a *perception aware of itself* as an event and as a creation. It is a perception which does not let itself 'be carried away', overestimating its power and forgetting its origin in the external world, as does intellectualist reflection, nor forget its constitutive and creative power, as does empiricist reflection. In this manner phenomenology proposes a continual renewal of perception, an endless process of creation which at the same time recognises and modifies its origin.

This notion of phenomenology as radical reflection, as a distinct kind of perception, can thus resolve one of the most fundamental problems of phenomenology as it is described by Merleau-Ponty:

141

All the misunderstandings of Husserl with his interpreters, with the existentialist 'dissidents' and finally with himself, have arisen from the fact that in order to see the world and grasp it as paradoxical, we must break with our familiarity with it and, also, from the fact that from this break we can learn nothing but the unmotivated upsurge [*jaillissement*] of the world. The most important lesson which the reduction teaches us is the impossibility of a complete reduction.

(*PhP*, xiv/xv, translation modified)

The phenomenological reduction, the bracketing of the natural attitude, does not reveal anything sensational. We only come to see the world's upsurge without having to do anything about it. But to conceive things in this manner would be to forget the role of the reduction as radical reflection, as a reflection which already makes up a part of perception. This 'unmotivated upsurge of the world' is not independent of the phenomenological reduction, since it needs it in order to appear, and, in a sense, in order to take place. Radical reflection grasps the unreflective, but it does so only by perceiving it, which already means, *to a certain extent*, constituting, inventing and creating it. This is why the reduction can never be completed, for the end of reduction would be the end of this perception as creative and renewed. This 'relearning to look at the world' is thus far from being a one-off event of learning, performed once and forever. It is an act of learning which takes an entire lifetime, which takes place every moment we perceive.

III

An example of the fashion in which reflection creates its own unreflective origin while still giving the impression that this origin has been there forever in a spontaneous upsurge, is given by Merleau-Ponty's distinction between two subjects, a transcendental subject and a primordial one. The transcendental subject is Cartesian, completely transparent to itself, and the primordial subject is the one which is obscure and opaque:

What for us is primary [*originaire*] consciousness is not a transcendental Ego freely positing before itself a multiplicity in itself, and constituting it throughout from start to finish, it is an *I* which dominates diversity only *with the help* of time, and for whom freedom itself is a destiny, so that *I* am never conscious of being the absolute creator of time, of composing the movement through which I live, I have the impression that it is the mobile entity itself which changes its position, and which effects the passage from one instant or one position to another.

(*PhP*, 276 n1/322 n47)

Freedom for this primary I is a destiny, so that one can ask in what sense it is still worthy of the name 'freedom'. But we must not understand the adjective 'primary' in its *chronological* sense, for this 'origin' is itself created by reflection, by an *I* which is more or less transcendental. The reflective *I* generates its origin which then becomes its 'destiny' in the face of which it can do nothing but passively accept it. Yet, it is only the violent act of reflection which discovers, perceives and invents this destiny, and the presumed passivity consequently proves to be nothing but appearance.

This complicated relationship between reflection and the unreflective, the transcendental subject and the primordial one, is further articulated by a parallel distinction between the *spoken cogito*, namely the cogito of objective world, and the *tacit cogito*, which expresses itself spontaneously and harmoniously by means of the body:

> Beyond the spoken cogito, the one which is converted into assertion [*enoncé*] and into essential truth, there lies a tacit *cogito*, myself experienced by myself. But this subjectivity, indeclinable, has upon itself and upon the world only a precarious hold [*prise glissante*]. It does not constitute the world, it divines the world round about it as a field not provided by itself; nor does it constitute the word, but speaks as we sing when we are happy; nor again the meaning of the word, which instantaneously emerges [*jaillit*] for it in its dealing with the world and other men living in it.
>
> (*PhP*, 403–4/469–70, translation modified)

We encounter here once again the unmotivated upsurge (*jaillissement*) of the world, or more exactly the unmotivated upsurge of the world's *meaning*, discovered by the phenomenological reduction as radical reflection. The crucial question here is what existence would this upsurge have *without* the act of reflection revealing it. What are the connections between the two subjects: the one which is transcendental or 'spoken',[5] *actively* and freely constituting its world, and the one which is primordial and tacit, almost *passively* assisting the upsurge of new meaning? If the omnipotent transcendental subject is an intellectualist illusion, and if the primordial subject is a phenomenological creation, doesn't it follow that the 'true' subject is neither one nor the other but somewhere *between* the two?

Moreover, it seems that it is in the interplay between the two subjects that freedom can be found. Merleau-Ponty affirms on the one hand that the transcendental Ego is a 'possibility of absence, the dimension of escape and freedom which reflection opens in the depths of our being' (*PhP*, 208/242), but on the other hand this reflective subject 'is based on the ground and the proposition of a life of pre-personal consciousness' (*PhP*, 208/242). The transcendental Ego is thus denounced as claiming to be the *only* constitutive principle of the human being, giving him or her an absolute freedom, but this does not imply that the primary subject, the primordial and pre-objective one, should replace this Ego, since we would then be able to understand neither how phenomenology can attain what seems to bypass it by definition, nor how the subject itself can acquire freedom. Once again, it is always through a certain *relationship* between constitution and pre-constitution, reflection and the unreflective, transcendental subject and primordial one, that we should look for the solution for both the methodological problem of phenomenology and the ethical and existential problem of the subject. In order better to understand the solution proposed to us by Merleau-Ponty, let us move now to the last chapter of the *Phenomenology of Perception*, entitled 'Freedom'.

IV

Merleau-Ponty opens the chapter with a critique of Sartre's notion of freedom, conceived as all or nothing: either freedom is absolute, in a decision taken by a completely autonomous consciousness (the 'for-itself'), or it is nil, due to human helplessness *vis-à-vis* exterior obstacles (the 'in-itself'). For Merleau-Ponty it is the bodily pre-objective experience which is supposed to surmount this dichotomy:

> Underlying myself as a thinking subject, who am able to make my place at will on Sirius or on the earth's surface, there is, therefore, as it were a natural self. .... In so far as I have hands, feet, a body, I sustain around me intentions which are not dependent upon my decisions and which affect my surroundings in a way which I do not choose.
>
> (*PhP*, 440/511)

Bodily experience precedes and determines any deliberate decision of thought, so that freedom is neither absolute nor nil:

> It is, therefore, true that there are no obstacles in themselves, but the self which qualifies them as such is not some acosmic subject; it runs ahead of itself in relation to things in order to confer upon them the form of things.
>
> (*PhP*, 441/512)

This 'compromise' of the interior and the exterior, the autonomous consciousness and the world in itself, does not only concern the strict field of perception, since 'there is something comparable present in all evaluations' (*PhP*, 441/512). The freedom we have is the freedom to perceive, to have a sense experience, to judge and to act, but this freedom is limited by our incarnate dealings with the world. These dealings seem to be done as if by themselves, apparently without any free choice, so that 'it is as if, on the hither side of our judgement and our freedom, someone were assigning such and such a significance to such and such a given grouping' (*PhP*, 440/511–12). We thus return once more to the primordial and 'operant' subject, participating in the

144

unmotivated upsurge of the world's meaning without being aware of that. It is this active-passive subject which seems to decide for us, which seems to supply significance and meaning to our life. But what freedom does such a quasi-tyrannical subject allow us? What contact does it maintain with the reflective one, conscious of its acts?

Merleau-Ponty suggests that the endowing of meaning is never done in a void, since it always has a *sedimented* background. He evokes the example of the inferiority complex, which, although it can be surmounted all at once, by a deliberate and active decision, is more likely to accompany the subject for a long time *against* his or her will, since it has become a privileged attitude acquired by sedimentation. This attitude shows that although the past is not a fate, it is the constant 'atmosphere of my present' (*PhP*, 442/514). The inferiority complex is thus a pre-objective atmosphere which does not let itself be easily destroyed by the power of thinking and deliberate decision. It is a tacit and silent layer, deeper than the 'conscious' and spoken one:

> We can see, beneath these noisy debates and these fruitless efforts to 'construct' ourselves, the tacit decisions whereby we have marked out round ourselves the field of possibility, and it is true that nothing is done as long as we cling to these fixed points, and everything is easy as soon as we have weighed anchor.
>
> (*PhP*, 438/509)

Deliberate decision, made in the objective world, will remain fruitless as long as we do not recognise its basis, namely the pre-objective world with its tacit decisions. We understand better now the significance of Merleau-Ponty's discovery of the pre-objective, for this discovery is the only means we have to weigh the anchor of our life, to free ourselves from decisions made against our will and from circumstances which we did not choose. But how shall we heave up the anchor? How shall we free ourselves? The answer is to be found in a certain *gesture* between the pre-objective and the objective world, a gesture described by Merleau-Ponty in his analysis of speech:

> Our view of man will remain superficial so long as we fail to go back to the origin, so long as we fail to find, beneath the chatter of words, the primordial silence, and as long as we do not describe the gesture which breaks this silence.
>
> (*PhP*, 184/214, translation modified)

The pre-objective domain seems to consist of a primordial silence, and yet the only access we have to it passes by *breaking* this silence. In consequence, does this silence have a real existence in itself, or is it only, once more, a myth invented by reflection? For Merleau-Ponty says only one page earlier, referring to the intellectualist notion of pure and silent consciousness, that 'in reality this supposed silence is alive with words' (*PhP*, 183/213), and these words are spoken, sedimented, and above all forgotten and repressed as such.

The pre-objective proves to be not only the domain of the upsurge of significance, but also the domain of what is sedimented, acquired and repressed. This is why Merleau-Ponty analyses in detail the phenomenon of repression, concluding that the body is a repressed 'inborn complex' (*PhP*, 84/97). Hence, in order to pass from the pre-objective as repressed to the pre-objective as an upsurge of significance, we should re-constitute the pre-objective. We should give it a fresh meaning by speech and by reflection, and it is only in this way that it becomes pre-objective as primordial and primary. Instead of subjecting ourselves to the acquired meaning of our life, we should effect this violent act, which, even if it arrives at nothing but an unmotivated upsurge of meaning, appropriates this upsurge while allowing it to proceed and to renew itself.

V

How then can we effect this step, how can we win back our freedom concretely, letting go of these fixed points of acquired experience? The example that Merleau-Ponty analyses here is that of proletarian revolution, and he describes three figures who participate in it: the factory worker, the nomad journeyman and the tenant of a farm. Revolution is indeed the conquest of freedom *par excellence*, but what freedom do these three figures have to free themselves? Are they first aware of their 'captivity'? Indeed, Merleau-Ponty tends to affirm the opposite:

> These situations do not imply any express evaluation, and if there is a tacit evaluation, it represents the thrust of a freedom devoid of any project against unknown obstacles; one cannot in any case talk about a choice, for in all three cases it is enough that I should be born into the world and that I exist in order to experience my life as full of difficulties and constraints – I do not choose so to experience it.
>
> (*PhP*, 444/516)

Revolution is thus motivated by a spontaneous 'thrust of freedom' which is neither explicit nor chosen. Is revolution then a process which takes place by itself, beyond the subject's will? Are there not any means to actively and deliberately influence it, changing our world? Merleau-Ponty, once more, tends to deny this possibility:

> It is not at all necessary that at any single moment a *representation* of revolution should arise. ... It is sufficient that the journeyman or the farmer should feel that he is on the march towards a certain cross-roads, to which the road trodden by the town labourers also leads. Both find their journey's end in revolution, which would perhaps

have terrified them had it been described and represented to them in advance.

(*PhP*, 445/517)

It is thus not a matter of an articulated and represented decision, but rather of a vague and implicit feeling which is not yet objectified. The free act, says Merleau-Ponty, is simply 'lived through in ambiguity' (*PhP*, 445/517). But what exactly is this 'free act'? And what does it mean to live through something in ambiguity? For, after all, in order to have a revolution, in order to 'feel that one is on the march' towards freedom, shouldn't one *decide* to move on, to make this step by a concrete *act*? Indeed, Merleau-Ponty admits the presence of the *agitators* in revolution, but he tends to minimise their role:

> [T]he slogans of the alleged agitators [*meneurs*] are immediately understood, as if by some pre-established harmony, and meet with concurrence on all sides, because they crystallize what is latent in the life of all productive workers.
>
> (*PhP*, 445/517)

Revolution does not have real leaders, since it already tacitly exists in the life of all those who participate in it. However, it is inevitable to notice that it is precisely these leaders or agitators who crystallise the meaning – initially latent – of revolution. Without them, wouldn't the workers still be captive to the passivity of their lives? Isn't the act of crystallisation exactly the kind of radical reflection we were looking for? Isn't it necessary in order to make the implicit meaning *appear*, constituting and creating it as such? What other sense would the word 'freedom' have?

VI

The pre-objective domain confronts us with the challenge to find freedom within the non-chosen acquired experience, activity within passivity and the personal within the impersonal anonymity:

> What then is freedom? To be born is both to be born of the world and to be born into the world. The world is already constituted, but also never completely constituted; in the first case we are acted upon, in the second we are open to an infinite number of possibilities. But this analysis is still abstract, for we exist in both ways *at once*.
>
> (*PhP*, 453/527)

Freedom is thus this movement and this oscillation between actively con-stituting the world and passively accepting it as given and as already con-stituted; between dynamically acquiring new meanings and statically getting

147

fixed in already acquired meanings. Neither all-objective nor all-pre-objective, freedom is the meeting point of the two:

> We choose our world and the world chooses us. What is certain, in any case, is that we can at no time set aside within ourselves a redoubt to which being does not find its way through, without seeing this freedom, immediately and by the very fact of being a living experi- ence, figure as being and become a motive and a buttress. Taken con- cretely, freedom is always a meeting of the inner and the outer ... and it deteriorates without ever disappearing altogether in direct propor- tion to the lessening of the *tolerance* of the bodily and institutional data of our lives.
>
> (*PhP*, 454/528, translation modified)

All that is constituted in our lives, all that which is perceived, becomes immediately an impersonal acquired experience which makes us forget the need to give it fresh meaning. This acquired experience can be objective, as it is in the case of language, or pre-objective, as it is in the case of the inferiority complex. But what is important here is less the distinction between the objective and the pre-objective than the ability to free oneself from the 'fixed points' in acquired experience, and the continuation of an ever renewed upsurge of meaning, thanks to this mysterious 'tolerance of the bodily and institutional data of our lives'. How can we maintain this toler- ance? How can we avoid the deterioration of our freedom? Merleau-Ponty answers:

> It is by being unrestrictedly and unreservedly what I am at present that I have a chance of moving forward ... I can miss being free only if I try to bypass my natural and social situation by refusing to take it up, in the first place, instead of assuming it in order to join up with the natural and human world. ... We need have no fear that our choices or actions restrict our liberty, since choice and action alone cut us loose from our anchorage.
>
> (*PhP*, 455–6/529–30)

After having understood that freedom is not to be found in deliberate deci- sion, and that 'one cannot in any case talk about a choice' (*PhP*, 444/516), we now learn that not only do we have the possibility to choose, but also that choice and action *alone* can free us from our anchorage. Indeed, we have already encountered this anchorage (which in both cases appears in French in plural: *ancres*), under the figure of tacit decisions and fixed points in the pre- objective world (*PhP*, 438/509). We shall note again that it is not by accepting the pre-objective as it is, but rather by breaking its silence, by making it appear, by recognising and assuming it, that this world can become a world of a continuous upsurge of meaning instead of serving as anchorage, as chains, as an impersonal meaning which imprisons us.

It is here that it seems crucial to re-introduce *radical reflection*, since what is this reflection if not the revelation of pre-objective meaning, 'revelation' which, as a matter of fact, *creates* this meaning? It lets the pre-objective appear by inventing it:

> Reflection does not follow in the reverse direction a path already traced by the constitutive act, and the natural reference of the stuff to the world leads us to a new conception of intentionality.
>
> (PhP, 243/283)

Doesn't it follow that radical reflection is already a form of constitution? Indeed, reflection must take into account its own foundation, the new intentionality discovered by Merleau-Ponty, the bodily and operant one, opaque to the presumably all-powerful reflection and constitution of the transcendental subject in Descartes or Husserl. Indeed, reflection must recognise that which escapes it by principle, but it does so precisely by constituting it *as* pre-objective and opaque. It joins this domain, it gives it its meaning, and in this way it frees it for a short time from the inaccessible darkness in which it has been captive.

Radical reflection as a principle of freedom seems moreover to be the only way to conceive how I can be 'unrestrictedly and unreservedly what I am at present', while still taking into account that 'to live a thing is not to coincide with it, nor fully to embrace it in thought' (PhP, 325/380, translation modified). In order to be what I am, I must recognise and assume my involvement in the world, but this involvement is nothing of a coincidence with the world. It is rather a matter of the *margin* between coinciding, being too close, and thinking, being too far away, and it is radical reflection which seems to maintain this balance, which seems to grasp the unreflective, precisely by reflecting upon it:

> True reflection presents me to myself not as idle and inaccessible subjectivity, but as identical with my presence in the world and to others, as I am now realizing it.
>
> (PhP, 452/525)

Radical reflection is *true* reflection, that is to say a reflection which unifies itself with the phenomenon at the same as time it changes its structure from the interior. In this way the significance of the thing can appear and the situation can take place. In this way I can gain my freedom, I can recognise the acquired experience which precedes me, at the same time as I transform it, re-create it, re-appropriate it.

This notion of radical reflection, one should admit, is very delicate. For like freedom, or rather *as* freedom, it is always confronted with the risk of forgetting its own creative act, pretending to attain the absolute pre-objective domain and failing to realise that reflection, like perception, is a constant movement, a perpetual play between proximity and distance, presence and absence:

> Just as reflection borrows its wish for absolute adequateness from the perception which causes a thing to appear ... so freedom flounders in the contradictions of commitment, and fails to realize that, without the roots which it thrusts into the world, it would not be freedom at all.
> (PhP, 456/530, translation modified)

We should read these lines with careful attention, since they capture the central theme of the *Phenomenology of Perception*. Reflection is here compared to freedom. Both have the tendency to try to transgress their limits, and so to deteriorate and to lose their vitality. Radical reflection could then become intellectualist or idealist reflection, whereas freedom could become a blockage in the acquired experience presenting the illusion of an absolute presence of me to myself. Reflection deteriorates exactly in the same manner as perception forgetting itself as an act of creation, whereas freedom loses its essence and becomes self-enclosure, ignoring its need of transcendence and projection in and of the world. In both cases, it is precisely the ideal of primordial, all-personal, interior and harmonious life that provokes this deterioration. It is perhaps the unmotivated upsurge of meaning which this ideal looks for, but we should not be misled by this upsurge. For it too proves to be nothing but play and continuous movement which must never stop, a process of come-and-go, a repeated intertwining of interior and exterior, presence and absence, pre-objective and objective. The wish to remain with only one of these poles – either an all-bodily life, primordial and harmonious, or an all-objective, reflexive and causal life – is precisely what harms freedom. It is against this secret wish that radical reflection must struggle. Indeed, reflection can get closer to the primordial layer, it can even, at certain times, touch it. But at the moment it does so it is no longer a matter of the primordial layer, but a reflective and re-constituted one, so that this whole process must begin once more. It is a matter of constitutive work which can never be completed, which fails in principle. But this failure is the only guarantee of freedom, since it is what reminds us of the distance, of the remote position we always hold facing things and of the reflection which is needed in order to give things fresh meaning.

Have we pushed Merleau-Ponty's theory too far, too much, or is it the philosopher himself who does so? We have seen how the *Phenomenology of Perception* closes with an appeal for another speech, the one of the hero who invents his or her own life. Yet just before making this appeal Merleau-Ponty remarks:

> Whether it is a question of things or of historical situations, philosophy has no other function than to teach us to see them clearly once

more, and it is true to say that it comes into being by destroying itself as separate philosophy.

(*PhP*, 456/530)

Radical reflection is no longer equivalent to 'philosophy', since it is a reflection which is already a perception *of* the world and *in* the world. As such, radical reflection can become the long and infinite way towards freedom. It is a way open to the philosopher, but also to every one of us who wishes to engage in it: to every perceiving subject.

Notes

1 The Smith translation, trying to give this citation from Saint-Exupéry a clear and coherent appearance, distorts the author's intentions in several places, especially by translating the French 'invention' by 'ingenuity'. The old English translation of *Flight to Arras* is unfortunately no better and I recommend consulting the original French *Pilote de Guerre* (Paris: Gallimard (Folio), 2005 [1942], 151–2).

2 Saint-Exupéry himself attributes these nouns to several *different* figures, one of which is the inventor looking for discoveries, but the very selective choice of citation made by Merleau-Ponty proves that for the philosopher all these figures find their place in one, namely the *hero*.

3 Merleau-Ponty evokes Saint-Exupéry's hero in his 1946 article 'Man, the Hero', where, once again, the hero is he or she who is facing death:

> Over Arras, in the fire of the anti-aircraft guns, when every second of survival is as miraculous as a birth, he feels invulnerable because he is *in* things at last; he has left his interior nothingness behind, and if he dies, it will be fully in the world.

> (*SNS*, 185, translation modified)

This praise of heroism (the article was originally entitled 'The Cult of the Hero') is certainly to be explained by the context of the immediate post-war period and the influence of Sartre, and yet it raises the question of the phenomenological enterprise of returning to the things themselves by developing the notion of being-in-the-world. One may deduce from the last citation that in order to be 'in things' and 'fully in the world' it is necessary to face death heroically. Yet, this paper aims to show precisely that not only is this heroism contextual, it also forms a part of phenomenology's necessary fictional dimension.

4 Once again, Smith's translation of 'une histoire racontée' by 'an historical account' is more than misleading. Merleau-Ponty plays here with the double meaning of the French word 'histoire', signifying both 'story' and 'history'. It is only by telling ourselves a certain story that we can assume our own history, and this has nothing to do with a detached 'historical account'. Cf. for instance Merleau-Ponty's discussion of the way children react to a story told to them (*PhP*, 401/466–7).

5 It is interesting to notice that Merleau-Ponty does not evoke the possibility of a *speaking* cogito, which would be more appropriate to the notion of the transcendental subject. This choice can be explained by the philosopher's effort to denounce the illusion of an omnipotent subject, the notion of a spoken cogito intending precisely to demonstrate the limits of reflection.

10

PHILOSOPHY AND NON-PHILOSOPHY ACCORDING TO MERLEAU-PONTY[1]

Françoise Dastur

I

'Philosophy and Non-philosophy': this title is borrowed from Merleau-Ponty himself, who entitled his last lecture series, transcribed and published by Claude Lefort in the mid-1970s, 'Philosophy and Non-philosophy since Hegel'. The expression 'non-philosophy', however, had already appeared in his 1958–9 lecture series on 'Philosophy today', as may be seen both from the summary which appeared in the yearbook of the Collège de France (*IPP*, 168), and from the lecture transcripts published in 1996 – *Notes de cours* (*NC*).[2] In these lectures, Merleau-Ponty defines the current era as 'our state of non-philosophy' (*NC*, 38), marked not only by the crisis of rationality but also by a whole range of 'cultural symptoms' in literature, painting, and music, which attest to the dawning of a 'fundamental thought' in artistic research (*NC*, 163) which is not 'explicit philosophy', as he states explicitly at the start of his 1960–1 lecture series entitled 'Cartesian ontology and ontology today'. In the 'philosophical void' which resulted from the collapse of German idealism after the death of Hegel, philosophy itself was called radically into question, and one might have considered that the thought of Kierkegaard, Marx, and Nietzsche constituted the 'nihilist conclusion' to the history of metaphysics (*NC*, 38). As Merleau-Ponty explains, we therefore find ourselves in a pivotal period, which witnesses at once the decay of 'official' philosophy and the rebirth of philosophy; a rebirth not just in art and literature, but also in the response to this non-philosophy offered by those such as Husserl and Heidegger who rendered philosophy itself problematic (*NC*, 66, 91). For Husserl, author of *The Crisis of European Sciences*, it was a matter of 'remaking a philosophy' at the end of the second half of the nineteenth century, a period which had witnessed the triumph of positivism, historicism, and psychologism, the 'academic forms' of antiphilosophy. Merleau-Ponty shows that Husserl achieves this by redefining philosophy as the reconquest of the lived world by means of a new kind of scientificity (NC, 79) which no longer allows one simply to identify philosophy with the theoretical attitude, but which rather demands that philosophy consider itself as a theoretical formation which starts from pre-theoretical life (NC, 84). Merleau-Ponty consecrates the greater part of his lectures on 'Philosophy today' to Heidegger, who proposes not so much to give a new meaning to the word philosophy, as to replace philosophy with thought, which means only to challenge philosophy in its 'constructive' and 'positive' form. 'If Heidegger's thought is no longer philosophy, no more is it extra-philosophical', as Beaufret writes in a passage from his 1958 preface to Heidegger's *Essays and Lectures* cited by Merleau-Ponty both in his 1958–9 and his 1960–1 lecture series (NC, 147, 163).

As in all Merleau-Ponty's work, it is the traditional figure of philosophy as overarching thought (*pensée de surplomb*) which is questioned in these last lectures (NC, 88). Very early in his career Merleau-Ponty became aware of the limits of philosophical thought and of the need to redefine the task of philosophy so that it might give an account of the opacity of the real. Already in his first book, *The Structure of Behaviour*, he declares that philosophy, insofar as it restricts itself to phenomena, 'returns to the evidences of naïve consciousness' (SB, 199), in a manner similar to that of transcendental idealism which, unlike classical idealism, guarantees that what is attained in perception is indeed the thing itself. However, Merleau-Ponty cannot follow Critical philosophy through to its conclusion in an intellectualist theory of perception, such as that defended by Léon Brunschvicg, the eminent representative of reflective philosophy and neo-Kantianism,[3] who states 'the universe of immediate experience contains not *more* than what science requires, but rather *less*', and considers that 'the mutilated and superficial world' of sensory experience cannot be dignified as a philosophical problem in its own right (Brunschvicg 1922, 446; cf. SB, 201). However, for Merleau-Ponty this does not mean that 'the philosophy of perception is ready-formed in life', for perceptual experience contains an 'ambiguous structure' which can lead just as easily to a realist philosophy which sees perception as generated by the world as to an idealist philosophy which sees in perception only a rough sketch of the science of the world. As Merleau-Ponty explains in the last pages of *The Structure of Behaviour*, in order to gain access to the originary experience of perception, we should not follow the natural movement of consciousness, but rather invert it, as Husserl does in his later philosophy when he shows that phenomenological reduction is less a return to the constitutive activities of that impartial spectator, the transcendental ego, than a return to the *Lebenswelt*, the lived world which constitutes the originary basis of all idealisation and of all science (SB, 219–20).

II

Merleau-Ponty's first truly metaphilosophical reflections, which aim to put the philosophical enterprise back at the heart of human experience, are to be found in his foreword to the *Phenomenology of Perception*, the manifesto of French phenomenology. The philosopher aims neither to give an explanation of the world, nor to discover its conditions of possibility, but simply to express that contact with the world which precedes all thought about the world. To do this, he must not interrupt the relationship which he, like all men, has with the world in ordinary life, but must simply suspend it, and take that distance from the world which the ancients termed 'wonder' and which is the true meaning of the famous phenomenological reduction. Husserl never ceased analysing this reduction, precisely because it must remain inherently incomplete, and because it cannot but lead to a recognition of that dependence of thought on unthought life which is, as Merleau-Ponty emphasises, 'its initial, constant, and final situation' (*PhP*, xiv/xvi – translation modified). The phenomenological *epoché*, far from invalidating our belief in the world, is in fact the authentic discovery of the world, since only the *epoché* can render accessible the natural attitude at the very moment when it suspends it, as is made clear by Eugene Fink (Fink 1933; 1974, 135), who was as we know a fundamental guide for Merleau-Ponty in his reading of Husserl.[4] For Merleau-Ponty this means that there is an insurmountable circularity between thought and life, in which experience always anticipates philosophy, and philosophy itself is only experience elucidated (*PhP*, 63/73). Reflection, the movement by which thought returns to itself, must recognise, in the unthought depths from which it comes, an 'original past, a past which has never been present' (*PhP*, 242/282), with which there is no possible correspondence. It is not surprising to see that the *Phenomenology of Perception* ends with the following words:

> Whether it is a question of things of or historical situations, philosophy has no other function than to teach us to see them truly once again, and it is true to say that this comes about when philosophy destroys itself as a separate subject.
>
> (*PhP*, 456/530, translation modified)

This echoes the young Marx's famous declarations in his doctoral thesis that 'the world as philosophical becoming is at the same time philosophy becoming world' (Marx 1971, 15) and that 'the accomplishment of philosophy is at the same time its loss', declarations on which Merleau-Ponty was to comment in his last lectures (*NC*, 329ff.), while underlining the difficulty of bringing about the chiasmus (intertwining) of philosophy and non-philosophy which is the true goal of dialectical thought.

At this point we must underline the close proximity of Merleau-Ponty's and Hegel's conceptions of philosophy, a proximity which explains why Merleau-Ponty dedicated most of his last lecture series to the end of the introduction to the *Phenomenology of Spirit*, which he reads in the light of Heidegger's long commentary in *Off the Beaten Track*. The figure of Hegel was always part of the landscape of Merleau-Ponty's thought, and he attended the celebrated lectures on the *Phenomenology of Spirit* given by Kojève between 1933 and 1939. Like all his contemporaries, Merleau-Ponty differentiates the late Hegel, the systematic thinker whose idealism we may reproach, from the Hegel of 1807, whom Merleau-Ponty unhesitatingly terms existentialist in his 1948 text on him, explaining that 'there is a Hegelian existentialism in the sense that for Hegel, man is not in the first instance a consciousness which possesses its own thoughts with clarity, but is a life given to itself and which seeks to understand itself' (*SNS*, 65). The *Phenomenology of Spirit*, then, describes man's efforts throughout history to link up with himself, beyond any of his successive determinations; in this respect the task of the philosopher is not to 'substitute himself for man's experiences' (*SNS*, 65), but simply to gather them together and decipher them. Hegel's conception of philosophy is readily recognisable here, a conception expounded in the first pages of his 1807 book, which Merleau-Ponty was to analyse in 1961. There is no need for the philosopher to intervene in order to bring natural experience to its truth, since natural experience is quite capable of examining itself, and all that is left to the philosopher is to 'watch what happens' (Hegel 1977, 54, translation modified). The philosopher is not the educator of humanity, which can gain access to knowledge all on its own, via the series of figures which lead it to absolute knowledge. As Hegel would write in 1821 in the preface to his *Philosophy of Right*, this means that philosophy 'always comes too late' and 'appears only when reality has already accomplished and finished its process of formation', as 'Minerva's owl takes flight only when dusk begins' (Hegel 1952, 12–13). Natural consciousness is already a kind of knowledge in itself; it is something more than pure life; as Hegel writes, it has 'the power to go beyond its immediate being' and 'surpass itself' (Hegel 1977, 51, translation modified). This implies that the philosopher's perspective is not exterior to him and that it constitutes in itself the theoretical dimension of natural consciousness. Was Hegel faithful to this conception of philosophy, which 'wants to be philosophy while being non-philosophy' (*NC*, 318), and which is developed not in opposition to its other, that is to say experience and life, but in the heart of them? Merleau-Ponty questions the Hegelian identification of philosophy and history as early as 1952, in 'In Praise of Philosophy', which is the text of his inaugural speech at the Collège de France. Merleau-Ponty believes that this identification is ultimately only a way of masking their conflict, since while Hegel continues to see philosophy as absolute knowledge, he sees history as something already accomplished rather than as an event which tears open the totality of the system from within. Merleau-Ponty concludes that it is ultimately the philosopher, insofar as he reserves 'the monopoly of meaning' for himself, who 'thinks and decrees the identity of history and philosophy, which means there is no such identity' (*IPP*, 49–50). The same criticism of Hegelianism is to be found in the 1960–1 lecture series: Merleau-Ponty shows that in the constitution of the system, at the moment when 'philosophy negates itself while formulating itself', by 'converting itself into contemplated meanings', the idea of a 'reciprocal envelopment' of life and thought is lost, so that the 'break' between them reappears. Hegel did not therefore 'succeed as he wished in linking philosophy and non-philosophy' (NC, 318).

In the aforementioned 1952 speech, and in his 1960–1 lecture series, Merleau-Ponty asks whether Marx was not more successful in maintaining the link between experience and philosophy, since he denied that thought possesses the 'exhaustive power' which characterises absolute knowledge, and strove to think 'the immanent meaning of interhuman events' (IPP, 53), by displacing the dialectic away from consciousness towards men. As Merleau-Ponty explains in 1961, Marx decisively criticises the claim philosophy makes 'to contain and possess its own contradiction', such that one ends by fabricating 'an illusory power to be everything' (NC, 341) under the name of knowledge. Marx sketches a truly dialectical philosophy in which opposites – nature/history, matter/idea, subject/object, philosophy/non-philosophy – are understood not as separate substances but as 'movements with no discernable discontinuity, in which the other is always implicated' (NC, 346). However Marx, like Hegel, fails to keep faith with his youthful intuitions. This explains why his successors have tended to localise the dialectic in nature itself, and 'this return to the positive' is also a return to the 'hidden meaning of history' which deprives men of the mastery of their destiny, and which Hegel called the 'cunning of reason' (NC, 352). Merleau-Ponty's last lecture ends abruptly with the conclusion that 'a separated philosophy always reappears in sheep's clothing', and that consequently we need 'a negation of the negation, which does not become ossified into negativism or positivism'. That is to say, we need a new way of thinking of the negative, the non of non-philosophy, which is precisely what Merleau-Ponty attempted to elaborate in The Visible and the Invisible. This way of thinking would focus not on the alternation of oppositions (the trap in which Hegel and Marx are both caught) but on their chiasmus, a chiasmus resulting not in an overcoming of these oppositions, but in their encroachment on each other's territory, and in the blurring of their respective limits. It would be a way of thinking based in the reversibility which Merleau-Ponty called 'ultimate truth' (VI, 155), and in the circularity, or return to oneself, which, in the same book, he terms 'flesh'. This thought does not require any 'synthesis', because it is founded precisely in the non-absolute character of the opposition between negative and positive, activity and passivity.[5]

In the first draft of the chapter 'Interrogation and intuition', published as an appendix to his lecture transcripts,[6] Merleau-Ponty emphasises that there are two ways in which philosophy may reach a deadlock: these are reflective coincidence, in which philosophy has an absolute overview (survol) of things and of ourselves, which are transformed thereby into ideal significations; and intuitive coincidence, which brings about a fusion of philosophy, and with it of ourselves, with the thing itself. This is the situation in which philosophy finds itself if it remains 'haunted by the ideal of absolute proximity'. Hence it must on the contrary recognise that it is 'essential to both the idea and the thing to be present at a distance, a distance which is not a hindrance to knowledge, but on the contrary guarantees it' (*NC*, 359). The 'hybrid mythology of the psyche' is born from the attempt to give positive reality to the gap which both separates us from and links us to things. To escape from this mythology we must stop opposing head-on the pure positivity of things deprived of value or quality and the pure negativity of spirit haunted by the ghosts of things, and must return to 'the indivisibility of the being and nothingness of which we are made' (*NC*, 363). Faced with the failure of this thought of absolute proximity, we must not declare the end of the age of philosophy; for Merleau-Ponty, we must rather see in this failure the possibility of a rebirth for philosophy, in which philosophy would learn that there is never anything more than a 'strange situation of partial coincidence' (*NC*, 365) between self and things, as between self and self. Merleau-Ponty declares that philosophy is taking posses-sion once again of its inalienable domain, the relationship of *Ineinander*, the mutual implication of self and things, of self and other, of the visible and the invisible (*NC*, 366). It is an implication in which the philosopher, too, as opposed to the *kosmos theoros*, is entangled (*NC*, 368). For the philosopher does not create the philosophical interrogation whose mouthpiece he is because, like every man, he is the crossroads of the seen (*visible*) and of the seer (*voyant*). This implies that he cannot extricate himself from his own ques-tioning, and that, like every man, he is only ever that 'X where being comes to itself, lives, or lives again' (*NC*, 372).

III

Merleau-Ponty had already developed the same idea of philosophy and the philosopher nearly ten years earlier in 'In Praise of Philosophy', in which he declares that 'what makes a philosopher is the movement which constantly leads from knowledge to ignorance, ignorance to knowledge, and which has a kind of restfulness in its movement' (*IPP*, 5). By this he means that philosophy is not a possession but an activity or movement which is not extinguished in the achievement of knowledge. The respite which can be found in formulating notions such as those of flesh or chiasmus must be understood not as inter-rupting the movement of thought, but as a resting place internal to that very movement. In a famous passage from the *Groundwork for the Metaphysics of Morals*, Kant describes the situation of philosophy as precarious, since it can find no foundation for ethics either in heaven or on earth (Kant 2002, 226). Similarly, Merleau-Ponty wishes to show that philosophy eludes both 'pro-methean humanism and the rival affirmations of theology' (*IPP*, 43). On the one hand, 'nothing is explicable through man', since man is a weakness, a 'hollow' in being, not a force or a positive entity; on the other hand, nothing is explained by theology, since theology gets rid of the problem by means of solutions 'which smother it'. This does not, however, mean that philosophy may simply identify itself with atheism, since 'to define philosophy as atheism misses the point of philosophy. Atheism is philosophy as seen by a theologian' (*IPP*, 46). Philosophy may neither affirm nor deny God, precisely because the thinker comes into being in the 'decisive moment' anterior to any distinction between the sensuous and the intelligible, the moment of the *birth* of the world, a moment when 'life is breathed into fragments of matter, words, and events by a meaning whose future contour they sketch but do not contain' (*IPP*, 46, translation modified).

For Merleau-Ponty, however, placing philosophy in such a dangerous negativity (he uses the word as early as 1952 – *IPP*, 46–7), as if it were suspended in a 'strange' void between heaven and earth, does not signify a return to the idea of a *philosophia perennis*. On the contrary, 'philosophy is in the midst of history; it is never independent of historical discourse' (*IPP*, 57). This does not mean, however, that philosophy passively endures its historical situation, but on the contrary that it helps change that situation by making it self-aware and 'giving it the opportunity to establish a relationship with other periods and other milieux, in which its truth appears' (*IPP*, 57). The appearance of the symbolic space of culture and society cannot be explained by a philosophy which goes no further than 'the alternation of *things* and *consciousnesses*' (*IPP*, 54), because this appearance presupposes that the contingent facts of nature be taken up by a will to expression which grants them new meaning and thus integrates them into a symbolism of which philosophy itself is part. The task of philosophy therefore consists in returning to the anonymous symbolic activity expressed by those various symbolic systems which are human institutions, and in scrutinising 'the symbolic power which the other symbolisms merely exercise' (*IPP*, 58, translation modified).

It is through a movement of reflection that philosophy finds the meaning which was instituted in history, and brings it to its truth. Philosophy itself is one symbolic system among many, but its peculiarity is that it has the power to 'measure' the others, a power analogous to that of the body itself, which is a 'measure'[7] of all the dimensions of the world. It is the dual nature of philosophy which is the key to its weakness, and the reason why 'philosophy is lame' (*IPP*, 58, translation modified): it is at once 'within' history and life, and in search of their origins; it is 'within' constituted meaning, and in search of the birth of constituting meaning. Philosophy is self-divided and is always in the grip of internal contradiction. For this reason Merleau-Ponty declares (unusually for a philosopher) that philosophy 'is never a *serious* occupation' (*IPP*, 58), if to be serious means to want only one thing at a time. Philosophy can never coincide with its own will; which implies that harbouring its own contrary within it, it can become tragic. But the *ironic* nature of philosophy's non-coincidence with itself does not mean that the philosopher, with ironic detachment, may opt out of history and sceptically refuse any kind of commitment: on the contrary, he is aware that the philosophical absolute holds court nowhere, that it is never 'elsewhere', and that it must precisely be defended in each thing that happens (*IPP*, 62). In so doing the philosopher recognises that he does not occupy a privileged position, and that he should not get ideas above his station as an 'ordinary' man. Merleau-Ponty thus concludes his inaugural lecture series by stating that the philosopher's 'dialectic' 'is simply a way of articulating what everyone knows', since 'man contains in silence all the paradoxes of philosophy' (*IPP*, 63–4, translation modified).

There is, then, neither opposition nor coincidence between philosophy and non-philosophy, or between philosophical and 'ordinary' life; each borrows from, encroaches on, and intersects with the other. Yet reflective philosophy is unaware of precisely this chiasmus which at once unites and differentiates philosophy and non-philosophy. Such a philosophy naively believes that the movement of reflection can recreate the spontaneity of intentional life in its totality, whereas in reality reflection can only ever give a retrospective reconstruction. In the texts he wrote during the last two years of his life, Merleau-Ponty calls for 'a kind of meta-reflection [*surreflexion*]' (*VI*, 38), with the goal of overcoming the naivety of the reflective operation. This does not, however, indicate a wish simply to abandon reflection, and philosophy with it. On the contrary, Merleau-Ponty's aim is to produce a reflection on reflection, capable of revealing its true nature as retrospective reconstruction, and hence to destroy the persistent illusion of an absolute reflection. A meta-reflection of this kind is needed to give an account of the genesis of philosophy itself, as Merleau-Ponty himself intended to do in the book eventually titled *The Visible and the Invisible* but which had previously been called *Genealogy of the True* and *The Origin of Truth* (cf. C. Lefort's 'editor's note', *VI*, xxxiv). He aimed to trace the genealogy of philosophy via non-philosophy, since he believed there to be no radical separation between the two. Sensuous experience (*expérience sensible*) is the location of truth, and the task of philosophy is to bring 'this still mute experience to the pure expression of its own meaning', as Husserl put it in a passage of the *Cartesian Meditations* which Merleau-Ponty often quoted (*VI*, 129).

According to Merleau-Ponty, philosophy has never yet spoken of the thought which is before thought, of the passivity which is the origin of activity, of the 'fact' that 'it is not I who make myself think, any more than it is I who make my heart beat' (*VI*, 221). The first relationship we have with the world is not active, nor is it a relationship of knowledge, rather, it is a primordial faith, or *Urdoxa* in Husserl's terminology, because consciousness must open itself to exteriority and *institute* a world with horizons, even before the constitution of the first object. Merleau-Ponty calls the world thus instituted 'wild' (*sauvage*) or 'vertical' (*VI*, 177), because it cannot be assimilated into the sum of objects, since they presuppose its existence. Similarly, he calls a being which cannot be assimilated into what tradition terms 'in itself' (*en-soi*), 'brute being' (*VI*, 167, translation modified) or 'vertical or wild being' (*VI*, 204). For Merleau-Ponty, the task of philosophy is to describe this vertical world and this wild being in terms of 'the pre-spiritual milieu without which nothing, not even the spirit, is thinkable' (*VI*, 204). As he emphasises, 'there is no rivalry or antinomy between *Lebenswelt* as universal Being, and philosophy as extreme product of the world: the latter discloses the former' (*VI*, 170, translation modified). This means that only the hyperculture which is philosophy can rediscover the world of silence which is the world of primordial life and nature. Merleau-Ponty's attitude does not indicate a form of naturalism but rather the subtle under-standing that we can only encounter nature in the very heart of culture. It would therefore be quite wrong to see a quest for some ontological integrity, lost in the course of the historical process, in Merleau-Ponty's enterprise of describing a brute or wild being. Such a mythology of the restoration of origins presupposes that a real fusion with these origins is possible, whereas in fact the experience of *rediscovered* immediacy is, essentially, the experience of a *return* to origins. It is the experience of only partial coincidence with origins, and of a necessarily distant relationship with an original state which can never be made present just as it was, and which can only retain its immediacy by opening itself to the dimension of its alteration and its revival to come. As Merleau-Ponty underlines, philosophy is 'the study of the *Vorhabe* of Being' (*VI*, 204), the study of the prepossession of being, which is not yet knowledge, but which knowledge always presupposes. Philosophy's interrogative experience of this pre-objective being can never take the form of fusion, but only of 'coincidence at a distance', of a 'gap' or something like a 'good error' (*VI*, 124–5, translation modified).

For Merleau-Ponty philosophy as the 'expression of experience which is mute in itself' is 'a creation which is at the same time a reinstatement of Being' (*VI*, 197, translation modified). It is consequently a strange product of history, a product which knows it is a product and aspires to surpass itself as such in order to find its origins, origins which it shares with all other productions of history. It is therefore a creation in a radical sense: a 'creation which is at the same time the only way to obtain an adequation' with that which is. In Merleau-Ponty's own words, 'being is *that which demands creation of us* in order that we should experience that being' (*VI*, 197).

Consequently, being is never directly experienced; we must take an oblique or lateral approach, and to know this is in itself a way into 'true philosophy'. True philosophy is able to 'understand why to go outside oneself [the cultural process of creation] is to return to oneself [a return to origins and to nature] and vice versa' (*VI*, 199, translation modified[8]). However, this means that 'true philosophy' is 'negative philosophy', in the same way that there is negative theology, because it is not possible to make a 'direct ontology' or to have a direct relationship with being, since being must, essentially, remain distant, and can only be reached through beings (*VI*, 179).

IV

We may now perhaps understand Merleau-Ponty's working note of November 1960, in which he indicates what philosophy ought to be. He proposes an understanding of philosophy based in the idea of chiasmus, according to which 'any relationship to being involves *simultaneously* taking and being taken' such that 'the act of taking is taken, *inscribed*, and inscribed in the very being it takes' (VI, 266). This simultaneity of active and passive involves the internal return to experience which Merleau-Ponty calls reversibility and which we may now also see at work in the act of philosophising. Hence, as he states, philosophy 'cannot be a total, active taking, an intellectual possession, because what there is to be grasped is a dispossession' (VI, 266). A dispossession which brings us back to our original passivity can only be understood as a return from activity to passivity, from taking to being taken, just as negative theology can only gain access to God when it accepts to say only what he is not. According to Merleau-Ponty this means that philosophy is not '*above* life, overlooking it', but 'beneath' it. Again, it is a question of the destitution of the *Kosmotheoros* and of any thought from on high (*pensée de survol*), which must lead us towards an entirely new idea of philosophy, in which thought is not a movement of elevation taking us 'beyond being' (as in transcendentalism), but in which thought implicates us in being and makes us plumb its depths. Philosophy is not only in itself an experience of chiasmus, but is an experience of chiasmus *as such*, insofar as chiasmus governs the *entire* gamut of experience, experience 'is the simultaneous test of the taking and the taken *in every domain*' (VI, 266, my italics). Understood in this way, philosophy is *praxis* as much as *theoria*, implication in being as much as thought about being: 'it is not stamped on the reverse face of the visible: it is on both sides', as Merleau-Ponty adds. Philosophy is therefore at once on the side of the invisible and the side of the visible, at once theory and practice, at once transcendental and empirical, ontological and ontic. For this reason Merleau-Ponty emphasises that there can no more be '*absolute* difference' between these two domains, than there can be an 'absolute invisible'. Consequently, neither is there an 'absolutely pure philosophical speech', since philosophy, 'like all literature', can only convey its meaning, the significations of things and of the world, 'via words' (VI, 266), and hence via the sensuous.

In this respect we must remember that philosophy, for Merleau-Ponty, is inseparable from literary expression, precisely because this latter is always 'indirect' (NC, 391[9]). Indeed, in the foreword to the *Phenomenology of Perception* he declares that 'true philosophy consists in learning to see the world anew' and that 'in this sense, the telling of a story may signify the world with as much "depth" as a philosophical treatise' (PhP, xx/xxiii, translation modified). In an article on 'Metaphysics and the Novel', written in the years following the publication of the *Phenomenology of Perception*, his clear understanding of the consequences of such a conception of philosophy is evident when he writes that 'the task of literature and that of philosophy can no longer be separated', since 'when one must give voice to the experience of the world', 'one may no longer flatter oneself that perfectly transparent expression is attainable', and philosophical expression takes on the same ambiguities as literary expression

(*SNS*, 28, translation modified). Because philosophy must take note of the implication of thought in the world it describes, philosophical discourse like literature as a whole is engaged in the experience of expression, which consists in allowing a world, of which the gesture of expression is itself part, to appear through the words. In *The Visible and the Invisible*, criticism of 'pure thought', of the autonomy of meaning from sensuous experience, leads to an understanding of the relation between ideality and visibility, better understood by Proust than by professional philosophers: 'No-one has gone further than Proust in establishing the relations between visible and invisible, nor in describing ideas not as the opposite of the sensuous, but as its inner form and its depth' (*VI*, 149, translation modified). It is because of what Proust says of Swann, not because of some philosopher's analysis, that we understand that

> there is a rigorous ideality to experiences which are experiences of the flesh: the moments of the sonata and the fragments of the luminous field adhere to one another by a cohesion without concept, of the same kind as that which joins the parts of my body, or my body and the world.
>
> (*VI*, 152)

However, although the philosophy of the sensuous *is* literature (one May 1960 working note carries the title 'The philosophy of the sensuous as literature' (*VI*, 252, translation modified), and although the sensuous is an 'inexhaustible treasure trove of things to say for the philosopher (that is, the writer)' (*VI*, 252, translation modified), the author of 'In Praise of Philosophy' never intended to transform philosophy into literature, for the peculiarity of philosophy, and its weakness, lies in its being that form of expression which can only come about when it relinquishes the attempt to coincide with what it expresses (*IPP*, 58).

Philosophy cannot overcome its ambiguity, which is at once an internal weakness or disability, and a virtue: it can never become an 'intellectual possession' of the world, a 'positive' philosophy in the sense of constituting a second order beyond the sensuous. It remains a 'negative philosophy'; as Merleau-Ponty declares in his last lecture series, paraphrasing Pascal, this means that 'true philosophy makes light of philosophy, and is aphilosophy' (*NC*, 275[10]). Even while it remains caught in the 'good' ambiguity of thought which sees the absolute not as something positive, but as the 'light of truth which appears in the layers of experience', like a 'watermark' seen through them, philosophy cannot formulate this ambiguity without transforming it into 'something said, a positive fact', and so making it disappear (*NC*, 320): such is the irony of philosophy.

Philosophy is consequently being's *inscription* – where being is understood as both subject and (genitive) object – and therefore it can never constitute a kingdom of pure significations. It necessarily possesses a *body*, precisely because the knowledge it attains cannot be separated from its sensuous moorings, and can only be attained through them. Likewise, philosophy cannot be considered independently of its historical appearance, its historical 'body'. From such a perspective, this historical body can no longer be thought of as that through which philosophy participates in the accidental; on the contrary it is what constitutes the very *being* of the idea. Consequently, there is no discourse capable of discussing ambiguity and reversibility as such: it is only possible to make them visible *through* philosophical experience and through philosophical speech and writing.

Notes

1 Translated by Marie-Elise Howells, including all quotations.
2 These lecture notes have not yet been translated into English.
3 Léon Brunschvicg (1869–1944) was a professor of the Sorbonne from 1909 to 1939, and during the inter-war years had a great influence over generations of students at the Ecole Normale Supérieure of the rue d'Ulm, Paris, both in his capacity as teacher there and as a member of the Agrégation examining jury.
4 Merleau-Ponty quotes Fink as early as 1934 in his grant application (*Le primat de la perception*, Grenoble: Cynara, 1989, 21 and 22) and it is known that as the first foreign visitor to the Husserl Archives in Leuwen in April 1939 he had the opportunity to meet Fink. In 1939 he read Fink's transcript of Husserl's 'L'origine de la géométrie' in 1939, and in 1942 the manuscript of the 'Sixième méditation', which he mentions in a note on the first page of *Phenomenology of Perception* (p. vii).
5 For Merleau-Ponty, this other conception of the negative was illustrated by the later Heidegger. For further information, see F. Dastur (2003).
6 Cf. NC, 31, where the editor of the *Notes de cours* explains that in his publication of *Le visible et l'invisible* Claude Lefort removed this text, which she publishes as an appendix, and replaced it with a later version, similar in theme to Merleau-Ponty's last lectures.
7 Cf. VI, 138: 'In our body, our senses, our sight, our capacity to understand speech and to speak, we have *measures* for being, dimensions to which we can refer it, but we have no relationship of correspondence or immanence' (translation modified).
8 Merleau-Ponty's exact words are as follows: 'True philosophy = understanding why to go outside oneself is to return to oneself and vice versa. Understanding this chiasma, this return. That is spirit.' ('La vraie philosophie = saisir ce qui fait que le sortir de soi est rentrer en soi et vice versa. Saisir ce chiasma, ce retournement. C'est là l'esprit.')
9 Merleau-Ponty says of this indirect expression that it 'does not reach a correspondence – intellectual possession – but rather gestures towards [*winkt*]'. This is an implicit allusion to a passage from Heidegger's interview with a Japanese man published in 1959 in *Unterwegs zur Sprache* where Heidegger explains that to gesture towards (*winken*) is the fundamental characteristic of all words (Heidegger 1971, 24ff., though in this translation *winken* is translated as 'to hint'); Merleau-Ponty refers to Heidegger's book in his 1959–60 lecture series entitled 'Husserl at the Limits of Phenomenology' (*HLP*, 39ff.).
10 Cf. Pascal, *Pensées*, 513, which ends 'to make light of philosophy is to truly philosophise' ('se moquer de la philosophie, c'est vraiment philosopher').

BIBLIOGRAPHY

Works by Merleau-Ponty (in chronological order)

The Structure of Behaviour (SB), trans. A. L. Fisher, Boston MA: Beacon Press, 1963. Translation of *La Structure du comportement*, Paris: Presses Universitaires de France, 1942.

Phenomenology of Perception (PhP), trans. C. Smith, London: Routledge, 1962. Translation of *Phénoménologie de la perception*, Paris: Gallimard, 1945.

Sense and Non-Sense (SNS), trans. H. L. Dreyfus and P. A. Dreyfus, Evanston IL: Northwestern University Press, 1964. Translation of *Sens et non-sens*, Paris: Nagel, 1948.

The Visible and the Invisible (VI), trans. A. Lingis, Evanston IL: Northwestern University Press, 1968. Translation of *Le visible et l'invisible*, ed. C. Lefort, Paris: Gallimard, 1964.

The Primacy of Perception and other essays (PofP), trans. J. M. Edie, Evanston IL: Northwestern University Press, 1964. This is a translation of essays published separately in French.

The Prose of the World (PW), trans. J. O'Neill, London: Heinemann, 1974. Translation of *La prose du monde*, ed. C. Lefort, Paris: Gallimard, 1969.

In Praise of Philosophy and other essays (IPP), trans. J. Wild, J. Edie and J. O'Neill, Evanston IL: Northwestern University Press, 1988. This is a translation of *Eloge de la Philosophie* (Paris: Gallimard, 1960) and *Résumés de cours, Collège de France 1952–60* (Paris: Gallimard, 1968).

Texts and Dialogues (T&D), eds H. Silverman and J. Barry, London: Humanities Press, 1992. This is a translation of essays published separately in French.

Notes de Cours (NC), Paris: Gallimard, 1996 (not translated into English).

Husserl at the Limits of Phenomenology (HLP), eds L. Lawlor and B. Bergo, Evanston IL: Northwestern University Press, 2002. This includes a translation of Merleau-Ponty's lecture notes 'Husserl aux limites de la phénoménologie' which were published in *Notes de cours sur l'origine de la géometrie de Husserl*, Paris: Presses Universitaires de France, 1998.

Other works

Austin, J. L. (1962) *Sense and Sensibilia*, London: Oxford University Press.

Baldwin, T. (2004) 'Editor's Introduction' to T. Baldwin (ed.) *Merleau-Ponty: Basic Writings*, London: Routledge.

Bates, E., Camaioni, L. and Volterra, V. (1976) 'Sensorimotor Performatives', in E. Bates, *Language and Context: The Acquisition of Pragmatics*, New York: Academic Press.

Bégout, B. (2000) *La généalogie de la logique: Husserl, l'antéprédécatif et le categorical*, Paris: Vrin.

Bennett, J. (1976) *Linguistic Behaviour*, Cambridge: Cambridge University Press.

Bruner, J. (1977) 'Early Social Interaction and Language Acquisition', in H. R. Schaffer (ed.) *Studies in Mother-Infant Interaction*, New York: Academic Press.

Brunschvicg, L. (1922) *L'expérience humaine et la causalité physique*, Paris: Alcan.

Butterworth, G. and Franco, F. (1993) 'Motor Development: Communication and Cognition', in L. Kalverboer, B. Hopkins and R. H. Gueze (eds) *A Longitudinal Approach to the Study of Motor Development in Early and Later Childhood*, Cambridge: Cambridge University Press.

Call, J. and Tomasello, M. (2005) 'What Chimpanzees Know About Seeing Revisited: An Explanation of the Third Kind', in N. Eilan, C. Hoerl, T. McCormack and J. Roessler (eds) *Joint Attention: Communication and Other Minds, Problems in Philosophy and Psychology*, Oxford: Oxford University Press.

Campbell, J. (1986) 'Conceptual Structure', in C. Travis (ed.) *Meaning and Interpretation*, Oxford: Blackwell.

Dastur, F. (2003) 'L'in-visible et le négatif chez le dernier Merleau-Ponty', in M. Cariou, R. Barabas and E. Bimbenet (eds) *Merleau-Ponty aux frontières de l'invisible*, Milan: Les Cahiers de Chiasmi International, no. 1, Mimesis.

Davidson, D. (2001) 'The Emergence of Thought', in D. Davidson, *Subjective, Intersubjective, Objective*, Oxford: Oxford University Press.

Derrida, J. (1973) *Speech and Phenomena*, trans. D. Allison, Evanston IL: Northwestern University Press. Translation of *Le voix et le phénomène*, Paris: Presses Universitaires de France, 1967.

——(1974) *Of Grammatology*, trans. G. Spivak, Baltimore MD: Johns Hopkins University Press. Translation of *De la grammatologie*, Paris: Minuit, 1967.

Diamond, C. (1995) 'Eating Meat and Eating People', in C. Diamond, *The Realistic Spirit: Wittgenstein, Philosophy, and the Mind*, Cambridge MA: MIT Press.

Dreyfus, H. (1972) *What Computers Can't Do*, Cambridge MA: MIT Press.

——(1999) 'The Primacy of Phenomenology over Logical Analysis', *Philosophical Topics* 27: 3–24.

——(2000) 'A Merleau-Pontyian Critique of Husserl's and Searle's Representationalist Accounts of Action', *Proceedings of the Aristotelian Society* 100, 3: 287–302.

Dreyfus, H. and Dreyfus, S. (1999) 'The Challenge of Merleau-Ponty's Phenomenology of Embodiment for Cognitive Science', in G. Weiss and H. F. Haber (eds) *Perspectives on Embodiment*, London: Routledge, 103–20.

Eilan, N., Hoerl. C., McCormack, T. and Roessler, J. (eds) (2005) *Joint Attention: Communication and Other Minds, Problems in Philosophy and Psychology*, Oxford: Oxford University Press.

Fink, E. (1933) 'La Philosophie phénoménologique d'Edmund Husserl face à la critique contemporaine', *Kant-Studien*.

——(1974) *De la phénoménologie*, Paris: Minuit.

Franco, F. (2005) 'Infant Pointing: Harlequin Servant of Two Masters', in N. Eilan, C. Hoerl, T. McCormack and J. Roessler (eds) *Joint Attention: Communication and*

Other Minds, Problems in Philosophy and Psychology, Oxford: Oxford University Press.

Gallagher, S. (1986) 'Body Image and Body Schema: A Conceptual Clarification', *Journal of Mind and Behavior* 7: 541–54.

——(1995) 'Body Schema and Intentionality', in José Bermúdez, Naomi Eilan and Anthony Marcel (eds) *The Body and the Self*, Cambridge MA: MIT Press, 225–44.

Glendinning, S. (1998) *On Being with Others: Heidegger-Derrida-Wittgenstein*, London: Routledge.

Glock, H. and Hyman, J. (1994) 'Persons and their Bodies', *Philosophical Investigations* 17: 2.

Gomez, J-C. (2005) 'Joint Attention and the Notion of Subject: Insights from Apes, Normal Children and Children with Austism', in N. Eilan, C. Hoerl, T. McCormack and J. Roessler (eds) *Joint Attention: Communication and Other Minds, Problems in Philosophy and Psychology*, Oxford: Oxford University Press.

Grice, H. P. (1989) *Studies in the Way of Words*, Cambridge MA: Harvard University Press.

Gurwitsch, A. (1979) *Human Encounters in the Social World*, Pittsburgh PA: Duquesne University Press.

Habermas, J. (1998) *Between Facts and Norms*, trans. William Rehg, Cambridge MA: MIT Press.

Harman, G. (1999) 'The Intrinsic Quality of Experience', in G. Harman, *Reasoning, Meaning, and Mind*, Oxford: Oxford University Press, 244–61.

Hart, H. L. A. (1961) *The Concept of Law*, Oxford: Clarendon Press.

Hegel, G. W. F. (1952) *Philosophy of Right*, trans. T. M. Knox, Oxford: Oxford University Press.

——(1977) *Phenomenology of Spirit*, trans. A. V. Miller, Oxford: Oxford University Press.

Heidegger, M. (1962) *Being and Time*, trans. John Macquarrie and Edward Robinson, New York: Harper & Row.

——(1971) *On the Way to Language*, trans. P. D. Hertz, London: Harper & Row.

Hobson, P. (2005) 'What Puts the Jointness into Joint Attention?', in N. Eilan, C. Hoerl, T. McCormack and J. Roessler (eds) *Joint Attention: Communication and Other Minds, Problems in Philosophy and Psychology*, Oxford: Oxford University Press.

Husserl, E. (1952–) *Husserliana*, Dordrecht: Kluwer (formerly The Hague: Martinus Nijhoff). Reference is made to the following volumes:

I. *Cartesianische Meditationen und Pariser Vorträge*, ed. S. Strasser, 2nd edn, 1973. Trans. Dorion Cairns, *Cartesian Meditations*, The Hague: Martinus Nijhoff, 1973.

III. *Ideen zu einer reinen Phänomenologie und Phänomenologischen Philosophie. Erstes Buch*, revised edn, ed. K Schumann, 2 vols, 1976. Trans. F. Kersten, *Ideas Pertaining to a Pure Phenomenology and to a Phenomenological Philosophy, First Book*, Dordrecht: Kluwer, 1982.

IV. *Ideen zu einer reinen Phänomenologie und Phänomenologischen Philosophie. Zweites Buch*, ed. M. Biemel, 1952. Trans. R. Rojcewicz and A. Schuwer, *Ideas Pertaining to a Pure Phenomenology and to a Phenomenological Philosophy, Second Book*, Dordrecht: Kluwer, 1989.

V. *Ideen zu einer reinen Phänomenologie und Phänomenologischen Philosophie. Drittes Buch*, ed. M. Biemel, 1952. Trans. T. E. Klein and W. E. Pohl, *Ideas Pertaining to a Pure Phenomenology and to a Phenomenological Philosophy, Third Book*, Dordrecht: Kluwer, 1980.

VI. *Die Krisis der europäischen Wissenschaft und die transzendentale Phänomenologie*, ed. W. Biemel, 1954. Trans. David Carr, *The Crisis of European Sciences and Transcendental Phenomenology*, Evanston IL: Northwestern University Press, 1970.

VII. *Erste Philosophie (1923 – 1924)*. *Erste Teil*, ed. R. Boehm, 1959.

IX. *Phänomenologische Psychologie*, ed. W. Biemel, 1962. Trans. (in part) J. Scanlon, *Phenomenological Psychology*, The Hague: Martinus Nijhoff, 1977.

XI. *Analysen zur passiven Synthesis*, ed. M. Fleischer, 1966. Trans. A. Steinbock, *Analyses Concerning Active and Passive Synthesis*, Dordrecht: Kluwer, 2001.

XIII–XV. *Zur Phänomenologie der Intersubjektivität. Erster Teil, Zweiter Teil, Dritter Teil*, ed. I. Kern, 1973.

XVI. *Ding und Raum*, ed. U. Claesges, 1973. Trans. R. Rojcewicz, *Thing and Space*, Dordrecht: Kluwer, 1997.

XVII. *Formale und transzendentale Logik*, ed. P. Janssen, 1974. Trans. (in part) D. Cairns, *Formal and Transcendental Logic*, The Hague: Martinus Nijhoff, 1969.

XXXIV. *Zur Phänomenologischen Reduktion*, ed. S. Luft, 2002.

——(1973a) *Logical Investigations*, trans. J. N. Findlay, London: Routledge.

——(1973b) *Experience and Judgement*, trans. J. S. Churchill and K. Ameriks, Evanston IL: Northwestern University Press.

Jeannerod, M. (1986) 'The Formation of Finger Grip During Prehension. A Cortically Mediated Visuomotor Pattern', *Behavioural Brain Research* 199: 99–116.

Kant, I. (2002) *Groundwork of the Metaphysics of Morals*, eds T. E. Hill and A. Zweig, Oxford: Oxford University Press.

Kelly, S. D. (2001) 'The Non-conceptual Content of Perceptual Experience: Situation Dependence and Fineness of Grain', *Philosophy and Phenomenological Research* 62: 601–8.

——(2004) 'Seeing Things in Merleau-Ponty', in Taylor Carman (ed.) *The Cambridge Companion to Merleau-Ponty*, Cambridge: Cambridge University Press.

——(forthcoming) 'Content and Constancy: Comments on Alva Noë', *Philosophy and Phenomenological Research*.

Kern, I. (1964) *Kant und Husserl*, The Hague: Martinus Nijhoff.

Kuhn, T. (1962) *The Structure of Scientific Revolutions*, Chicago IL: University of Chicago Press.

Lee, Nam-In (1993) *Edmund Husserls Phänomenologie der Instinkte*, Dordrecht: Kluwer.

Lepore, E. and Smith, P. (2006) *The Oxford Handbook to Language*, Oxford: Oxford University Press.

Levinas, E. (1969) *Totality and Infinity: An Essay on Exteriority*, trans. Alphonso Lingis, Pittsburgh PA: Duquesne University Press.

Lewis, C. I. (1946) *An Analysis of Knowledge and Valuation*, La Salle IL: Open Court.

Lewis, D. (1969) *Convention*, Cambridge MA: MIT Press.

Marx, K. (1971) *Early Texts*, ed. D. McLellan, Oxford: Blackwell.

McDowell, J. (1986) 'Singular Thought and the Extent of Inner Sense', in P. Pettit and J. McDowell (eds) *Subject, Thought, and Context*, Oxford: Clarendon Press, 137–68.

——(1994) *Mind and World*, Cambridge MA: Harvard University Press.

Mensch, J. (1988) *Intersubjectivity and Transcendental Idealism*, Albany NY: State University of New York Press.

Milner, A. D. and Goodale, M. A. (1995) *The Visual Brain in Action*, Oxford: Oxford University Press.

Moran, D. (2000) *Introduction to Phenomenology*, London: Routledge.

Moreland J. P. (1998), 'Should a Naturalist be a Supervenient Physicalist', *Metaphilosophy* 29.

BIBLIOGRAPHY

Mulhall, S. (2005) *Philosophical Myths of the Fall*, Princeton NJ: Princeton University Press.
Noë, A. (2004) *Action in Perception*, Cambridge MA: MIT Press/Bradford Books.
Pappas, G. S. (1987) 'Berkeley and Immediate Perception', in *Essays on the Philosophy of George Berkeley*, ed. E. Sosa, Boston MA: D. Reidel, 195–213.
Peacocke, C. A. B. (1989) 'Perceptual Content', in J. Almog, J. Perry and H. Wettstein (eds) *Themes from Kaplan*, New York: Oxford University Press, 297–329.
——(1986) 'Analogue Content', *Proceedings of the Aristotelian Society* 60: 1.
Primozic, D. T. (2001) *On Merleau-Ponty*, Belmont CA: Wadsworth.
Reddy, V. (2005) 'Before the "Third Element": Understanding Attention to Self', in N. Eilan, C. Hoerl, T. McCormack and J. Roessler (eds) *Joint Attention: Communication and Other Minds, Problems in Philosophy and Psychology*, Oxford: Oxford University Press.
Roessler, J. (2005) 'Joint Attention and the Problem of Other Minds', in N. Eilan, C. Hoerl, T. McCormack and J. Roessler (eds) *Joint Attention: Communication and Other Minds, Problems in Philosophy and Psychology*, Oxford: Oxford University Press.
Russell, B. (1959) *The Problems of Philosophy*, Oxford: Oxford University Press.
Sartre, J-P. (1958) *The Transcendence of the Ego: An Existentialist Theory of Consciousness*, trans. F. Williams and R. Kirkpatrick, New York: Farrar, Straus & Giroux.
Searle, J. R. (1983) *Intentionality*, Cambridge: Cambridge University Press.
——(1992) *The Rediscovery of the Mind*, Cambridge MA: MIT Press.
——(1995) *The Construction of Social Reality*, New York: The Free Press.
Sellars, W. (1963) *Science, Perception and Reality*, London: Routledge.
Smith, A. D. (2002) *The Problem of Perception*, Cambridge MA: Harvard University Press.
——(2003) *Husserl and the Cartesian Mediations*, London: Routledge.
Sperber, D. and Wilson, D. (1986) *Relevance: Communication and Cognition*, Cambridge MA: Harvard University Press.
Steinbock, A. J. (1995) *Home and Beyond: Generative Phenomenology after Husserl*, Evanston IL: Northwestern University Press.
Todes, S. (2001) *Body and World*, Cambridge MA: MIT Press.
Tomasello, M. (1995) 'Joint Attention as Social Cognition', in C. Moore and P. Dunham (eds) *Joint Attention: Its Origins and Role in Development*, Hillsdale NJ: Lawrence Erlbaum.
——(1999) *The Cultural Origins of Human Cognition*, Cambridge MA: Harvard University Press.
Valberg, J. J. (1992) 'The Puzzle of Experience', in Tim Crane (ed.) *The Contents of Experience: Essays on Perception*, New York: Cambridge University Press, 18–47.
Welton, D. (1983) *The Origins of Meaning*, The Hague: Martinus Nijhoff.
Werner, H. and Kaplan, B. (1963) *Symbol Formation*, Hillsdale NJ: Lawrence Erlbaum.
Wiggins, D. (1998) 'Truth, Invention, and the Meaning of Life', in D. Wiggins, *Needs, Values, Truth*, Oxford: Clarendon Press.
Wild, J. (1963) 'Foreword', to J. Wild, *Structure of Behaviour*, trans. Alden L. Fisher, Cambridge MA: Beacon Press.
Woodward, A. (2005) 'Infants' Understanding of the Actions Involved in Joint Attention', in N. Eilan, C. Hoerl, T. McCormack and J. Roessler (eds) *Joint Attention: Communication and Other Minds, Problems in Philosophy and Psychology*, Oxford: Oxford University Press.
Wrathall, M. (2000) 'Background Practices, Capacities, and Heideggerian Disclosure', in M. Wrathall and J. Malpas (eds) *Heidegger, Coping, and Cognitive Science*, Cambridge MA: MIT Press.

INDEX

169

Related titles from Routledge

In the Name of Phenomenology
Simon Glendinning

The attempt to pursue philosophy in the name of phenomenology is one of the most significant and important developments in twentieth century thought. In this bold and innovative book, Simon Glendinning introduces some of the major figures in the phenomenological inheritance of philosophy and demonstrates that its ongoing strength and coherence is to be explained less by what Maurice Merleau-Ponty called the 'unity' of its 'manner of thinking' and more by what he called its 'unfinished nature'.

Beginning with a discussion of the nature of phenomenology, Glendinning follows the shifting sequence of launches and re-launches of phenomenology that are elaborated in key texts by Husserl, Heidegger, Sartre, Merleau-Ponty, Levinas and Derrida. Focusing on the different ways in which each philosopher has responded to and transformed the legacy of phenomenology, Glendinning shows that the richness of this legacy lies not in the formation of a distinctive movement or school but in a remarkable capacity to make fertile philosophical breakthroughs through self-interruption and deviance. Important topics such as the nature of phenomenological arguments, the critique of realism and idealism, ontology, existentialism, perception, ethics and the other are also closely examined. Through a re-evaluation of the development of phenomenology Glendinning traces the ruptures and dislocations of philosophy that, in an age dominated by science, strives constantly to renew our understanding of ourselves and our place in the world.

Clearly and engagingly written, *In the Name of Phenomenology* is essential reading for students of phenomenology and contemporary philosophy.

ISBN10: 0-415-22337-7 (hbk)
ISBN10: 0-415-22338-5 (pbk)

ISBN13: 978-0-415-22337-9 (hbk)
ISBN13: 978-0-415-22338-6 (pbk)

Available at all good bookshops
For ordering and further information please visit:
www.routledge.com